Cheap Speech

CHEAP SPEECH

HOW DISINFORMATION
POISONS OUR POLITICS—
AND HOW TO CURE IT

● ● ●

RICHARD L. HASEN

Yale

UNIVERSITY PRESS

New Haven and London

Published with assistance from the Mary Cady Tew Memorial Fund.

Yale University Press books may be purchased in quantity for
educational, business, or promotional use. For information, please e-mail
sales.press@yale.edu (U.S. office) or sales@yaleup.co.uk (U.K. office).

Set in Gotham & Adobe Garamond type by
Integrated Publishing Solutions.
Printed in the United States of America.

Library of Congress Control Number: 2021944800
ISBN 978-0-300-25937-7 (hardcover : alk. paper)

A catalogue record for this book is available from the British Library.

10 9 8 7 6 5 4 3 2

For the Heroes
Who Were Injured Defending the U.S. Capitol
during the January 6, 2021, Insurrection and Who Assured
We Had a Fair and Safe 2020 Presidential Election

Contents

Contents

Acknowledgments

I began exploring the ideas in this book at a symposium, "Distorting the Truth: 'Fake News' and Free Speech," held by the *First Amendment Law Review* at the University of North Carolina School of Law on October 27, 2017. I further developed the ideas delivering the Richard J. Childress Memorial Lecture at St. Louis University School of Law on October 11, 2019, a part of a symposium titled "American Election Law in a Post-Truth World." Events of January 6, 2021, at the U.S. Capitol unfortunately verified many of the fears I expressed in those earlier writings.

I then received a leave in fall 2020 to complete work on the book thanks to the very generous support of the John S. and James L. Knight Foundation and Craig Newmark Philanthropies. Additional support for research came from the University of California, Irvine, School of Law.

As always, I benefited greatly from the expertise and wisdom of symposium participants and of generous readers of both those original articles and this current draft. I thank the following people who provided very useful comments and suggestions: Floyd Abrams, Bob Bauer, Joe Birkenstock, Ted Boutrous, Bruce Cain, Anupam Chander, Guy Charles, Erwin Chemerinsky, Bobby Chesney, Danielle Citron, Julie Cohen, Ron Collins, evelyn douek, David Ettinger, Chad Flanders, Ned Foley, Howard Gillman, Rebecca Green, Sarah Haan, Daniel Hemel, Steve Kay, David Kaye, Justin Levitt, Michael Morley, Derek Muller, Brendan Nyhan, Norm Ornstein, Nate Persily, Rick Pildes, Ann Ravel, Charlotte Stanton, Brad Smith, Dan Tokaji, Eugene Volokh, and Sonja West. Thanks also to my University of California, Irvine, colleagues who participated in a faculty workshop, as well as colleagues at the Georgetown University Law Center who participated in a workshop when I was a visitor. Thanks as well to the anonymous reader for Yale University Press. Although the book is much improved thanks to these comments, I take full responsibility for remaining errors.

Thanks to Bill Frucht of Yale University Press, whose judgment and editing skills are second to none, to Karen Olson at the Press for help with all manner of logistical issues, to Margaret Otzel and Ann Twombly for excellent production assistance, and to my agent, Melissa Flashman, whose smarts and initiative helped bring this book to life.

University of California, Irvine, School of Law Dean Song Richardson ensured that I had all the resources I needed to complete this project, and she provided enthusiastic encouragement all along the way. Thanks as well to Mary Ann Soden and Dennis Slon, who assisted in obtaining the financial support for this work.

Hannah Bartlett, Kayley Berger, Julia Jones, and Anna Setyaeva provided excellent research assistance. Stacy Tran provided professional and terrific administrative assistance. Erin Hiebert assisted in the preparation of this book's illustrations, and Ellen Augustiniak, Jeff Latta, Dianna Sahhar, and Christina Tsou provided first-rate library support.

Most of all, I thank my wife, Lori Klein, for her unwavering support, sage advice, love, and patience.

I gratefully acknowledge permission to reprint parts of these works:

Cheap Speech and What It Has Done (To American Democracy), 16 First Amendment Law Review 200 (2018)

Deep Fakes, Bots, and Siloed Justices: American Election Law in a Post-Truth World, 64 St. Louis University Law Journal 535 (2020)

Election Meltdown: Dirty Tricks, Distrust, and the Threat to American Democracy 75–80, 83–87 (Yale University Press 2020)

Thanks to Thomas Kennedy for permission to republish his tweet about mailboxes in Wisconsin and to Bruce Mittlesteadt for permission to republish his photograph of the mailboxes that appears in the tweet. And thanks to Matthew Mulligan for assisting in determining the origin of the photograph.

Rick Hasen
Studio City, California
June 2021

Cheap Speech

Clear and Present Danger

The greatest spreader of election disinformation in the 2020 U.S. presidential election season was not a group of Russian hackers operating out of a boiler room in St. Petersburg or a shady political operative deploying anonymous Twitter bots. It was the president of the United States, Donald J. Trump.

Trump's spreading over social media of the "Big Lie" that he had won an election he actually had lost decisively to Joe Biden led to the January 6, 2021, invasion of the U.S. Capitol and violent insurrection by Trump supporters just as Congress was in the middle of confirming Biden's victory in the Electoral College. The invasion put the lives of Vice President Mike Pence and the congressional leadership in danger, and it left 4 Trump supporters dead and 146 law enforcement officers injured. One officer died of apparent natural causes a day after being sprayed with chemicals by protesters, two died by suicide shortly after the insurrection, and two more died by suicide by mid-August 2021. A slightly more successful operation causing the death of American political leadership could have resulted in political upheaval, led to possible military intervention in the transfer of power, and brought down American democracy itself.[1]

Hours later, after D.C. police and the National Guard helped restore order, Congress resumed the vote counting. Despite the melee demonstrating the real-world danger of the Big Lie, 138 Republican House members and 7 Republican senators nonetheless voted to object to the counting of Pennsylvania's Electoral College votes for Biden though there was no evidence of malfeasance or significant error in the state's vote counting. After having weakly labeled some of Trump's false speech about election integrity during the election season, Twitter and Facebook suspended—or "deplatformed"—Trump's social media accounts right after the insurrection, citing the potential for further violence. A week after the insurrection, the House impeached Trump for inciting it, and in February 2021, weeks after Trump left office, 57 senators, including 7 Republicans, voted to convict him, ten votes short of the necessary two-thirds majority. A conviction would have paved the way for a vote to disqualify Trump from running for future office and dealt a big blow not just to Trump but to Trumpism.[2]

The 2020 election season was nothing short of bizarre. It was held during the COVID-19 pandemic, in which tens of millions of Americans voted by mail to avoid unnecessary personal contact with others who could infect them. The massive shift to remote balloting demanded a Herculean effort among election administrators, a major public service campaign to ensure that voters knew how to fill out their ballots accurately and return them on time, and hundreds of millions of dollars in private philanthropic funding (including $350 million from Facebook's Mark Zuckerberg) to keep the election system afloat.[3]

In the summer, when the pandemic had claimed about 150,000 American lives, Trump repeatedly blasted out to his 84 million Twitter followers (and to millions more on Facebook and other forms of social media) false statements about the fairness and security of voting by mail—a method that has been employed since the Civil War and that he, his family, and his associates have regularly used in past elections. Trump even voted by mail in the 2020 primaries, using a third party to return his ballot to Florida election officials (a form of "ballot harvesting" he railed against).[4]

Trump made over 90 statements and tweets in the first half of 2020 about the supposed insecurity of voting by mail, calling the procedure "RIGGED!" and "CORRUPT." And these were just a fraction of the 713 statements and tweets between 2012 and mid-2020 in which he called election procedures and voting into question. By one count, nearly a quarter of Trump's 6,081 Facebook posts during 2020 contained misinformation or extreme rhetoric about the election, COVID-19, or his critics.[5]

He was able to communicate his ideas directly to the public without having to rely on television or radio to amplify his statements, and despite numerous fact checks and articles debunking them. He made his relentlessly repeated unsubstantiated claims even though voter fraud in the contemporary United States is rare, and even though the five states that regularly conduct elections entirely by mail see very low rates of fraud. Harvard researchers writing less than a month before the 2020 election found Trump at the center of a campaign sharing his false claims about voter fraud, using his perch as the president to spread false election information not only on social media but through major media outlets such as the Associated Press and major television networks, which picked up his comments as news. A comprehensive study by the Election Integrity Partnership found Trump at the top of a group of twenty-one prominent right-wing and conservative personalities and entities that were the overwhelming source of election disinformation spread on social media before and after Election Day.[6]

The shift to significant use of vote-by-mail ballots forced by COVID-19, and the refusal of some Republican legislatures to update the rules for processing these ballots before Election Day, caused predictable—and predicted—delays in some states' reporting enough election results to allow news organizations to project a winner. This meant the winner of the 2020 presidential election was unknown on

Election Night and even the next morning. Worse, because Trump had discouraged his supporters from voting by mail by falsely claiming the process was rife with fraud, and because mail-in ballots took longer to process, we experienced a significant "blue shift" in the reporting of results, when predominantly Democratic votes were tallied later in the process. Trump was ahead by 14 percentage points among counted ballots on Election Night in Pennsylvania, when in-person votes were counted first, but Biden eventually won the state by over 80,000 votes as election officials later processed mail-in ballots and included them in the totals.[7]

By the Saturday after Election Day, it was apparent that Joe Biden had sufficient leads in enough states to win the presidency by an Electoral College margin of 306 to 232. Rather than concede the race once the outcome became clear and news networks had called it for Biden, Trump repeatedly and falsely claimed victory—even a "landslide"—arguing that the reported results were marred by fraud, pointing in part to his ephemeral Election Night leads, based on only partial vote counts in key states.[8]

He and his allies brought dozens of suspect lawsuits across the United States calling the election results into question, but once in court, his lawyers did not present any real evidence of significant voter fraud anywhere in the United States. When his lawsuits began to fail, he called on Republican state legislatures to thwart the will of the people by selecting phony slates of Trump electors for the Electoral College. He tried to pressure the Georgia secretary of state to "find" 11,780 votes— one more vote than Biden's margin of victory—to flip the results to Trump. He leaned on Republican governors and the U.S. Department of Justice to help in his effort to declare the results fraudulent. About three weeks after the election Trump, without conceding, allowed the transition process to begin while still falsely claiming voter fraud.[9]

Despite consistent losses in the courts and state legislatures, Trump

Donald J. Trump ✓
@realDonaldTrump

000

...AND I WON THE ELECTION. VOTER FRAUD ALL OVER THE COUNTRY!

⚠ Multiple sources called this election differently

Ⓣ **The New York Times** ✓ @nytimes · Nov 17

President Trump received 10.1 million more votes across the U.S. than he received four years ago, including in areas with a majority of Hispanic voters. nyti.ms/35HqH5P

Show this thread

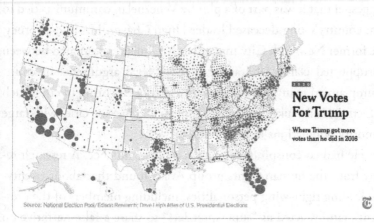

2020
**New Votes
For Trump**

Where Trump got more
votes than he did in 2016

Source: National Election Pool/Edison Research; Dave Leip's Atlas of U.S. Presidential Elections

---

5:31 AM · Nov 18, 2020 · Twitter for iPhone

54.6K Retweets   **10K** Quote Tweets   **246.4K** Likes

💬   ↻   ♡   ⬆

*Screenshot of a now-deleted Donald J. Trump tweet, Nov. 18, 2020, with
Twitter label (archived at https://web.archive.org/web/20201205081925
/https://twitter.com/realDonaldTrump/status/1329054683441278977)*

doubled down on his inflammatory rhetoric, convincing millions of his supporters that Biden had stolen the election. #StopTheSteal, a phrase borrowed from Trump's ally Roger Stone's efforts to prophylactically undermine the results of the 2016 presidential contest between Trump and Hillary Clinton should Clinton have won, became the Trumpist rallying cry. Within three weeks of the election, Trump had made at least four hundred false claims of voter fraud on social media. He repeatedly called the election stolen or rigged. He spread false statements about voting machines flipping votes for Biden. Sidney Powell, a short-lived member of Trump's legal team, bizarrely suggested that it was part of a plot by Venezuelan communists tied to that country's long-deceased leader Hugo Chávez. His lead attorney, the former New York City mayor Rudy Giuliani, alternated between unsupported claims of fraud and poor legal arguments in court. Trump aimed many of his scurrilous attacks on voting in cities such as Detroit, Milwaukee, and Philadelphia, Democratic cities with large minority populations in swing states.[10]

He had co-conspirators and a receptive audience. A research report from the human rights group Avaaz found that about twenty-five leading right-wing personalities, including members of the president's family, acted as "superspreaders" to share a false narrative on social media about election fraud having cost Trump the presidency. The Election Integrity Partnership report showed that some disinformation about the election's being stolen flowed from these superspreaders down to mass audiences; others flowed bottom-up, as conservative influencers seized on out-of-context reports from ordinary Americans about supposed election irregularities to make a claim for widespread election malfeasance. Most Republican leaders, such as Senate Majority Leader Mitch McConnell, conspicuously refused to refute these unsupported fraud allegations, saying Trump had the right to present his claims in court (even though it was quickly clear

Donald J. Trump ✔
@realDonaldTrump

Biden can only enter the White House as President if he can prove that his ridiculous "80,000,000 votes" were not fraudulently or illegally obtained. When you see what happened in Detroit, Atlanta, Philadelphia & Milwaukee, massive voter fraud, he's got a big unsolvable problem!

⚠ This claim about election fraud is disputed

7:56 AM · Nov 27, 2020 · Twitter for iPhone

25.1K Retweets   **7.3K** Quote Tweets   **95.8K** Likes

💬   🔁   ♡   ⬆

Screenshot of a now-deleted Donald J. Trump tweet, Nov. 27, 2020, with Twitter label (archived at https://web.archive.org/web/20201211212108 /https://twitter.com/realDonaldTrump/status/1332352538855747584)

that those claims were frivolous). Others embraced the false claims. As CNN's Donie Sullivan reported, a Republican member of the Wayne County, Michigan, Canvassing Board "who temporarily blocked certification of Detroit's results shared election conspiracy theories on Facebook." The board member "also shared a racist post equating President Obama to an Islamic terrorist that was on Facebook for a DECADE."[11]

Social media companies, including Twitter and Facebook, had to deal with Trump's unprecedented attacks on the integrity of the election system. Back in the spring of 2020, Twitter slapped a label on a pair of Trump's vote-by-mail tweets, in which he accused California of allowing fraud through mail-in balloting. But instead of directly saying the tweets were false, Twitter directed users to "get the facts about mail-in ballots." Users clicking on Twitter's accompanying link saw facts rebutting the president's claims and an explanation by the company stating: "We added a label to two @realDonaldTrump Tweets about California's vote-by-mail plans as part of our efforts to enforce our civic integrity policy. We believe those Tweets could confuse voters about what they need to do to receive a ballot and participate in the election process." But it did not label or remove similar tweets by Trump that offered more general false statements about the insecurity of voting by mail.[12]

In response to Trump's Facebook post stating that "Mail-In Voting, unless changed by the courts, will lead to the most CORRUPT ELECTION in our Nation's history! #RIGGEDELECTION," Facebook added a label reading, "Get official voting info on how to vote in the 2020 US Election at usa.gov." The label did not direct voters to a fact check or state that Trump's tweet was false or unsupported by facts. The website usa.gov just provided information about voter registration. The label may have even suggested to some readers that the site was endorsing Trump's message and providing a path for getting more information about it. As the election progressed, the platforms experimented with additional labels and with requiring users to click through before seeing some content in which Trump made false claims about election integrity. Facebook's internal data reportedly showed that the labels did not appreciably deter the sharing of Trump posts. And Facebook let false information about voter fraud overall get shared with millions of readers during the 2020 election. The company seemed unable or unwilling to keep up with deliberately or inadvertently false information about elections, spread millions of times by users.[13]

As the 2020 election season came to its dramatic end, and as Trump refused to concede, Facebook temporarily tweaked its algorithm—the set of rules Facebook's computers use to determine the content that users receive. Rather than show users just the stuff they wanted to see as driven by their data profile and what they had already clicked on—potentially including unreliable content from right-wing Breitbart or left-wing Occupy Democrats—the company favored more reputable sources such as CNN, the *New York Times,* and NPR. But this "calmer, less divisive Facebook," as the *New York Times* called it, was short-lived, temporarily employing an algorithm designed only for the "break [the] glass" moment when Trump and others fundamentally challenged the election's integrity on social media. Facebook soon restored its original algorithm, feeding up falsehoods and bile.[14]

Meanwhile, Trumpist television viewers shopped around for simpatico content during the period before the insurrection and Congress's final votes formalizing the results. Some of these viewers turned against Fox News, the network known generally for boosting Trump and Republicans. Fox had quickly recognized Biden as president-elect once its decision desk had called the race for him in mid-November 2020, and Fox News debunked some of Trump's voter fraud claims even as some of its opinion shows gave them oxygen. Trump supporters attacked Fox's pundit Tucker Carlson for demanding that Trump's lawyer Sidney Powell provide evidence of her unhinged voting machine claims involving an international communist conspiracy. Some Trumpists abandoned Fox for its competitors Newsmax and One America News Network (OANN), which at first uncritically parroted Trump's election claims. Perhaps to win back its defecting audience, on Thanksgiving 2020 Fox broadcasted in full a Trump fusillade of falsehoods about the election, including the blatant lie that hundreds of thousands of fraudulent votes were cast in every state. Lies shared by the networks over the weeks after the election eventually led to defamation lawsuits brought by voting machine companies against the networks, some of their hosts, and the lawyers Powell and Giuliani, alleging billions of dollars in damages from the false claims that the companies' voting machines fraudulently manipulated election results. The three networks walked a tightrope between giving viewers what they wanted and seeking to avoid liability.[15]

Beginning weeks before Congress's ceremonial counting of the Electoral College votes, after states had confirmed those votes for Biden in mid-December, Trump began inviting his supporters to Washington, D.C., through social media for a "wild" #StopTheSteal protest on January 6. As the House Managers for Trump's second impeachment trial explained in a brief:

> On December 19, [Trump] tweeted: "Statistically impossible to have lost the 2020 Election. Big protest in D.C. on January 6th. Be there, will be wild!" On December 26, he tweeted: "If a Democrat Presidential Candidate had an Election Rigged & Stolen, with proof of such acts at a level never seen before, the Democrat Senators would consider it an act of war, and fight to the death. Mitch & the Republicans do NOTHING, just want to let it pass. NO FIGHT!" Fourteen minutes later, he tweeted again: "The 'Justice' Department and the FBI have done nothing about the 2020 Presidential Election Voter Fraud, the biggest SCAM in our nation's history, despite overwhelming evidence. They should be ashamed. History will remember. Never give up. See everyone in D.C. on January 6th." And on January 1, he tweeted: "The BIG Protest Rally in Washington, D.C., will take place at 11.00 AM on January 6th . . . StopTheSteal!" That same day, Kylie Jane Kremer, the head of Women For America First—a group that had helped organize the Second Million MAGA March on December 12 (which ended in 4 stabbings and 33 arrests)— tweeted a link to the website "Trumpmarch.com." At the top of the post she added, "the cavalry is coming Mr. President!"

President Trump retweeted her post, responding, "A great honor!"[16]

After giving an incendiary speech on January 4 in Georgia in which Trump again falsely claimed that Democrats stole the election, that "you can't let it happen," and that "we're going to fight like hell, I'll tell you right now," Trump further pushed the rally on social media on January 5, the day before Congress was set to confirm the Electoral College votes. Trump tweeted: "Washington is being inundated with people who don't want to see an election victory stolen by emboldened Radical Left Democrats. Our Country has had enough, they won't take it anymore! We hear you (and love you) from the Oval Office. MAKE AMERICA GREAT AGAIN! . . . I hope the Democrats, and even more importantly, the weak and ineffective RINO section of the Republican Party, are looking at the thousands of people pouring into D.C. They won't stand for a landslide election victory to be stolen. @senatemajldr @JohnCornyn @SenJohnThune."[17]

As January 6 neared, Trump had turned to attack his own vice president, Mike Pence. Pence had a ceremonial role before Congress in opening the envelopes containing the Electoral College votes from each state, but Trump pressured Pence publicly and privately to manipulate the process and declare him the winner. Pence made it known he would not do that.[18]

Trump addressed a January 6 rally with thousands of his supporters in person in Washington, D.C., on the Ellipse near the Capitol, claiming again that the election had been rigged. He told his supporters to march to the Capitol and said he would join them there. He told the rallygoers: "We fight like hell. And if you don't fight like hell, you're not going to have a country anymore." He posted video of his rally on social media. Trump did not go to the Capitol building despite saying he would, but his supporters did, some of

Donald J. Trump ✔
@realDonaldTrump

(Follow) ⌄

Peter Navarro releases 36-page report alleging election fraud 'more than sufficient' to swing victory to Trump washex.am/3nwaBCe. A great report by Peter. Statistically impossible to have lost the 2020 Election. Big protest in D.C. on January 6th. Be there, will be wild!

10:42 PM - 18 Dec 2020

67,273 Retweets **219,973** Likes

◯ 31K   ⇄ 67K   ♡ 220K

*Screenshot of a now-deleted Donald J. Trump tweet, Dec. 18, 2020
(archived at https://web.archive.org/web/20201220160229/https://
twitter.com/realdonaldtrump/status/1340185773220515840)*

whom he inspired to violence. According to a federal indictment of a Capitol invader named Kelly Meggs, "The self-described leader of the Florida chapter of the [right-wing militant group] Oath Keepers," in late December "Meggs wrote in a Facebook message, 'Trump said It's gonna be wild!!!!!!! It's gonna be wild!!!!!!! He wants us to make it WILD that's what he's saying. He called us all to the Capitol and wants us to make it wild!!! Sir Yes Sir!!! Gentlemen we are heading to DC pack your s***!!' He went on to state, '[W]e will have at least 50–100 OK there.'"[19]

Facebook "Groups" played a key role in the organizing for the January 6 activities and in spreading election disinformation. The Election Integrity Partnership report described how a Facebook "STOP THE STEAL" Group grew to 320,000 users in less than one day until Facebook shut it down and users were forced to join smaller, similar groups. Facebook knew its Groups feature could help facilitate violence. According to the *Wall Street Journal:* "The company's data scientists had warned Facebook executives in August [2020] that what they called blatant misinformation and calls to violence were filling the majority of the platform's top 'civic' Groups, according to documents The Wall Street Journal reviewed. Those Groups are generally dedicated to politics and related issues and collectively reach hundreds of millions of users. The researchers told executives that 'enthusiastic calls for violence every day' filled one 58,000-member Group, according to an internal presentation. Another top Group claimed it was set up by fans of Donald Trump but it was actually run by 'financially motivated Albanians' directing a million views daily to fake news stories and other provocative content."[20]

Some of Trump's most ardent supporters overwhelmed U.S. Capitol Police and stormed the building, entering several parts of the Capitol, including the Senate chamber where Pence had been presiding over a claim of objections brought by a group of senators led by Republican Senator Ted Cruz and some Republican House members against the results in Arizona. As some of the protesters chanted, "Hang Mike Pence!" and others invaded the office of Speaker of the House Nancy Pelosi, the mob was in some cases seconds away from confronting and perhaps harming or even killing American political leaders. One police officer lost an eye, and others suffered broken ribs or spinal disks and concussions. Invaders tased one officer so many times that he had a heart attack. Three Capitol police officers were dead within days of the riot.[21]

Well after Trump learned of the breach of the Capitol, while the insurrection was in full swing and Pence's safety uncertain, Trump tweeted again against Mike Pence: "Mike Pence didn't have the courage to do what should have been done to protect our Country and our Constitution, giving States a chance to certify a corrected set of facts, not the fraudulent or inaccurate ones which they were asked to previously certify. USA demands the truth!" After being implored by Republican leaders to call for his violent supporters in the Capitol to stand down, Trump issued a few tweets calling on his supporters to stay peaceful. Hours later, he posted a new video on social media. As the House Mangers for Trump's impeachment trial in the Senate described it: "The next action that President Trump took—while the violence persisted and escalated—occurred more than three hours from the start of the siege. At this point, he released a scripted video that included a call for 'peace' and 'law and order,' and instructed his followers, 'you have to go home now.' But even in that video, President Trump continued to provoke violence, telling his supporters— who were *at that very moment* committing violence inside the Capitol and terrorizing Members of Congress—that the election was 'stolen from us.' He added that '[i]t was a landslide election and everyone knows it, especially the other side.' He concluded by telling the violent insurrectionists: 'We love you, you're very special. . . . I know how you feel. But go home and go home in peace.'"[22]

Additional law enforcement officers arrived at the Capitol and restored order after a few-hour delay that may have been caused by Trump's not immediately authorizing the National Guard's deployment. Congress came back into session and the vote counting resumed. Despite the day's remarkable events demonstrating the threat to American democracy, Missouri's Republican Senator Josh Hawley joined with House members to lodge a frivolous objection against counting Pennsylvania's Electoral College votes for Biden, triggering an additional round of separate voting in the Senate and House. The challenge failed, just as the earlier Arizona challenge had, and after three o'clock in the morning of what was now January 7, Congress finished its work of accepting all the Electoral College votes submitted by the states and Washington, D.C., as valid. Pence declared Biden the winner. Georgia state authorities began investigating Trump for potential criminal election law violations in seeking to alter the official vote count.[23]

In the wake of the insurrection, first Twitter and then Facebook suspended Trump from their platforms, citing the danger of continued violence. Deplatforming came after months of internal and external struggle, and almost no punishment had been doled out to Trump beforehand as the Big Lie spread. Deplatforming led Trump supporters to new outlets, including Parler, a Twitter-like competitor favored by those on the right. As Parler continued to allow dissemination of election disinformation and calls for violence following the insurrection, hosting companies, including Amazon, suspended Parler's service, knocking the platform out for weeks until it found a new host. Apple and Google removed the Parler app from their app stores, making the platform harder to access. Months later, the "Oversight Board" that Facebook created to independently review its content-moderation decisions affirmed the company's decision to deplatform Trump in the wake of Trump's posts involving the election and the Capitol violence. The board sent the issue back to Facebook to adopt rules for determining if and when Trump's suspension from the platform should end. Facebook then announced that Trump's ban would last for at least two years and that he would be restored to the platform only if the risk to public safety had receded.[24]

Trump's flood of dangerous electoral lies in the run-up to and aftermath of the 2020 election could not have surprised these companies. The 2016 election season had seen an explosion of disinformation and political manipulation aimed at influencing the presidential election, some spread by the Russian government. One of the most pernicious Russian activities was an attempt to suppress the votes of African Americans, who were overwhelmingly likely to vote for Hillary Clinton; the Russians posted anti-Clinton material on social media accounts meant to appear as representing the views of African American citizens. In the wake of public criticism for their inaction that year, the platforms had pledged to move more aggressively to counter bad conduct. Facebook promised to remove posts demonstrating "coordinated inauthentic behavior," such as the Russians' "Blacktivist" network of 2016.[25]

The Russians appear to have been minor social media players in 2020, but Representative Adam Schiff, head of the House Intelligence Committee, suggested the existence of clandestine Russian government efforts in 2020 to amplify Trump's false claims about voting by mail. Much of that Russian activity, if it was happening, did not break American law.[26]

The content decisions of the platforms in the 2020 election season were as momentous as they were unregulated. As private companies, they could decide how prominently, if at all, to share the president's and others' posts. They could demote the posts so that they received little coverage or highlight them as they wished, undeterred by any government oversight or disclosure.

The algorithms by which the platforms decided which candidates and posts to highlight, link, or demote were a black box. Even inadvertent choices could influence voter decisions. A BuzzFeed investigation published in August 2020 found that Instagram, a social media site owned by Facebook, favored Trump over his 2020 Democratic rival, Joe Biden, when users searched for the candidates' names. "For at least the last two months," BuzzFeed reported, "a key Instagram feature, which algorithmically pushes users toward supposedly related content, has been treating hashtags associated with President Donald Trump and presumptive Democratic presidential nominee Joe Biden in very different ways. Searches for Biden also return a variety of pro-Trump messages, while searches for Trump-related topics only returned the specific hashtags, like #MAGA or #Trump—which means searches for Biden-related hashtags also return counter-messaging, while those for Trump do not." The company blamed a "technical error."[27]

The platforms were in a difficult spot. On the one hand, they faced enormous pressure not to repeat the mistakes of 2016 and allow false, misleading, and foreign-sourced polarizing social media posts to influence election outcomes. On the other hand, conservatives had been accusing them of censorship or favoring liberal viewpoints when they went after Trump and other public figures on the right for objectively false statements. The evidence showed that if anything, Facebook had a bias in favor of not removing or demoting false information posted by conservatives and Trump supporters. Facebook senior officials overrode the company's internal rules, which would have punished some prominent conservative sites for repeatedly sharing misinformation. If conservatives or Trump social media users were spreading more false information, then a fair system would remove more of those users' content.[28]

Even if Twitter and Facebook had committed to removing demonstrably false statements about the mechanics of voting from the beginning of the 2020 election season, many of Trump's pre-election statements, like his #RIGGEDELECTION post, were perhaps not *lit-*

erally false: Trump was making a prediction—although surely unsupported by evidence—about what would happen with mail-in balloting in the 2020 election. The First Amendment does not limit the platforms, which are private companies, from including or excluding whatever content or viewpoints they want, but it was unclear where they should draw the line. They could aim to weed out "voter suppression." But if Trump's tweet is seen as an effort at voter suppression, lots of posts aimed at discouraging partisans from supporting their candidates might be swept into that definition too, which would require the platforms to make difficult and frequent judgment calls.

Allowing robust debate during an election season is an important American value. Even if Congress passed a law mandating that the platforms remove false statements by politicians, and even if the courts upheld such a law as permissible under the First Amendment (both dubious propositions), who would decide if Trump's posts were "false" and merited removal? Legislation barring false candidate speech could be dangerous to American democracy.

How to deal with Trump's voting tweets was a much harder question than how to police false posts related to COVID-19. The platforms removed content from both Trump and his son Donald Trump Jr. that promoted false virus information. The president's posts included false statements he made on Fox News about the danger of the virus to children; Trump Jr. linked to a video containing false COVID-19 treatment information. In the case of COVID-19, the platforms could rely on verifiable medical information. Voting issues are more contested.[29]

And even if the platforms made a conscious decision to remove demonstrably false information, they showed they either would not or could not deal with issues in real time and at scale. In July 2020 Facebook took more than thirteen hours to remove a video posted by the right-wing website Breitbart falsely claiming that COVID-19 could be prevented with hydroxychloroquine. It got millions of views during that time. Twitter temporarily suspended the account of Donald Trump Jr. for sharing that false information with his millions of followers. At the time, Facebook included Breitbart as one of its "trusted" sources of news despite the right-wing website's record of concocting and amplifying false information.[30]

If Facebook could not quickly deal with scientifically false information about the virus, how could it decide in real time what to do about debatable election misinformation? What would Twitter do if on the eve of an election someone posted a doctored video purportedly showing one of the presidential candidates collapsing during some kind of health crisis or making racist comments? Did the platforms wait too long to deplatform Trump, risking the health of American democracy, or is removal of a political leader a kind of private "censorship" that the powerful companies should not have been allowed to undertake?

Welcome to the world of cheap speech.

The Lost Promise of "Cheap Speech"

In a remarkably prescient article in a 1995 *Yale Law Journal* symposium titled "Emerging Media Technology and the First Amendment," a UCLA law professor, Eugene Volokh, looked ahead to the coming Internet era. The article, "Cheap Speech and What It Will Do," predicted the rise of streaming music and video services such as Spotify and Netflix, the emergence of handheld tablets for reading books, the demise of classified advertising in the newspaper business, and more generally how the dramatically decreased costs of disseminating written, audio, and visual content, which Volokh termed "cheap speech," would create radical new opportunities for readers, viewers, and listeners to custom-design what they read, see, and hear, while undermining the power of intermediaries, including publishers and bookstore owners.[31]

Volokh found these changes exciting and democratizing. Understandably, his predictions were not perfect—for example, he thought we would be using high-speed printers to print out columns from our favorite newspaper columnists, and he grossly underestimated how cheap speech would wreck the newspaper business. And despite his optimism, he also saw some dark sides, such as the lowering of costs for hate groups like the Ku Klux Klan to organize and share ideas. But his overall picture of the coming cheap speech era was positive. Volokh asked: "Will listeners do a better job of informing themselves than the intermediaries have been doing? When the media aren't there to help set a national agenda, or to give people a common base of information to argue from, will people be able to deliberate together? I think the answer to both questions is yes, but others . . . disagree."[32]

Two and a half decades later, the picture of what cheap speech has done and is likely to do—in particular to American democracy—is considerably darker. No doubt cheap speech has increased convenience, dramatically lowered the cost of obtaining information, and spurred the creation and consumption of content from radically diverse sources. But the economics of cheap speech have undermined the mediating and stabilizing institutions of American democracy, including newspapers and political parties, a situation that has had severe social and political consequences for American elections. In place of media scarcity we now have a media firehose that has diluted trusted sources of information and led to the rise of "fake news"—falsehoods and propaganda spread by domestic and foreign sources for their own political and pecuniary purposes. The demise of local newspapers sets the stage for increased corruption among state and local officials.[33]

Rather than improving our politics, cheap speech makes political parties increasingly irrelevant by allowing demagogues to appeal directly and repeatedly at virtually no cost to voters for financial and electoral support, with incendiary appeals and often with lies. Social media can both increase intolerance and overcome collective action obstacles, allowing for peaceful protest but also supercharging polarization and raising the danger of violence, as we saw with the January 6, 2021, insurrection.[34]

The decline of the traditional media as information intermediaries has transformed—and coarsened—social and political communication, making it easier for misinformation and vitriol to spread. Political campaigns go forward under conditions of voter mistrust and groupthink, increasing the potential for foreign interference and domestic political manipulation through ever more sophisticated technological tools. These dramatic changes raise important questions about the conditions of electoral legitimacy and threaten to shake the foundation of democratic governance.

Cheap speech—speech that is both inexpensive to produce and often of markedly low social value—raises deep concerns whether disseminated on social media, search engines, news cable channels, or otherwise. Platform technology allows politically and morally objectionable manipulation of the information used for voter choice. Viral anonymous speech, spread partly through "bots"—automated programs that communicate directly with users—lowers the accountability costs for sharing false information and manipulated content. It deprives voters of valuable information to judge the credibility of the messages directed at them. Platforms gather an unprecedented amount of intrusive data on people's backgrounds, interests, and choices, which allows campaigns to "microtarget" advertising, such as by sending one set of messages to older white male voters and another to young African American women. The practice drives profits for the platforms, but it can also fuel polarization and political manipulation. Political operatives may deploy microtargeting for negative messaging intended to depress voter turnout. The platforms' design may encourage extremism through the algorithms used to offer voters additional, more worrisome content similar to what they or their social media friends and contacts have chosen. Those who can control platform content may help one candidate and hurt another. Platforms influence elections when they make choices about whether to promote or remove content, including false content.

Cheap Speech and the First Amendment

The Supreme Court's current First Amendment doctrine did not cause the democracy problems associated with the rise of cheap speech, but it may stand in the way of reform, especially with the new conservative supermajority now in control. Most of the Court's conservative justices are inconsistent libertarians. Justice Clarence Thomas, for example, believes virtually all campaign finance laws violate the First Amendment, but he recently suggested that the government could force social media platforms to carry content from Trump and other politicians with whom they don't want to be associated.

The Court's jurisprudence may stymie efforts to limit foreign money flowing into elections, including money used to propagate disinformation. And the Court's reluctance to allow the government to regulate false political speech could block laws aimed at requiring social media sites to curb false information about when, where, and how to vote. The Court might even stand in the way of data privacy rules that could protect voters from manipulative, targeted messages. And that same Court may uphold rules requiring social media platforms to carry politicians' messages encouraging violence.

Much of the Court's First Amendment doctrine is premised on an outmoded "marketplace of ideas" model in which citizens debate ideas publicly and the truth rises to the top. Whether this marketplace vision ever accurately represented political speech in the United States—and today many First Amendment scholars believe it never did—it does not do so now. Promoters of conspiracism such as QAnon flourish on the web. Many people disbelieve basic scientific evidence, such as that about the spread of COVID-19 and the means to combat it. Millions of Republican voters believe, despite all reliable evidence, that the 2020 election was stolen from Donald Trump. Voters have a harder time distinguishing legitimate news and analysis from propaganda and lies. Voter confidence in traditional media is deteriorating, especially among voters on the right. Much communication now takes place in private social media groups, where counterspeech and fact checking are impossible. The marketplace of ideas is experiencing market failure.

The Supreme Court's reluctance to allow regulation of most political speech is partly right; First Amendment doctrine serves as a bulwark against government censorship and oppression that might be undertaken in an ostensible effort to battle "fake news." We do not want the cure to be worse than the disease, despite the serious problems with the marketplace approach. Some adjustments nonetheless seem not only necessary but urgently so.

Some shifts in First Amendment doctrine would help citizens ascertain the truth and also bolster stabilizing and mediating institutions, preserving both the fairness of elections and American democracy itself. But there is reason to worry the current Supreme Court will not recognize the need for a shift in legal doctrine.

Nevertheless, there is precedent for the Court's changing its understanding of the First Amendment over time. In the early twentieth century, the Court gave the government great leeway to limit the speech of those who advocated revolution and other radical ideas. Justices Oliver Wendell Holmes and Louis Brandeis pushed back against this extensive government power to curtail antigovernment speech, arguing that the First Amendment permitted the government to limit such speech only if it presented a "clear and present danger" to the public welfare. In 1969, in *Brandenburg v. Ohio,* the Supreme Court built on Holmes and Brandeis's previous minority view to impose a stronger speech-protective standard, holding that the government could not proscribe inflammatory political speech unless it was directed to incite or produce "imminent lawless action." That allowed for a great deal of political speech that otherwise might have been chilled.[35]

The shift in the First Amendment doctrine expressed in *Brandenburg* was right at the time because of the importance then—and now—of dissent against government action, whether about going to war or dealing with a pandemic. The government should not be able to muzzle those who would argue for radical change in government and society, short of threatening imminent violence to get there.

The clear and present danger we face today, however, is not simply government censorship. While we cannot dismiss the risk of censorship as an unintended consequence of reform, the greatest danger today is a public that cannot determine truth or make voting decisions that are based on accurate information, and a public susceptible to political manipulation through repeatedly amplified, data-targeted, election-related content, some of it false or misleading. The events of January 6, 2021, show that incendiary rhetoric spread on social media can fuel a real-life political insurrection and undermine confidence in fair elections. Modern First Amendment doctrine should reflect radically changed circumstances, albeit duly sensitive of the real dangers posed by government regulation.

The collapse of the economic market for reliable journalism, especially on the local level, and the emergence of a disinformation era have undermined voters' ability to make informed decisions and opened the door to what some call voter suppression. We must consider the extent to which it is possible, given these new conditions and in a way consistent with a realistic appreciation of the First Amendment, to change election laws to bolster democratic self-governance. Some legal changes are necessary but not sufficient to sustain our democracy. Especially if the Supreme Court rejects some of these necessary changes under its First Amendment doctrine, saving American democracy will also require private action such as donation models to support local journalism and consumer pressure on social media and search companies to rein in election disinformation.

Many of the questions raised in this book have a precursor of sorts in the debate over the desirability and constitutionality of laws regulating money in politics. In the past, Congress and other legislative bodies imposed limits on election funding, such as barring corporations and labor unions from contributing directly to candidates, and these limits faced First Amendment challenges in court. Some believe that efforts to limit big money in politics not only have been futile but have exacerbated political ills such as polarization by fueling less accountable outside groups. I draw on lessons learned from the campaign finance fights, including unintended consequences, in suggesting the kinds of change we require now. We need to consider explicitly how to avoid changes that would make the situation worse.

We also need to recognize how knotty the problems are. For example, many—although not all—American voters believe that the government should be allowed to bar foreign interference in U.S. elections in order to preserve the interest in democratic self-government. Under this interest, "We the People," and not outsiders, should debate who can best lead our country, states, and communities. It is easy to say under this principle that the Russian government should not masquerade as African American voters to persuade real Americans not to vote for Hillary Clinton as president. It is quite another to say that the *Guardian*, a British newspaper, should not be allowed to place an advertisement on Facebook enticing American readers to read its editorial about who would make the best U.S. president. Crafting a law that prohibits some foreign election-related speech but allows other speech is tough. Line-drawing problems and slippery slopes are everywhere in the cheap speech world. I try to confront these difficulties head-on.

Another problem is figuring out which reforms can actually work. For example, in the chapters below I advocate enhanced disclosure rules. But disclosure works only if voters update their views on the basis of additional credible information, and some social science evidence indicates that especially during a period of hard polarization like our current one, emotional attachments, motivated reasoning, and negative partisanship may swamp accurate information. I try not to oversell the proposals, and I advocate multiple paths forward in the hope that at least some will be successful.

Chapter 2 of this book describes how the cheap speech era has threatened American democracy. It considers problems such as the loss of voter competence and decreasing officeholder accountability stemming from the demise of local newspapers; foreign interference in American elections; the rise of misinformation and disinformation both generally and related specifically to voting, and the asymmetric inflation of false information on the American right; the increased conspiracy theory acceptance and potential for election-related violence; a rising tide of anonymous campaign activity; the ways in which social media enables polarization; the escalation of demagoguery and the potential for corruption as political parties and traditional media weaken; and the threat of algorithmic manipulation through and by social media platforms. It explains how many of these problems have been exacerbated by the current hyperpolarized period in American politics and have also exacerbated that polarization, and it seeks to separate problems with American democracy caused primarily by polarization from those caused primarily by the rise of cheap speech, recognizing that the two phenomena are interacting synergistically.

Chapter 3 asks what law can do to fix American democracy. There is no single answer because cheap speech causes multiple problems. After first explaining that running a sound and fair election system can dilute the potency of disinformation about the election process itself, it surveys potential fixes that are consistent with a democracy-enhancing reading of the First Amendment. Fair and transparent election administration, which raises none of the First Amendment problems discussed elsewhere in this book, is the most important step to counter false information about election integrity.

Other measures to ameliorate the harmful effects of cheap speech that do implicate First Amendment concerns include increased disclosure of the funders of both online ads and mass, coordinated online activities aimed at influencing elections; labeling deep fakes and other synthetic media as "altered"; tightening the ban on campaign expenditures by nonmedia foreign persons, entities, and governments; enacting a narrow ban on empirically verifiable false election speech about when, where, and how people vote (but not barring campaign speech about candidates' positions); supporting private lawsuits for defamation that may deter some false statements about elections; prohibiting microtargeting of political advertising; and potentially adopting more radical laws that might limit platform bias, such as requiring disclosure about algorithmic discrimination for or against candidates, applying antitrust law to break up some of the larger companies into smaller ones, and even barring advanced data collection by the platforms entirely.

I reject proposed laws that directly mandate platform evenhandedness or "fairness," by requiring the platforms to carry speech of all politicians or that ban speech that some believe counts as "voter sup-

CLEAR AND PRESENT DANGER

pression," except those covered by the false election speech prohibition. Such laws would be overly broad and impossible to administer, and they would put too much discretion to police speech in the hands of government actors. They do more harm than good.

I also evaluate my proposed reforms in light of the debate over the meaning of the First Amendment. I explain how the Supreme Court's outmoded free speech doctrine could stymie efforts to save American democracy from the cheap speech era, and how to best interpret the First Amendment to respond to current challenges while preserving public and virtual space as arenas for robust political debate.

Passing new laws and reforming Supreme Court doctrine are not enough. Chapter 4 takes up solutions to the problems of cheap speech that go beyond what the law can do. That discussion is necessary not just because I expect that some of the changes I advocate might not be enacted or could be blocked by the Supreme Court, but also because even implementing all the changes suggested in chapter 3 would not be enough. There must also be private action, including pressure on social media companies and other platforms to make changes in response to serious democracy problems caused by cheap speech, even deplatforming political figures, such as Trump, in extreme circumstances. Some of these changes are off-limits to governments because of the First Amendment—but platforms may adopt them voluntarily. These include subsidizing and bolstering real, and especially local, investigative journalism efforts and a concomitant effort to minimize the reach of counterfeit news sites; strengthening and building reliable intermediaries and institutions that engage in truth telling and can counter the tsunami of election disinformation; and inculcating the values of truth, respect for science, and the rule of law.

Chapter 4 concludes by explaining that the battle over election disinformation and other social ills for American elections caused by the emergence of cheap speech ideally requires both legal and private actions. Without adequate legal change approved by the Supreme Court, private actions may fail to protect American democracy. The matter is urgent, and the stakes could not be higher.

Other Problems

It is important that I say something about what this book is not. I come to these questions from the point of view of someone who has long studied American election law and related First Amendment issues. I am not an expert on social media or technology, and I do not purport to be able to explain exactly *how* technology might be harnessed in the future to influence elections and American democracy. A broad understanding of the scope of technological change is enough for my arguments. I also do not deal with non-speech-related technological dirty tricks that may influence elections, such as foreign or domestic actors hacking into voter registration databases or voting machines.[36]

I do not weigh in on other key questions about the intersection of cheap speech and society, such as the loss of privacy and the potential for government to rein in the nonconsensual sharing of sexual images. I enter the debate over the immunity provided to Internet service providers under Section 230 of the Communications Decency Act only to the extent that it bears on American democracy and election law. I do not analyze the national security implications of deep fakes or other synthetic media, again except to the extent they may undermine American elections.[37]

These are all vital issues, better explored by those with relevant expertise. This book asks only: How does cheap speech threaten fair American elections, and what can we do about it? This is more than enough to try to get right.

2

More Speech, More Problems

The Market for Lemons

In 1970 the *Quarterly Journal of Economics* published a twelve-page article by the economist George Akerlof called "The Market for 'Lemons.'" Akerlof, who later shared a Nobel Prize for this work, looked at how information asymmetries could adversely affect economic markets, and what to do about the problem. His leading example was the market for used cars.[1]

Using the kind of plain English no longer found in economics journals, Akerlof explained that buyers shopping for a used car have difficulty determining whether a seller is offering a reliable used car or a "lemon." The seller knows the car's quality from experience. Potential buyers, lacking such knowledge, make lower offers, discounting the offering price by the probability that the car will be unreliable. The depressed price for used cars caused by the information asymmetry drives better-quality cars out of the market because potential sellers who own high-quality used cars are less willing to sell them at a lower price. With a higher proportion of lemons now in the market, buyers discount their offers even more, and the downward spiral continues. Akerlof proposed some ways out of this "market failure," which I take up later in the book.

In the cheap speech era, the market for political information is coming to resemble Akerlof's used car market. Bad information is driving out good, and voters discount all information as potentially unreliable. This market failure undermines basic conditions of democratic governance: voters must be able to get enough reliable and accurate information about the state of the world to permit them to vote in line with their interests and values and have confidence in a fair and impartial election system.

How did we get here? Why is it that the flood of speech facilitated by the Internet and social media revolution does not always promote better decision making by voters? Isn't more speech always better for voters?

There is no doubt that the rise of the Internet and social media has had many free speech benefits. We worry much less about media consolidation and scarcity of information than we did when there were just three main broadcast television networks and a handful of local newspapers in each area. Today, readers and viewers receive information from vastly more, and more diverse, sources. It is possible to make one's ideas available to a huge audience without being wealthy or an employee of a large media corporation. Information that was once available only at a world-class library is now at our fingertips with a smartphone, a computer, or even a watch. New sources of ideas and information can benefit democracy.[2]

But this communications revolution has also produced significant downsides, the most important the demise of the business model that supported newspapers and news reporting. As classified advertising and other forms of advertising moved from newspapers to the Internet, and from the Internet to social media, newspapers lost their key source of revenue. Some elite national outlets, such as the *New York Times,* successfully adapted to a subscription-based model and are thriving financially, but many local newspapers, which have trouble generating enough money from subscriptions and have seen advertising revenue plummet, have closed or drastically cut back their operations. Hedge funds purchased some legacy newspaper chains and effectively dismantled the news organizations or sold off key assets, such as a newspaper's physical building. Some areas of the country are now "news deserts," with no local newspaper coverage at all.[3]

In 2001 the journalism industry employed some 411,800 people. By 2016 the number had fallen below 174,000. In 2019 alone about 7,800 American journalists were laid off or offered a buyout, and things got much worse during the COVID-19 pandemic. These latest losses are on top of a tremendous decline in the industry as a whole; another study found that journalism jobs fell 23 percent from 2008 to 2017, and 65 percent over the last two decades. Journalists lost their jobs at a faster rate than coal miners.[4]

The advertising money that once supported newspapers is now flowing to digital media platforms, mostly Facebook and Google. According to reporting by the *Guardian,* between 2000 and 2015 newspaper print advertising revenue declined from $60 billion to $20 billion per year. "In constant 2014 dollars, advertising revenues [for newspapers in 2014] were $3.6 billion (and 18%) below the $20 billion spent in 1950, 62 years ago." Meanwhile, Google and Facebook collected 59 percent of digital advertising revenue in 2019 and were on track for a $77-billion year in advertising revenues before the pandemic hit. Amazon is beginning to increase its market share as well.[5]

The *Washington Post* columnist (and former *New York Times* public editor) Margaret Sullivan wrote in her book *Ghosting the News* that though much attention has been focused on the fake news problem, the crisis in local journalism is happening quietly: "Some of the most trusted sources of news—local sources, particularly local newspapers—are slipping away, never to return." There is little reason to expect local television stations, even if they continue to survive, to do the kinds of investigative journalism that local newspapers once conducted.[6]

This collapse of journalism has enormous implications for American democracy. A recent *Journal of Politics* article by Danny Hayes and Jennifer Lawless concluded that without strong local coverage, voters tend to be less politically engaged and less likely to share opinions about candidates and representatives. A 2020 survey by Gallup and the Knight Foundation showed that "Americans who follow local news closely are more likely to vote in local elections and to feel attached to their communities. They are less likely to say that 'people like me don't have any say in what the government does.'" As Leonard Downie Jr. and Michael Schudson argue, "What is under threat is independent *reporting* that provides information, investigation, analysis, and community knowledge, particularly in the coverage of local affairs."[7]

These analyses flag the obvious problem with the decline of (especially local) journalism: the loss of relevant information for voters. Without journalists making freedom-of-information requests, attending government meetings, following up on tips from whistleblowers, and generally keeping an eye on government, much information valuable to voters will never see the light of day. As we will see, this can lead to an increase in political corruption and a lack of officeholder accountability.

But voters also face a more complex and less obvious problem. At the same time that the Internet killed journalism's business model, it dramatically lowered the cost of disseminating unreliable information, or social media lemons. Less and less are news media playing the critical curating role of the trusted intermediary. There is no modern-day equivalent of someone like CBS News's Walter Cronkite, the mid-twentieth-century television anchor who could convey accurate information in ways that most Americans could accept. In current times of political polarization, when a television newscaster or the *New York Times* said that then-President Trump was lying about the danger of voting by mail, many people who have a favorable view of Trump disbelieved the reporting despite the lopsided evidence on the question. Worse, it was so easy to find news and opinion outlets that would parrot Trump's views that most of these people never even looked at the *Times* or non-right-wing television to begin with. They heard only that voting by mail was rife with fraud and never heard the evidence to the contrary.

Today, any tech-savvy person can create a website that looks as legitimate and impressive as the news site of a bona fide media organization employing rigorous journalistic standards. The ease of sharing social media posts or tweets allows the viral spread of false information, both inadvertent *mis*information and intentional *dis*information.[8]

Some political outfits have even set themselves up as "news" organizations, using sites that are aimed at convincing voters to vote a certain way but that contain just enough news to evade both social media platform rules about political advertising and campaign finance rules requiring political committees to register with the Federal Election Commission and report their expenditures and contributions. Take the activities of the group Acronym, a Democratic-oriented political group whose affiliated company Shadow was responsible for creating the failed app used in the botched 2020 Iowa caucuses. Another Acronym affiliate, Courier Newsroom, established what look like local news sites but are actually propaganda sites providing content to be shared on social media to boost moderate Democrats.

Acronym is taking advantage of the implosion of local news sites. Rather than re-create viable local news media with an emphasis on trustworthiness, Acronym's goal, according to an internal memo posted by Vice News, is to provide shareable viral pseudo–"news content" to boost its preferred candidates. A Politico analysis in July 2020 found that "Courier has spent over $1.4 million on Facebook ads this election cycle, mostly to promote its flattering articles and videos about more than a dozen endangered House Democrats at the top of the Democratic Party's priority list this November, according to Facebook's political ad tracker." Without a hint of irony, a Fox News story describes Courier as a "liberal, dark-money-funded" organization.[9]

Tara McGowan, CEO of Acronym, troublingly told Vice News that "Courier journalists have full editorial independence. Asked whether they had license to report freely on Democratic politicians or were tasked with, as the [internal memo] says, 'Reach[ing] voters with strategic narratives + information year-round,' she said, 'I don't know what the difference between the two is.'" In other words, the goal here is promoting certain Democratic candidates and not providing fair and accurate information to voters when accuracy conflicts with promotion. McGowan appeared to simply assume that accurate information inevitably helps Democratic candidates.[10]

Conservatives seem to be ahead of liberals in creating fake news organizations. Brian Timpone, a former news reporter, created a network of 1,300 sites that were disguised as local news sites but actually were one big pay-to-play operation. The network paid journalists as little as three to thirty-five dollars per story to write positive articles for conservative clients, Republican candidates, and think tanks. The clients paid specifically for positive coverage, but the financial arrangements were not disclosed. As the *New York Times* explained: "While Mr. Timpone's sites generally do not post information that is outright false, the operation is rooted in deception, eschewing hallmarks of news reporting like fairness and transparency. Only a few dozen of the sites disclose funding from advocacy groups. Traditional news organizations do not accept payment for articles; the Federal Trade Commission requires that advertising that looks like articles be clearly labeled as ads."[11]

It gets worse. As social media companies started cracking down on attempted Russian interference in American elections, Russians in 2020 shifted to hiring actual American journalists to write stories as freelance writers, or "stringers," for their publications. They consistently urged progressive voters not to support the Democratic nominee, Joe Biden. According to the *Washington Post*, "Facebook said the operatives created fictitious personas on Facebook to direct people to a new site called Peace Data, which billed itself as a 'global news organization' whose goal was 'to shed light on the global issues and raise awareness about corruption, environmental crisis, abuse of power, armed conflicts, activism, and human rights.'" According to the *Post*, "One of the journalists who wrote columns for Peace Data . . . said that an editor reached out to him through a direct message on Twitter in July offering $200 per article. He said he pursued the opportunity in part because he had lost his job in the pandemic. He wrote articles about the conspiracy-theory movement QAnon, the coronavirus, and U.S. militarism's role in climate change. The journalist, who said he considers himself a socialist, said he had not been informed by Facebook and had no idea that the website, while appearing disorganized, was run by a Russian group."[12]

As barriers to entry into media space have dropped, the public's trust in traditional media has fallen, and social media has emerged as an ideal vehicle for delivering falsehoods and propaganda disguised as news. The 2020 Gallup and Knight Foundation public opinion survey of media attitudes found that 81 percent of Americans believe that the news media are "critical" or very important for democracy. Yet a majority troublingly see "a great deal" or a "fair amount" of bias in news coverage, which they attribute to reporters misrepresenting the facts or making them up entirely. And there is a huge partisan divide on attitudes toward the media. "Two-thirds of Republicans (67%) have a 'very' or 'somewhat' unfavorable opinion of the news media, compared to 20% of Democrats and 48% of independents."[13]

Americans also worry about misinformation. According to the

same survey, 74 percent of respondents "say the spread of misinformation online is 'a major problem'"; "seventy percent . . . want to see major internet companies find ways to exclude false/hateful information online," and "more Americans say it is harder (60%) rather than easier (38%) to be well-informed because of all the sources of information available. In 2017, 58% said it was harder to be informed." The worry about misinformation is well-founded. Studies demonstrate that websites containing misleading content often succeed in misleading Americans, especially when the misinformation supports a reader's or viewer's ideological predispositions.[14]

Professors Hunt Allcott and Matthew Gentzkow explained the social costs of virally spread false information: voters and consumers are worse off when they believe false statements because the information environment makes it harder for them to choose high-quality candidates. Voters also may become subject to the lemons effect and discount all information as potentially fake, reducing the incentives for journalists and others to produce truthful, useful information.[15] Misinformation about the integrity of the election process is especially dangerous because an election depends on the losers' accepting the election results as legitimate, agreeing to recognize the winners, and gearing up for the next fair election.

A recent study by Michael Thaler showed that people overestimate the truth of news reports that are in line with their preexisting beliefs, discount those that are contrary to those beliefs, and overestimate their ability to tell true from false statements. Other studies offer a bit more hope that people can separate some truthful statements from false statements, and that targeted fact checking may help a little. But it is a constant battle against a flood of misinformation; a 2020 report from the online advocacy organization Avaaz found 3.8 billion views on Facebook of misleading health content during a one-year period, peaking during the COVID-19 pandemic. "The report found that content from 10 'superspreader' sites sharing health misinformation had almost four times as many Facebook views in April 2020 as equivalent content from the sites of 10 leading health institutions, such as the World Health Organization and the Centers for Disease Control and Prevention." Another study showed that fact checks reduce belief in misinformation but don't stop people from spreading it, at least on Twitter.[16]

This lemons effect seems exacerbated by inaccurate or broad warnings about misinformation. For example, former President Trump's repeated labeling of accurate reporting about him and his administration as "fake news" may have convinced some voters that most or all information is inaccurate rather than singling out Trump's falsehoods.[17]

The very prevalence of the term *fake news* today shows the concept's reach. Professor Brendan Nyhan and his coauthors found that general warnings to beware of misinformation may cause voters to doubt the veracity of both truthful and false information.[18]

There is much we do not know about how the flood of false information affects voter perceptions, and it is important not to overstate the current effects of an avalanche of Internet and social media fake news. For example, claims that fake news swung the 2016 U.S. presidential election from Hillary Clinton to Donald Trump are unproven and unlikely.

Still, what we know is bad enough. Many traditional journalistic outlets, especially local ones, have collapsed or are in danger of being scaled back to irrelevance; barriers to entry for producing slick, objective-looking false information have fallen dramatically; the flood of false information is hitting American voters at the same time that confidence in legitimate media is falling; and people are most likely to fall for false information when it lines up with their preexisting ideological preferences.

From Disinformation to Violence

The ease with which all types of information can now flow on social media means that some false information is spread innocently and widely. It takes only one mouse-click to share a link, tweet, or story containing unverified information with potentially thousands (or, in the case of celebrities, millions) of others. False information and rumors had spread in social circles long before there was an Internet, but never with the speed and reach possible now. Lies spread faster and more virally than the truth on social media.[19]

Consider a 2020 photograph of stacked mailboxes outside a company called Hartford Finishing in Hartford, Wisconsin. Hartford Finishing has a contract with the U.S. Postal Service (USPS) to repaint old mailboxes, which is hardly nefarious. But the picture spread virally on the left in August 2020 as news reports circulated of a claimed Trump administration effort to pressure USPS to slow down mail service to deter 2020 mail-in balloting during the pandemic. The picture originated with a Hartford resident, Bruce Mittlesteadt, who posted the picture on Facebook because he was concerned about USPS manipulating mail delivery to affect the election. After hearing about the work at the plant refurbishing mailboxes, he wrote that it was probably a "nothing sandwich." The picture nonetheless went viral.[20]

According to the website PolitiFact, the picture appeared in a Reddit post with the caption "Whole thing looks terrible." That posting was followed by tweets of the picture explicitly tying the mailbox stack to a supposed "massive voter suppression" effort, and eventually by Facebook posts containing a screenshot of one of the tweets furthering the message. Hundreds of thousands of people, including the actress Jeri Ryan, shared the message on social media and millions of viewers saw it. PolitiFact rated the voter suppression claim connected to those mailboxes as "false."[21]

It is unclear how many sharers of the image really believed it was

Thomas Kennedy
@tomaskenn

Photo taken in Wisconsin. This is happening right before our eyes. They are sabotaging USPS to sabotage vote by mail. This is massive voter suppression and part of their plan to steal the election.

5:16 PM · Aug 14, 2020 · Twitter Web App

73K Retweets   **7.8K** Quote Tweets   **126.3K** Likes

Thomas Kennedy tweet, Aug. 14, 2020, with a photograph taken by Bruce Mittlesteadt (available at https://twitter.com/tomaskenn /status/1294427812670124033?s=12, archived at https://web.archive .org/web/20210126105623/https://twitter.com/tomaskenn /status/1294427812670124033) (reprinted with permission of Kennedy and Mittlesteadt)

part of a voter suppression effort. Thomas Kennedy, a progressive activist working in Florida who wrote a widely circulated tweet with the picture, told me in an interview that "Trump admitted to undermining USPS to make it harder to vote by mail. If there are people raising alarm it's because they gave the image of impropriety. Maybe a pandemic when we need expanded vote by mail is not the time to be refurbishing and removing mailboxes." When I mentioned that the picture in fact was not part of a plot to slow down the postal service, he added, "I just want people to understand my intention isn't to mislead people. I'm just concerned and scared."[22]

As Kennedy's statements show, some people on the left probably shared the image because they were already predisposed to believe from President Trump's other incendiary statements and actions—especially his statements that he was wary of fully funding the postal service because it could aid in expanded mail-in balloting—that he intended to suppress the vote during a pandemic.[23]

But we cannot discount the possibility that some people shared the image and a voter suppression message deliberately to mislead people about the election or undermine voter confidence in the results. Innocent misinformation may influence elections, but intentionally spread false information is the much greater danger. This *disinformation* violates democratic norms that people should not be lied to about politically relevant facts, and it tests the marketplace of ideas under conditions with serious stakes.[24]

The false information about the Wisconsin mailboxes may seem relatively unimportant, but disinformation can be deadly, such as when public figures shared false information about how COVID-19 spreads or how to prevent or cure it. Political disinformation can be dangerous too. Ridiculous claims that Hillary Clinton and other Democrats were running a child sex ring out of the Comet Ping Pong pizza parlor in Washington, D.C., led to a 2016 shooting with an AR-15 rifle by someone who believed the false statements and wanted to save children's lives. As the *New York Times* put it, "Fake News Brought Real Guns." Fortunately, no one was shot in that incident.[25]

Four years after the "Pizzagate" false statements were repeatedly debunked, they took on new life among conspiracy-minded QAnon followers and spread virally on new platforms such as TikTok. Some of the pop star Justin Bieber's 130 million social media followers believed that when he touched his beanie in an online video, he was sending a secret signal that he had been the victim of Pizzagate child abuse. The *Times* reported that "there was no evidence that Mr. Bieber had seen that message. But the pop star's innocuous gesture set off a flurry of online activity, which highlighted the resurgence of one of social media's early conspiracy theories. Viewers quickly uploaded hundreds of videos online analyzing Mr. Bieber's action. The videos were translated into Spanish, Portuguese and other languages, amassing millions of views. Fans then left thousands of comments on Mr. Bieber's social media posts asking him if he was safe. Within days, searches for 'Justin and PizzaGate' soared on Google, and the hashtag #savebieber started trending."[26]

While the Justin Bieber–Pizzagate connection might seem comical, the issues grew more serious when congressional candidates started embracing QAnon-type conspiracy theories, and President Trump not only refused to condemn them but courted their adherents, calling them people who "love our country." Millions of people now regularly share false QAnon theories, including a core belief that Donald Trump has been fighting a "deep state" made up of Democratic politicians, government bureaucrats, and others committed to pedophilia. Some QAnon adherents have resorted to violence, and the Federal Bureau of Investigation (FBI) has branded the group a domestic terrorist threat. The *Washington Post* reported: "Individuals who had posted in support of QAnon or otherwise expressed their devotion to it, according to police, have been arrested in at least 10 incidents, including two murders, a kidnapping, vandalism of a church and a heavily armed standoff near the Hoover Dam." A May 2021 poll conducted by Public Religion Research Institute and the Interfaith Youth Core found that "15 percent of Americans say they think that the levers of power are controlled by a cabal of Satan-worshiping pedophiles, a core belief of QAnon supporters. The same share said it was true that 'American patriots may have to resort to violence' to depose the pedophiles and restore the country's rightful order," according to a *New York Times* article titled "QAnon Now as Popular in U.S. as Some Major Religions, Poll Suggests." The *Times* article drew a straight line from Trump's online untruths to the huge uptick in those believing QAnon conspiracies.[27]

Although the political valence of things could change in the future, disinformation appeared to be a particular problem on the far right. A New York University study found that "politically extreme sources tend to generate more interactions from users. In particular, content from sources rated as far-right by independent news rating services consistently received the highest engagement per follower of any partisan group. Additionally, frequent purveyors of far-right misinformation had on average 65% more engagement per follower than other far-right pages." And a study out of Germany found a correlation between the posting of anti-refugee sentiment on Facebook and violent attacks on refugees. Things move easily from the screen to the streets.[28]

One particular form of disinformation spreading mostly on the right—unsupported claims of widespread voter fraud—is especially threatening to the legitimacy of American elections and democratic stability. A political science study conducted in the aftermath of the 2018 U.S. midterm elections showed that "exposure to claims of voter fraud reduces confidence in electoral integrity, . . . especially among

Republicans and individuals who approve of Donald Trump's performance in office. Worryingly, exposure to fact-checks that show these claims to be unfounded does not measurably reduce the damage from these accusations." Similarly, a study in the aftermath of the 2020 election found that exposure to Trump tweets attacking the legitimacy of the election caused Trump supporters to lose confidence in the fairness and legitimacy of the election (though, thankfully, it did not also increase support for political violence). "The results suggest that unsubstantiated claims of voter fraud undermine the public's confidence in elections, particularly when the claims are politically congenial, and that these effects cannot easily be ameliorated by fact-checks or counter-messaging."[29]

A Reuters/Ipsos poll taken a week and a half after the 2020 election showed that about half of all Republicans believed the false claim that Donald Trump had rightfully won the election against Joe Biden but that it was stolen from him by voter fraud: "68% of Republicans said they were concerned that the election was 'rigged.' . . . Altogether, 55% of adults in the United States said they believed the Nov. 3 presidential election was 'legitimate and accurate,' which is down 7 points from a similar poll that ran shortly after the 2016 election. The 28% who said they thought the election was 'the result of illegal voting or election rigging' is up 12 points from four years ago. The poll showed Republicans were much more likely to be suspicious of Trump's loss [in 2020] than Democrats were when Hillary Clinton lost" in 2016. According to surveys by Bright Line Watch, in October 2020, a month before the election, 56 percent of Trump supporters believed the national vote would be fairly counted. By mid-November 2020, after Trump's loss and his continued false claims about fraud, the number of surveyed Trump supporters believing the vote was fair plummeted to 28 percent. And time did not cause the false beliefs to dissipate. A May 2021 Reuters/Ipsos poll found 53 percent of Republicans believed that Trump was the "true President," and 56 percent believed the 2020 election was tainted by illegal voting.[30]

The shift was no surprise. In the immediate aftermath of the 2020 election, supporters of Donald Trump turned away in droves from even their trusted sources of news, such as Fox News, to new media and social media platforms that fed them lies explaining away Trump's loss as due to voter fraud. As Twitter and Facebook excluded the most irresponsible voices claiming election fraud and slapped labels on others, some Trump supporters fled to the new social website Parler, backed financially by the conservative Mercer family. This divorce from reality and bifurcation of content, as the Internet researcher Renée DiResta put it, "also raises the possibility that, among those who gravitate to niche platforms like Parler, the discussion may grow even more extreme. People who sincerely believe that a CIA supercomputer changed votes for Biden in swing states did not do an about-face and accept him as the duly elected president on Inauguration Day. A persistent belief that the new president is illegitimate could cause political violence." During the counting of the 2020 ballots, many election officials in places such as Arizona faced threats of violence.[31]

All this unhinged conspiracism culminated in the January 6, 2021, attack on the U.S. Capitol as Congress counted the Electoral College votes from the 2020 presidential election. The events, described in detail in the last chapter, demonstrated the power and danger of unmediated false messages about election integrity by a political leader. Trump's statements were not just cheap talk to explain away his loss in both the Electoral College and the popular vote to his opponent, Joe Biden. They were messages that his most ardent supporters heard as a literal call to arms and for political intervention against the peaceful transition of power.

A bipartisan Senate Intelligence Committee report issued in June 2021 faulted U.S. intelligence officials for failing to identify the magnitude and seriousness of the threat of violence on January 6 coming from online sources. Melissa Smislova, acting undersecretary, Office of Intelligence and Analysis at the Department of Homeland Security, told senators, "A lesson learned from the events of January 6th is that distinguishing between those engaged in constitutionally protected activities from those involved in destructive, violent, and threat-related behavior is a complex challenge. For example, domestic violent extremists may filter or disguise online communications with vague in[n]uendo to protect operational security, avoid violating social media platforms' terms of service, and appeal to a broader pool of potential recruits. Under the guise of the First Amendment, domestic violent extremists recruit supporters, and incite and engage in violence. Further complicating the challenge, these groups migrate to private or closed social media platforms, and encrypted channels to obfuscate their activity. We must develop the tools to overcome this challenge if we are to effectively address the rising levels of violence perpetrated by those who are inspired by domestic extremist ideological beliefs." Similarly, Jill Sanbord, the assistant director of the Counterterrorism Division of the FBI, told senators that she was uncertain of the FBI's authority to monitor social media threats of violence, given the First Amendment: "Under our authorities, because being mindful of the First Amendment and our dual-headed mission to uphold the Constitution, we cannot collect First Amendment–protected activities without sort of the next step, which is the intent" to engage in acts of violence.[32]

The Deep Fakes Threat

As bad as things seem now, disinformation is poised to become a much larger problem in future elections. Repetition, made ever easier on social media, increases the likelihood a voter will accept a false claim. As technology improves, it is quickly getting easier, even for those without great technical sophistication, to use artificial intelligence (AI) technology to create synthetic media (more commonly known as "deep fakes"). Such audio and video clips can be manipulated using machine learning and AI and can make a politician, celebrity, or anyone else appear to say or do anything the manipulator wants. Within a few years, any politician could be "shown" making a racially derogatory remark, engaging in sexual misconduct, or suddenly falling ill on the eve of an election. We will no longer be able to trust what we see and hear.[33]

Fake textual material will grow as well. As DiResta points out: "In time, operators far less sophisticated than the Russian government will have the ability to robo-generate fake tweets or op-eds. The consequences could be significant. In countries around the world, coordinated propaganda campaigns in print as well as social media have sown social unrest, pushed down vaccination rates, and even promoted ethnic violence. Now imagine what happens when the sources of such postings are untraceable and the supply is essentially infinite."[34]

The lemons problem is likely to accelerate with AI-generated mass disinformation and as deep fakes improve in technical sophistication, making it harder for humans to differentiate true from false images without technical help. The effect also seems to be more pronounced among younger people, who are more prone to suspect the veracity of online content. Professor Nyhan worries that false videos might have more serious effects on our ability to make sound decisions than false written statements, given how human cognition works. And the researchers Cristian Vaccari and Andrew Chadwick found that deep fakes did not deceive users into believing the fake videos were true so much as they increased uncertainty and distrust in news on social media and fueled "generalized indeterminacy and cynicism."[35]

Foreign Interference and Domestic Copycats

Disinformation and polarizing social media posts coming from foreign sources were a major focus of attention in the 2016 and 2020 elections, and the volume of foreign interventions is likely to increase dramatically in coming years. This is so for both political and pecuniary reasons. But by 2020, many of the foreign tactics seen first in 2016 had spread to domestic sources of disinformation.

As part of its effort to influence the 2016 presidential election and U.S. politics, Russia undertook an extensive propaganda effort, which included publishing negative stories about Hillary Clinton and U.S. interests as well as inflaming passions and spreading false stories aimed at influencing the outcome of the election in Trump's favor. "For example," PolitiFact reported, the Russian news website Sputnik "published an article that said the [John] Podesta email dump included certain incriminating comments about the Benghazi scandal, an allegation that turned out to be incorrect. Trump himself repeated this false story" at a campaign rally.[36]

Sources allied with the Russian government paid at least $100,000 to Facebook to spread election-related messages and false reports to specific populations (microtargeting), including aiming certain false reports at journalists who might be expected to spread the misinformation. Russian and other sources also used automated bots to spread and amplify false news across social media platforms such as Facebook and Twitter.[37]

A joint report issued in January 2017 by the Central Intelligence Agency (CIA), FBI, and National Security Agency confirmed Russian attempts to influence the outcome of the 2016 elections, create instability, and favor Trump over the Democratic candidate, Hillary Clinton: "We assess Russian President Vladimir Putin ordered an influence campaign in 2016 aimed at the US presidential election. Russia's goals were to undermine public faith in the US democratic process, denigrate Secretary Clinton, and harm her electability and potential presidency. We further assess Putin and the Russian Government developed a clear preference for President-elect Trump. We have high confidence in these judgments."[38]

To foment American political unrest, Russia's Internet Research Agency (IRA) used a variety of social media platforms, including Facebook, YouTube, Twitter, Pinterest, and especially Instagram. Over 30 million users shared IRA-created content on Facebook and Instagram between 2015 and 2017. In perhaps the most brazen example of Russian social media manipulation, in May 2016, as reported by NPR, "two groups of demonstrators faced off outside the Islamic Center in Houston Texas. On one side stood people drawn by a Facebook group called Heart of Texas. It had 250,000 followers. The group's tagline was folksy—homeland of guns, barbecue and your heart. They were there to demonstrate against the purported Islamization of Texas. On the other side were people who were also drawn by a Facebook group— United Muslims of America. It had 328,000 followers. Tagline—I'm a Muslim, and I'm proud. They were on the streets to save Islamic knowledge." Russian operatives had established both Facebook groups, for a grand total of $200.[39]

Special Counsel Robert Mueller's investigation into Russian interference in the 2016 election revealed "dozens of U.S. rallies organized by the IRA" in the run-up to the election, beginning with a "confederate rally" in November 2015.[40]

What stood out more than anything else in Russia's social media efforts was its focus. Although they did much to foment social media unrest in general by highlighting divisive issues such as immigration, foreign affairs, and gay rights, Russian government agents devoted disproportionate resources to convincing African Americans to stay home and not vote for Hillary Clinton. As a December 2018 report by the social media analysis firm New Knowledge put it: "While other distinct ethnic and religious groups were the focus of one or two Facebook Pages or Instagram accounts, the Black community was targeted extensively with dozens." On YouTube, "by far the most content was related to Black Lives Matter & police brutality: 1063 videos split across 10 different channels (59% of the channels, 96% of the content)." They used not just bots but also humans, who took on American personas to make direct contact with activists in the United States. They created an ecosystem around the "Black Matters" brand (a name suspiciously similar to the unrelated Black Lives Matter), curating linked accounts to ensure that African American readers trusted the site and heard its messages repeated across multiple sites.[41]

A report by Oxford University researchers for the Senate Intelligence Committee noted that "messaging to African Americans sought to divert their political energy away from established political institutions by preying on anger with structural inequalities faced by African Americans, including police violence, poverty, and disproportionate levels of incarceration. These campaigns pushed a message that the best way to advance the cause of the African American community was to boycott the election." For example, "attacks on Clinton and calls for voter disengagement were particularly clear [on a Russian Facebook page called] Blacktivist during September, October, and November 2016, with statements such as 'NO LIVES MATTER TO HILLARY CLINTON. ONLY VOTES MATTER TO HILLARY CLINTON' (Blacktivist, 29 October 2016), another one argu[ing] that black people should vote for Jill Stein (Blacktivist, 7 October 2016), or not vote at all, with the claim: 'NOT VOTING is a way to exercise our rights' (Blacktivist, 3 November 2016)." According to NBC News, Russian operatives who had participated in the 2016 election interference were, as late as 2018, still looking for new ways to foment racial discord, "including a suggestion to recruit African Americans and transport them to camps in Africa 'for combat prep and training in sabotage.' Those recruits would then be sent back to America to foment violence and work to establish a pan-African state in the South, particularly in South Carolina, Georgia, Alabama, Mississippi and Louisiana."[42]

Russia's IRA also disseminated "voter fraud" memes aimed at right-wing groups, suggesting that minorities would try to steal the election for Clinton. The most-shared IRA-sourced Facebook post mentioning Hillary Clinton during the election season showed a picture of a group of Latinos waiting in a long line, with the meme: "Like if you agree only U.S. citizens should be allowed to vote." According to New Knowledge: "There were 109 posts devoted to creating and amplifying fears of voter fraud; the overwhelming majority of them targeted right-wing audiences. 71 were created in the month leading up to election day, and made claims that certain states were helping Sec. Clinton win, that militia groups were going to polling places to stop fraud (called for volunteers to participate), that civil war was preferable to an unfair election or the election of Sec. Clinton, that 'illegals' were overrepresented in voter rolls in Texas and elsewhere, or were voting multiple times with Democratic Party assistance. . . . The prevalence of this narrative suggests they may not have expected Trump to win; regardless, they intended to incite violence if he did not."[43]

It is easy for those who opposed Donald Trump in 2016 to blame Russian interference for Clinton's loss. But the picture is more complex, and the specific claim that Russian *social media activity* swung the 2016 election is speculative and unsupported. In a close election one may point to many factors that might have pushed Trump over Clinton in the three states of Michigan, Pennsylvania, and Wisconsin (which Trump won by a combined 70,000 votes). But compared to what others were doing, Russian social media activities in 2016 were small-scale. A $100,000 total buy in Facebook ads is a fraction of what the presidential campaigns were spending every day. The Clinton campaign spent $768 million in total, and the Trump campaign $398 million; the Center for Responsive Politics estimated overall spending on the 2016 elections at $6.5 billion. Facebook's former security chief, Alex Stamos, believes the microtargeted ads from the Trump campaign were probably much more influential than Russian social media activities.[44]

It seems much more possible that a different Russian activity—stealing and leaking internal Democratic Party communications—affected the outcome. Although the documents spread rapidly on social media, that scandal did not depend primarily on cheap speech. It is likely that similar leaked documents would have received extensive news coverage in earlier eras on radio, on television, and in newspapers.[45]

But if Russian social media activities did not swing the 2016 election to Trump, they had a profound psychological effect on the conduct of the 2020 election, especially among those on the left stung by the Mueller investigation's failure to bring Trump down on charges of collusion with Russia. As investigations into 2016 Russian interference continued through 2020, civil rights organizations focused on Russian suppression of African American voters and pressured Facebook, Twitter, and other social media companies to police such efforts more aggressively in 2020. Facebook began planning in August 2020 what to do if Donald Trump lost the election and sought to cast doubt on the results.[46]

House and Senate Democrats also pushed intelligence officers to reveal more about 2020 election interference coming from Russia. Those officials said little more in August 2020 than that Russia, China, and Iran were trying to interfere in the election; Russia favored Trump's victory and China favored his defeat. In October 2020 intelligence officials blamed Iran and Russia for new attempts at interference, including a Russian attempt to probe voter registration databases once again. Iran was accused of threatening Democratic voters with emails purportedly coming from the white supremacist group Proud Boys to warn them against voting for Trump, a tactic that Trump's Director of National Intelligence John Ratcliffe sought to portray as an effort to hurt Trump's electoral chances. In March 2021, well after the 2020 election season, the *New York Times* reported that U.S. intelligence officials revealed that "President Vladimir V. Putin of Russia authorized extensive efforts to hurt the candidacy of Joseph R. Biden Jr. during the election last year, including by mounting covert operations to influence people close to President Donald J. Trump. . . . Besides Russia, Iran and other countries also sought to sway the election, the report said. China considered its own efforts but ultimately concluded that they would fail and most likely backfire, intelligence officials concluded. A companion report by the Justice and Homeland Security Departments also rejected false accusations promoted by Mr. Trump's allies in the weeks after the vote that Venezuela or other countries had defrauded the election."[47]

By 2020 the foreign threat seemed to fade compared to disinformation bearing a Made in America label. In a 2017 special U.S. Senate race in Alabama, supporters of the Democratic candidate, Doug Jones, acting without Jones's knowledge or cooperation, used fake social media accounts purporting to be from conservative Republicans to try to convince these key voters to abstain from voting for Jones's Republican opponent, Roy Moore. Moore was a controversial former state supreme court justice who was accused of having inappropriate relationships with teenage girls when he was in his thirties. Jones went on to beat Moore, although there is no proof that the disinformation campaign was responsible for a Democrat's narrow and improbable victory in deep-red Alabama.[48]

The pro-Trump business group FreedomWorks backed an online effort in 2020 by a new, shadowy group called Protect My Vote that used an image of the basketball star LeBron James to try to discourage African American voters from voting by mail. James was active in promoting voting rights and combating voter suppression, and the use of his image to discourage voting seemed designed to pervert his efforts. Facebook removed the page containing the postings after a *Washington Post* inquiry. According to the *Post:* "The Facebook page in question, Protect My Vote, had purchased more than 150 ads on the platform by the time it was removed. Viewed hundreds of thousands of times in August, the ads appeared to be designed to tap into anxiety about the integrity of the voting system to convince Americans in battleground states where minority turnout could be decisive that mail balloting is not reliable. The paid posts featuring an image of James misconstrued a quote from the basketball star, falsely suggesting that when he condemned polling closures as 'systemic racism and oppression,' he was linking those closures to the expansion of opportunities to vote by mail." The group behind the Facebook ads used the website URL protectthevote.com, which was confusingly similar to the protectthevote.net website used by a consortium of groups that work to protect people's voting rights.[49]

Google did even worse than Facebook in dealing with the ads, waiting five days after a *Washington Post* inquiry before deciding not to remove them. "A Google spokeswoman, Charlotte Smith, declined to answer specific questions about the ads or explain how they complied with the company's policies, saying only in an emailed statement: 'We have zero tolerance for ads that employ voter suppression tactics or undermine participation in elections. When we find those ads, we take them down.'" According to the *Post,* Google inexplicably did not classify the ads as "political," which "made it difficult to discern the size of the ad buy or the precise geographical scope of the campaign."[50]

Google's YouTube service was perhaps the worst offender among the larger social media companies in allowing foreign and domestic sources of election disinformation to remain online without so much as a warning label on much of the content. According to Bloomberg News: "One YouTube video claiming evidence of voter fraud in Michigan has more than five million views. Another posted by Trump was selectively edited to appear as if Biden is endorsing voter fraud. That has over 1.6 million views. One of the [clips from One America News Network (OANN)] was watched 142,000 times in seven hours on Monday, while the other got 92,000 hits in that time."[51]

Disinformation also spread heavily through encrypted messaging apps such as WhatsApp and WeChat, especially among immigrant communities, which have been more likely to communicate through these apps. And this disinformation spread without any ad targeting, as occurs on social media. KQED and ProPublica reported just before the 2020 election: "At least two dozen groups on the Chinese-owned social media app WeChat have been circulating misinformation that the U.S. Department of Homeland Security is 'preparing to mobilize' the National Guard and 'dispatch' the military to quell impending riots, apparently in an attempt to frighten Chinese Americans into staying home on Election Day. The misinformation, which takes the form of a photo of a flyer and is in both English and Chinese, also warns that the government plans to impose a national two-week quarantine and close all businesses." Meanwhile, "in private messaging apps and social media, Spanish-speaking residents in South Florida have been exposed to a barrage of deceptive claims—a voter disinformation tactic that could last until Election Day. The latest example is an anonymous message that emerged in WhatsApp chats this week that threatens Spanish-speaking supporters of President Donald Trump. . . . The message includes threats to burn down their houses if Trump does not concede the election."[52]

Polarization and Asymmetric False Information

Russian social media efforts in 2016 and those of domestic copy-cats in 2020 depended on exploiting existing fissures in American politics and society. If Americans were not deeply divided on issues such as immigration, LGBTQ rights, voting rights, Black Lives Matter, abortion, taxes, guns, and other subjects, the IRA would never have been able to rile people up and organize rallies and counter-rallies with a $200 expenditure to create Facebook group pages. The IRA parlayed this existing social fragmentation to influence election outcomes.

The polarization of American politics is no secret. Social media helps fuel it, and polarization increases the relevance of social media as a device for reinforcing political views. For those who are the most politically engaged—far more than for other users—social media can create a kind of echo chamber in which the people one follows and the links one clicks help assure that one sees only the messages that are consistent with one's existing worldviews. These algorithm-driven echo chambers may harden the views of those who are already moving to the extremes, making political compromise more difficult among the most politically active and aware users. In the United States, this problem appears to be significantly greater among the politically active on the right. And with the growth of separate sites like Parler, which cater specifically to the right, the echo chamber risk increases.[53]

It would be a mistake to attribute American polarization primarily to the rise of cheap speech. The modern era of polarization predates the rise of cheap speech and has many causes, including the realignment of the political parties following passage of the Civil Rights Act of 1964 and the Voting Rights Act of 1965. And disentangling polarization's effects on the corrosion of American democracy from the effects of cheap speech is difficult. But cheap speech helps fuel polarization by reinforcing existing worldviews, reducing the search costs of finding like-minded people and online content, and lowering the barriers for confrontation. The closure of local newspapers also increases polarization by "nationalizing" the news that people follow, making people view political issues through a red-blue lens. Voters in a polarized atmosphere take their cues from elites and are more susceptible to believing incorrect information. People band together with compatriots and hurl insults and threats on social media that they would be wary to make in person (except perhaps in a rally or crowd), contributing to disrespect for the other side. In some corners of the web, hate speech has driven out almost all other communication. Negative partisanship has become a major force in American politics, aided by a system of amplified communication that facilitates rivalries, confrontation, and dissemination of falsehood.[54]

Social media fuels both partisanship and disinformation, but it has done so asymmetrically. During the 2016 elections, more false information spread on the right than on the left, such as the false story that the pope had endorsed Donald Trump for president (which had 960,000 Facebook engagements). Allcott and Gentzkow's study of fake news articles on social media during the 2016 election found about three times as many pro-Trump fake news articles as fake pro-Clinton articles; the pro-Trump articles were shared 30.3 million times on Facebook compared to 7.6 million shares of pro-Clinton fake news. Similarly, a study by Andrew Guess and his coauthors showed that "almost 6 in 10 visits to fake news websites came from the 10% of people with the most conservative online information diets."[55]

An important study by Yochai Benkler, Robert Faris, and Hal Roberts revealed a mostly closed conservative media ecosystem in which Fox News, Breitbart, and many other online players feed into one another, creating an alternative universe not only of opinions but of facts. The authors found that about 30 percent of the American public were plugged into this ecosystem and were regularly rejecting scientific facts. Fox News exists primarily as a cable television station and only secondarily as a website, but cheap speech helped fuel its popularity in both places. The expansion of American viewing habits from broadcast television to cable television to social media distributed across a variety of platforms created openings for Fox News's success that would not have been possible in an earlier era. The problems only expanded in the 2020 election, as Donald Trump and his superspreader social media supporters fanned the flames of a false story of a vast voter fraud conspiracy to explain his loss to his opponent, Joe Biden.[56]

Although the Benkler, Faris, and Roberts study predates the COVID-19 pandemic, beliefs about the pandemic differed within this ecosystem. Republicans and conservatives, taking their cues from Trump's public statements, were less likely to believe the virus was a serious threat and less likely to agree to wear a mask in public despite evidence that masks could lessen their chances of contracting the disease. These divergent beliefs sometimes became a matter of life and death.[57]

The reasons for this asymmetry are many, but much of the problem stems from shifting American demographics and cultural values, which activated the Republican Party's white, non-college-educated base. Unhappiness with cultural shifts and bad news drove *demand* for false information. During the COVID-19 pandemic, which took place under Donald Trump's watch, there was strong demand on the right for stories affirming that the virus was not as bad as reported, that deaths were lower than reported, and that a treatment like hydroxychloroquine, which Trump repeatedly touted, would actually work despite the scientific consensus at the time that it was ineffective and dangerous. Along similar lines, the best way to explain Donald Trump's loss in the 2020 election was to say that it was "stolen" or "rigged."[58]

As Benkler, Faris, and Roberts put it, "Somewhere between 25 and 30 percent of Americans willingly and intentionally pay attention to media outlets that consistently tell that audience what it wants to hear, and what that audience wants to hear is often untrue." False information spreads for social and psychological reasons. Cailin O'Connor and James Owen Weatherall note the strong human desire to be accepted by others in one's social circles: "In some cases we are prepared to deny our beliefs, or the evidence of our senses, to better fit in with those around us." This conformity bias is well documented and applies regardless of intelligence or education.[59]

Without irony, true negative stories about Trump were dismissed by some on the right as fake news. This is no coincidence. As Nathaniel Persily put it, "Regimes that feed on distrust in elite institutions, such as legacy media and establishment parties, have found the online environment conducive to campaigns of disinformation and polarization that both disrupt the old order and bring new tools of intimidation to cement power."[60]

Political entrepreneurs with a profit motive parlay grievances into eagerly absorbed content and conspiracy theories telling people what they want to hear and providing a sensationalist supply that spurs further demand. The demand can then further radicalize the supply. Whitney Phillips and Ryan Milner argue: "Conspiracy entrepreneurs *are also radicalized by their audiences,* whose appetite for all that increasingly reactionary content are both whetted and sated by algorithms. Content that meets the audience's growing need for conspiracy theories is rewarded by clicks and likes and comments and shares and subscriptions, generating revenue for the content creator." Or, as the journalist Ezra Klein writes: "Fox News doesn't get Facebook shares by reporting on some banal comments made by Bob Casey, the understated Democratic senator from Pennsylvania. It focuses on Minnesota Representative Ilhan Omar, a liberal, confrontational Muslim

American who wears a hijab and speaks with a soft, Somalian accent. Similar dynamics hold on MSNBC and, honestly, everywhere in the media."[61]

Fox News is an extremely profitable enterprise, earning Rupert Murdoch and the network's other owners nearly $2 billion per year. In June and July 2020, it was the most-watched network in prime time on cable or broadcast television.[62]

The problem of a market for fake news is asymmetric, but the left is hardly immune to conspiracism. Although there were plausible reasons initially to be concerned that the Trump campaign colluded with Russian agents to help Trump beat Hillary Clinton during the 2016 presidential campaign, the Mueller Report found no evidence of such collusion—though it did find plenty of evidence of the Russians independently seeking to help Trump. Evidence that the Russian government held compromising information about Trump contained in the "Steele Dossier"—a report commissioned by Democrats for opposition research on Trump using a former British intelligence agent and later published by BuzzFeed—has similarly been discredited. Yet to this day, many on the left take claims of collusion and *kompromat* as conclusively proven rather than debunked. Such messages flourish on prominent liberal social media accounts and liberal media outlets like MSNBC.[63]

Even comically produced fake news can be profitable. During the 2016 election season, a group of young Macedonians spread a huge amount of pro-Trump fake news as a way of making money on social media advertising. A false story from one of the Macedonians saying Hillary Clinton would be indicted in 2017 got 140,000 shares and comments on Facebook, generating income of up to $2,500 per day. An American from Clearwater, Florida, started a fake news site as a joke and gained one million views in two weeks.[64]

The asymmetry in false information on the right has led to an unsurprising series of events. Under public pressure after the 2016 election to address the spread of false information, platforms such as Facebook and Twitter began offering fact checks, labeling certain information as false, and taking other steps to deal with the problem. Because more false speech appears on the right than on the left, more conservatives than liberals have seen their speech regulated by the companies. This in turn sparked a conservative backlash against the platforms on the ground that they were "censoring" conservative speech, when in fact the platforms were emerging as new intermediaries to help voters tell fact from fiction. This fact-checking role has led to calls from the right to require the platforms to be more even-handed. But the more the platforms check facts and police content, the more they drive those on the right to alternative sources, which offer false information that conforms to their worldviews. When Fox News was not radical enough in supporting Trump's false conspiracy theories about the 2020 election's being stolen, Trump supporters, at the president's urging, shifted to Newsmax and OANN.[65]

Weak Parties

One might think that with sky-high rates of political polarization, and especially with the rise of negative partisanship and the ease of reaching people on social media, political parties would draw millions of supporters and be stronger than ever in the cheap speech era. Instead, we are in an era of intense partisanship and weak political party organizations, a combination that opens the door to candidate demagoguery and a loss of accountability.

Political parties have weakened in the United States for complex reasons far afield from this book's focus, but the rise of cheap speech has accelerated the process. Briefly put, political parties in the early part of the twentieth century relied on masses of people and organized labor, funded in many American cities through patronage jobs—giving people employment in exchange for kickbacks. Campaigns moved from being labor-intensive to capital-intensive as television became a prime means for candidates to compete for votes, and as patronage faded with the rise of civil service protections and court decisions outlawing the practice.[66]

With the evolution of technology and law, political parties have struggled to dictate the choice of party nominees. Television allowed candidates to communicate directly to voters, and mass appeal became key to electability as more states moved to choosing their candidates through direct party primaries that allowed voters affiliated with the party—and sometimes nonmembers—to vote for party nominees rather than relying on party bosses and smoke-filled rooms.[67]

Campaign-finance reforms adopted in the early 2000s, aimed at limiting corruption, made it harder for parties to raise funds as court decisions opened up the fund-raising of nonparty outside groups such as Super PACs. The result was that these outside groups, which were less accountable to the parties, had greater resources to spread their messages. Eventually, these groups became shadow campaign organizations that boosted single candidates for office, further freeing the candidates from the need for party money.[68]

Cheap speech has fueled candidate-centered politics and candidate demagoguery in two distinct ways. To begin with, as Donald Trump's electoral success has shown, candidates and elected officials may now communicate directly to voters and others on social media. Not only can they reach an audience of millions at any time with no notice; the statements they make, no longer mediated by journalists, are subject to little resistance and no fact checking. Before his account was suspended, Trump could tweet a falsehood and journalists and others could fact-check it in a separate tweet, post, or article, but Trump's tweet stood on its own, able to be shared without context.

Those predisposed to believe Trump were likely to believe him and reject any fact checking.

There is no way in an earlier era that Trump could have persistently pushed his messages about voter fraud and election rigging to a huge audience. Journalists would have pushed back and would not have allowed the repetition and amplification of incendiary and sometimes false information now available to a candidate through much more diverse mass and social media. The virality of social media posts today has no earlier analogue.

Cheap speech also has facilitated a funding boom from small donors, many of whom are motivated by intense polarization. Before the rise of the Internet and social media, it was expensive to solicit small contributions to campaigns. Aside from formal fund-raisers and dinners, campaigns used direct mail, which was effective but expensive. Today it takes just a handful of clicks for a candidate to ask for a few dollars from a voter and for the voter to provide it. The ease of giving, combined with intense polarization, provides the recipe for extreme campaigns fueled by armies of intensely partisan small donors. It is no wonder that it is the Matt Gaetzes and the Alexandria Ocasio-Cortezes of the world, rather than the moderates, who are fund-raising darlings.[69]

By allowing campaigns to be funded through small-donor contributions, cheap speech allows candidates to bypass both political parties and the media, which no longer act as gatekeepers. It strengthens the fringes. We see more candidates whose extremist positions are counterproductive for a party's overall goals or antithetical to the party's values. Marjorie Taylor Greene, a one-time QAnon supporter, won a U.S. House seat in Georgia, and Laura Loomer, an Islamophobic conspiracy theorist, won the Republican nomination in Florida's twenty-first congressional district. A Democratic-controlled Congress stripped Greene of her committee assignments in light of her apparent support of violence against Democrats. She's since been a fund-raising juggernaut, raising over $3 million in the first three months of 2021 (compared to the impressive but much lower $728,000 that AOC raised in the first quarter of 2019).[70]

The Liar's Dividend

The potential for candidate demagoguery should rise as the cheap speech era endures and as deep fakes build in technical sophistication. More candidates will rely on what Danielle Citron and Robert Chesney have called the "Liar's Dividend": the decreasing possibility that any image of a politician or celebrity is genuine "make[s] it easier for liars to avoid accountability for things that are in fact true."[71]

Once again, Donald Trump provides a potent example. On October 7, 2016, in the heat of the 2016 election season, the *Washington Post* revealed the *Access Hollywood* tape. In the video, the *Post* reported: "Donald Trump bragged in vulgar terms about kissing, groping and trying to have sex with women during a 2005 conversation caught on a hot microphone, saying that 'when you're a star, they let you do it.' . . . The video captures Trump talking with Billy Bush, then of 'Access Hollywood,' on a bus with the show's name written across the side. They were arriving on the set of 'Days of Our Lives' to tape a segment about Trump's cameo on the soap opera."[72]

The video drew immediate condemnation across the political spectrum and brought predictions of the Trump campaign's collapse. Yet the campaign did not collapse. One reason may be what came right after the tape leaked: the leak by Russian government operatives of embarrassing emails from DNC officials.[73]

Trump was "extremely upset" about the *Access Hollywood* tape, according to his former aide Hope Hicks. Yet after issuing a rare apology one day after the video's release, Trump did something extraordinary: he suggested it was fake. The *New York Times* reported that Trump told a senator and an adviser a year after his apology that the tape was not authentic and that he was looking to hire someone to ascertain whether the voice on the tape was actually his.[74]

It is hard to know how many believed Trump's denials: people know what they saw and heard. Even Trump's press secretary at the time, Sarah Sanders, would not weigh in to defend him. Although there is no known polling on the question, it would not be surprising if many of Trump's supporters now believed the *Access Hollywood* recording was a fake. One such supporter, interviewed by CNN a year after Trump took office, said Trump's words were "taken out of context. . . . He talked about what was possible in the world of celebrities. . . . He's not that kind of man."[75]

There is good reason to believe that future politicians who wish to lie about what they have been caught doing or saying on tape will have more plausible deniability. The proliferation of AI-generated deep fakes gives them the full advantage of the Liar's Dividend. As Trump has said in the context of sexual harassment allegations, the strategy is "deny, deny, deny." Denial becomes easier as social media lemons increasingly flood the market, leading many to reject true, damaging information on the ground that its authenticity is unprovable.[76]

Trump further parlayed the Liar's Dividend into political advantage by continuously labeling as "fake news" negative but truthful stories about him. He used the term *fake news* 940 times on Twitter from 2016 through his deplatforming in January 2021. In June 2017, to take a very typical instance, he tweeted: "The Fake News Media has never been so wrong or so dirty. Purposely incorrect stories and phony sources to meet their agenda of hate. Sad!" This strategy makes it even harder for journalists and others to communicate to voters that there is truth and falsity in the world, and that there is a fair and accurate way to identify stories that have no basis in reality.[77]

A Rise in Corruption

The rise of cheap speech has done more than just weaken already weak political parties and boost candidates not reliant on their parties for support who can more easily lie and engage in demagoguery. It also undermines candidates' accountability for corrupt acts.

Candidate corruption is inhibited by an active press, and it thrives when a strong press is absent. This explains why members of Congress are much less likely than state and local officials to be found to have engaged in bribery and other forms of corruption. We should expect that the demise of local newspapers has led to an increase in the amount of state and local corruption, which is mostly covered by local professional journalists, and research suggests that this is so.[78] In an insightful *American Economic Review* article, Felipe Campante and Quoc-Anh Do examined the hypothesis that public corruption in a state is greater when the state capital is relatively far from the state's population centers. They found that "isolated capital cities are robustly associated with greater levels of corruption across [U.S.] states, in line with the view that this isolation reduces accountability." "Newspapers cover state politics more when readers are closer to the capital, voters who live far from the capital are less knowledgeable and interested in state politics, and they turn out less in state elections." Further, they find that "isolated capitals are associated with more money in state-level campaigns, and worse public good provision." So corruption is relatively high, as measured by federal prosecutions for public corruption in states like New York, where the state capital, Albany, is relatively far from its greatest population center, New York City.[79]

Campante and Do's model shows that government honesty and

accountability are driven in part by media coverage. The media cover state politics less intensely when state capitals are isolated, and readers in such states consequently read less news about state politics. Voter turnout in state elections is lower in states with isolated capitals as well, perhaps because voters believe they do not have enough information to cast intelligent votes or because there is no news of scandal to give voters a reason to vote. The lack of accountability creates an opening for corruption.

The authors' findings on campaign finance are especially interesting. Campaign contributions are higher in states with isolated capitals, and donations in those states are dominated by people who live closer to those isolated capitals. The authors speculate that "with lower media scrutiny and reduced involvement by voters, an isolated capital opens the way for a stronger role of money in shaping political outcomes."

What Campante and Do find occurring with isolated capitals will increasingly apply across the board; as state and local news coverage diminishes and as candidate accountability and voter turnout decrease, expect corruption and the influence of money on politicians to increase. A recent study by Pengjie Gao, Chang Lee, and Dermot Murphy in the *Journal of Financial Economics* shows what is ahead: after a local newspaper's closure, municipal borrowing costs went up; "our results indicate that local newspapers hold their governments accountable, keeping municipal borrowing costs low and ultimately saving local taxpayers money." With the watchdog gone, corruption grows.[80]

Manipulation of and by the Platforms

We have already seen that misinformation and disinformation can crowd out good information; that technology improvements will make it ever harder for voters to separate truth from falsity; that unscrupulous politicians recorded doing something wrongful or embarrassing will be able to cash in on the Liar's Dividend to obscure their involvement; that political parties will be weakened further and candidates more extreme and less accountable will be strengthened, raising the potential for increased demagoguery and corruption; and that foreign and domestic actors can exploit American political polarization through social media to achieve both political ends and financial profit. Many of these trends are amplified by the nature and architecture of social media platforms, which raises the risk of greater social manipulation of elections on the platforms and of bad conduct by the platforms themselves.

To begin with, social media platforms make influencing elections a profoundly different matter from what it was in past decades. Radio and television news and advertising remain important, especially when the advertising is channeled on live news or sports programming that individuals cannot skip over. But social media is growing in importance as a means of reaching voters. Two-thirds of eighteen- to twenty-four-year-olds now report that their main source of news is the Internet, whereas about one-quarter name television. Almost seven in ten American adults use Facebook; three-quarters of them use it at least once daily. Tens of millions are interacting with one another on other social media platforms, including Twitter, YouTube, Snapchat, Instagram, Reddit, and TikTok.[81]

The eyeballs and ears focused on social media are magnets for those looking to influence voting decisions. Much of this politicking is desirable from the standpoint of democratic elections: a candidate, party, or group posts truthful information about a candidate's views or some facts about the world; those who agree and disagree then share and comment on the information.

But social media platforms are not simply the twenty-first-century version of the public square. Even putting aside issues of misinformation and disinformation, platform technologies allow greater manipulation of voter information. Automated bots can increase the virality and reach of content. Anonymity and pseudonymity are relatively easy to achieve, at least initially, lowering the accountability costs for spreading false information and manipulated content, and depriving voters of the means to judge the credibility of the messages that they see. As Persily puts it: "The internet's 'bot' problem is a consequence of the privileging of online anonymity. Not only can it be impossible to determine who is speaking to you online, but it is becoming increasingly difficult to discern whether such speech comes from a human being at all."[82]

Anonymity of ad sponsors has become a major issue. Young Mie Kim and her colleagues studied 5 million digital ads on issues such as immigration, guns, and LGBTQ rights appearing on Facebook in the 2016 election season. They found that more than half came from individuals and groups that had no legal obligation to report their activities and identities to the Federal Election Commission (FEC). "Almost half of the groups were classified in the 'suspicious' category, some of which (20% of the 'suspicious' groups) turned out to be Russian-linked groups. . . . The volume of ads run by non-FEC groups (nonprofits and astroturf/movement groups) was almost 4 times larger than that of FEC groups."[83]

The companies, which gather a great deal of data on people's backgrounds, interests, and choices, allow campaigns to microtarget advertising. Campaigns can, for instance, send one set of tailored election-related messages to white, non-college-educated males in rural Wisconsin and another set to women of color in southwestern cities. Microtargeting lets campaigns speak out of both sides of their mouths and avoid accountability. Facebook lets candidates and political groups choose their characteristics or set of people to reach, and then Facebook will use its "look-alike" feature to send the same messages to people whom Facebook's algorithm identifies as having profiles similar to those chosen by the candidates or groups paying for advertising.[84]

The Young Mie Kim study showed that in the hotly contested 2016 presidential election, "the most targeted states with divisive issue campaigns—Pennsylvania and Wisconsin—overlapped with those usually considered strong for Democratic candidates, yet turned to Trump with a razor-thin margin." As Benkler, Faris, and Roberts put it, microtargeting "threatens to undermine the very possibility of a democratic polity" by allowing those who pay for access to "highly refined data" to "get . . . its users to want, believe, or do things." Both those authors and Facebook's former security chief, Alex Stamos, attribute the Trump campaign's unlikely success in 2016 to its extensive use of microtargeting on Facebook.[85]

As the Russian activities in 2016 demonstrated, microtargeting may also be used to depress voter turnout. A Senate Intelligence Committee report later described this phenomenon: "The use of messaging to sway voter sentiment is not a new development. However, it is now enabled by advanced data analytics and algorithmic targeting, the globally expansive reach of social media, and user-generated data and personal information that is often unwittingly provided or illicitly obtained." Different companies aspired to provide microtargeted social media messaging for the 2016 Trump campaign. The Israeli-based cyber intelligence company Psy Group pitched the campaign on a plan to target minority communities, suburban female voters, and undecided voters with covert messaging on social media. The campaign itself did not engage that group, but a Trump ally, George Nader, later paid them over $1 million for undisclosed activities. The Trump campaign did hire Cambridge Analytica, which engaged in microtargeting for the campaign in a way that violated Facebook's terms of service and users' privacy. Facebook later faced a record $5 billion fine, and the leaders of Cambridge Analytica faced additional penalties, for privacy breaches related to the data mining with which they targeted voters for political messages.[86]

In the 2020 election season, the Trump campaign used a mobile app that did more than push microtargeted advertising to the person downloading the app. As part of its terms of service, the app requested users' permission to download their contact lists, which allowed the campaign to target those who never signed up for campaign messaging. The company that the campaign partnered with on the app engaged in an extensive data-mining operation reminiscent of Cambridge Analytica's tactics. When app users provide access to the phone numbers of their contacts, the campaign could then match the numbers to detailed platform data to serve up more ads.[87]

The microtargeting problem is twofold, as Anthony Nadler, Matthew Crain, and Joan Donovan explain: "Unlike campaigns of even a decade ago, data-driven advertising allows political actors to zero in on those believed to be the most receptive and pivotal audiences for very specific messages while also helping to minimize the risk of political blowback by limiting their visibility to those who might react negatively."[88]

The platforms' design also may encourage greater electoral extremism through the algorithms used to recommend and uprank content. Automated systems monitoring a user's engagement with content will suggest additional content that follows similar patterns. And users can easily share content with like-minded people, pushing content further into people's feeds. The goal may be noble—give people what they want—but studies show that this can lead platform users to more extreme content, thereby turning someone who is just curious about a conspiracy theory such as QAnon into a true believer. As the tech journalist Will Oremus puts it: "The more personalized, the more democratized, the more optimized for engagement and agnostic to truth value our mass media become, the more we can expect wild conspiracies to infiltrate mainstream politics and culture."[89]

Virally spread disinformation and misleading messages can be especially problematic on encrypted messaging apps such as WhatsApp. These services allow sending the equivalent of group or individual text messages hidden from public view, making it impossible for those outside the apps to track the activity. The lack of transparency from encryption creates additional openings for undetected foreign and domestic interventions in U.S. campaigns. Though this secrecy problem has emerged in countries more dependent on WhatsApp than the United States, by 2020 it had spread to the Latin American communities in South Florida. Politico reported a "fucking crazy" explosion of disinformation aimed at this community in the run-up to the 2020 election. Among the conspiracy theories spread on WhatsApp: "George Soros directs a 'deep state' global conspiracy network. A Joe Biden win would put America [under the] control of 'Jews and Blacks.' The Democratic nominee has a pedophilia problem."[90]

And then there are the platforms' algorithms, deeply sophisticated computer programs that even platform engineers themselves do not fully understand. We cannot eliminate the possibility that rogue actors working at a platform, or even those who control the platforms themselves, could manipulate algorithms or policies to help one candidate and hurt another. Consider the example from the 2020 campaign described earlier in this book, of Instagram presenting users searching for information on Joe Biden with links to positive stories about Trump, but returning no positive Biden material for users searching for Trump. Facebook, which owns Instagram, attributed the problem to a technical "glitch," but no law prevents platform owners from choosing to favor one candidate over another, or one set of ideas over another.

Search engines present a related problem. Google has a commanding lead in this arena, and its algorithms could be tweaked easily to favor or hide different kinds of information about candidates. Indeed, the algorithms already make choices about what to show, for example, when someone searches for "Biden voter fraud." No law would stop a search engine from promoting or denigrating a candidate or require it to announce such manipulation.

We do not even have a good handle on how big an issue this is. A key problem with determining the extent of influence search engines and social media companies command is that most platforms limit researchers' access to the data that could inform us about user habits and the influence of platform architecture on voter choice.[91]

Platforms influence elections when they make choices about whether to promote or remove content, including content that could deter people from voting. Early researchers were able to show that Facebook could boost voter turnout by letting users know that their close friends had reported voting. There are probably parallel ways to depress voting. These choices inevitably raise questions about platform policy goals, which reflect the values of those who control the platform. As Persily wrote, platform managers' "decisions as to which communications to allow on these platforms are more important than government speech restrictions. Their rules as to disinformation, hate speech, incitement, or threats, for example, may 'govern' more speech than the laws on the books, especially given that their automated filters have capacity to 'preemptively regulate' in ways unavailable to government speech restrictions."[92]

In the 2020 election season, as conservative content came to dominate public-facing Facebook pages in the United States, news leaked from within the company that Facebook had relaxed its rules on removing misinformation in order to keep conservative pages on the platform. NBC News reported that pages associated with "Breitbart, former Fox News personalities Diamond and Silk, the nonprofit media outlet PragerU and the pundit Charlie Kirk" were flagged by Facebook's outside fact checkers as containing misinformation. Flagging of misinformation leads Facebook internally to give the pages a number of "strikes"; with enough strikes, a page can get demoted and lose the ability to collect certain advertising revenue. Despite the strikes, senior management declined to impose sanctions on these pages, perhaps from fear of adding to the charge that it was anti-conservative. BuzzFeed reported that the Facebook employee who sounded the alarm about the preferential treatment for right-leaning sites was fired. It later reported that Facebook's CEO, Mark Zuckerberg, personally intervened to reverse Facebook's decision to block dissemination of false and inflammatory material by Alex Jones of InfoWars. Zuckerberg said he did not see Jones as a hate figure.[93]

Platform decisions also can have unintended consequences. When Donald Trump falsely suggested in an August 2020 tweet that drop boxes for mail-in ballots were not "Covid sanitized," Twitter waited five hours before placing a warning label on the content, saying that it included false health and voting information. Facebook did nothing with the post the day it appeared. The delay and controversy generated much more coverage of Trump's tweet, spreading its content to a wider audience and adding to voter uncertainty about the fairness of the 2020 election.[94]

The Cheap Speech Revolution

Cheap speech is fundamentally changing how candidates campaign, how elected officials and political parties act, how voters receive political and electoral information, how foreign and domestic

← **Tweet**

 Donald J. Trump ✔
@realDonaldTrump

ₒₒₒ

This Tweet violated the Twitter Rules about civic and election integrity. However, Twitter has determined that it may be in the public's interest for the Tweet to remain accessible. Learn more

So now the Democrats are using Mail Drop Boxes, which are a voter security disaster. Among other things, they make it possible for a person to vote multiple times. Also, who controls them, are they placed in Republican or Democrat areas? They are not Covid sanitized. A big fraud!

4:25 AM · Aug 23, 2020 · Twitter for iPhone

View Quote Tweets

Screenshot of a now-deleted Donald J. Trump tweet, Aug. 23, 2020, with Twitter label (archived at https://web.archive.org/web/20201201224219 /https://twitter.com/realDonaldTrump/status/1297495295266357248)

actors seek to influence voter choice, and how those voters make their choices. It is also affecting voter confidence in the fairness and integrity of the election process itself.

Strictly in terms of volume, voters are exposed to more speech and information than ever before. It is likely that the rise of cheap speech has hurt voters more than it has helped them and that we are fast approaching a market for information lemons, but that does not mean we should—or even can—solve the resulting problems by passing laws limiting speech. Doing so would undermine some fundamental American values and a key part of our democracy: the benefits of robust and uninhibited political debate. It also raises the tricky question of who, in a society animated by distrust, would do the regulating and how they would do it.

How, then, can we address the problem of cheap speech in a way that respects the twin ideas of giving voters the tools they need to make choices that are consistent with their interests and values, and yet avoiding the danger of speech restrictions? Part of the answer lies in new laws backed by an updated understanding of the First Amendment. But changes in law and constitutional interpretation are not enough: there is much else that Americans must do to preserve both robust debate and an atmosphere that lets voters make free and informed choices.

3

What Can Law Do?

We have seen the problems cheap speech has caused and will cause for American elections and democracy, most importantly by exposing voters to massive amounts of misinformation, disinformation—including manipulated synthetic media—and microtargeted political propaganda. In this environment, honest information intermediaries face competition from disinformation upstarts, and demagogic candidates have an advantage. Platforms both can be manipulated by bad actors and can manipulate voter opinion themselves without regulation or even detection. In the worst-case scenario, as the 2020 election demonstrated, demagogic political leaders can use disinformation to rile up at least thousands of followers, interfering with the peaceful transition of power after elections and threatening democratic governance itself.

Cheap speech's debilitating effects on intermediaries such as political parties, combined with the dismal economics of local journalism, mean that elected officeholders are more apt to get away with corruption, and voters are less likely to have the information they need for voting in ways that are consistent with their interests and preferences. False and misleading messages spread especially easily through social media platforms, allowing campaigns and political operatives to rely on highly personalized data to pay for targeted messages likely to appeal to our worst tribal instincts. And false speech specifically about the integrity of American elections can undermine one of the key requirements of a democracy: that those on the losing side of an election accept the results as legitimate.

One potential answer to these problems is that the market will correct itself, and that if voters want better information, they will demand it and the market eventually will supply it. The economist George Akerlof, in his "Market for 'Lemons'" piece, recognized that creative marketers could correct the information asymmetry affecting the used car market. He noted that "private institutions may arise to take advantage of the potential increases in welfare which can accrue to all parties. By nature, however, these institutions are nonatomistic, and therefore concentrations of power—with ill consequences of their own—can develop."[1]

The used car market illustrates the side effects of entrepreneurs stepping up to alleviate a market failure. Some people still negotiate directly with a private car owner for a sale, taking a risk that they might buy a lemon. But nowadays, firms like CarMax, which obtain superior knowledge about the quality of used cars, can act as middlemen and reduce risks, buying used cars from sellers at a deep discount and selling them at a markup along with a short-term warranty. The CarMax model lessens the risk of information asymmetry, but at a cost: middlemen dealers make extra profits that take money out of the hands of both buyers and sellers, even as information about equilibrium car pricing flows more freely online than it did before the cheap speech era. Still, risk-averse buyers and sellers see the situation as win-win: they lessen uncertainty even at some financial cost.[2]

No doubt, facing an electoral choice, some voters too demand reliable information and are willing to pay for it: witness the transition of national news organizations such as the *New York Times* into supersized online news organizations dependent much more on subscriptions than advertising. In Akerlof's terms, this "concentration of power" has its own "ill consequences": Ben Smith, BuzzFeed's former editor in chief and now a *New York Times* media columnist, devoted his first column to arguing that the *Times* was becoming like Facebook and Google, a "digital behemoth crowding out the competition."[3]

Further, the *Times* model has not worked to save local journalism, as Margaret Sullivan's *Ghosting the News* argues, and its reporting does not seem to have made a dent in the thinking of those on the American right who view everything the *Times* produces as "fake news" unless it happens to momentarily line up with the interest of Donald Trump or other like-minded leaders. That trend is the result of a long-term project on the right to denigrate legitimate journalism as biased against conservatives, one that accelerated under Trump.

So long as people continue to demand false information, the cheap speech market will abundantly supply it. The lemons problem persists despite the *Times* and other reputable national journalistic outlets. Indeed, in a sense the problem is worse than the one Akerlof described. It is as if there is a segment of the automobile market that not only tolerates but actually demands lemons while rejecting reliable cars. Imagine that the sport of demolition derby were so widespread that it took up a significant share of the used car market—in which case Akerlof's lemons problem wouldn't exist at all. It suggests that curing the market failure will depend in part on turning voter preferences against lemons.[4]

The undeniably high quality of journalism at the *Times* and its competitors also does nothing to solve the problems of manipulation by and through platforms like Facebook and YouTube, or to curb the ability of demagogic politicians to use these platforms for their advantage. Some people who are fed up with Facebook's failure to police disinformation have deactivated their accounts, but the platform has not seen many defectors, in part thanks to the popularity of its Groups feature, and it remains profitable at a level most news organizations can only dream of.[5]

Akerlof's other proposed solution to the lemons problem was that "in some cases, governmental intervention may increase the welfare of all parties."[6] This has not worked all that well in the used car market. Many states have "lemon laws" that require manufacturers to buy back new vehicles that suffer a certain number of mechanical failures within a certain period after purchase. Whether because of the political power of used car dealers or for some other reason, only a few states, such as New York, provide lemon protection for used cars. And even New York's protection is limited to a subset of used cars sold by dealers. It doesn't apply to individuals who sell their own cars.[7]

Government intervention in the information market is much trickier than in the used car market, both because of the potential for unintended political consequences and because of the strong history of protection for political speech under the First Amendment. The relevant part of that amendment protects against government "abridg[ment]" of "the freedom of speech." Although those words are brief, the Supreme Court has decided many cases explaining how that right is protected, leading to a number of complex and sometimes contradictory pronouncements. In practice, the Court has often had to balance free speech rights against government interests. The government can punish someone for falsely yelling "Fire!" in a crowded movie theater, to take the paradigmatic-if-tired example, because in this context the government's interest in preventing injury is so high, and the value of false speech in this context is so low.[8]

In recent years, the Court has become especially protective of some kinds of speech claims, including challenges to government action to limit money in political campaigns and to police false political speech. The conservative supermajority may well reject new regulation, and some regulations already upheld, such as those requiring the disclosure of information about who has funded certain kinds of political speech, may face new judicial hostility.

Before turning to the interventions and the possible constitutional hurdles before them, it is worth pausing to ask a question: If the First Amendment were no impediment to regulation, which laws would work best to deal with cheap speech problems for voters? This thought experiment quickly reveals the dangers of overregulation, principally that the cures to the problem may end up depriving voters of important information they need to make informed voting decisions and ironically can facilitate other forms of voter manipulation. In other words, even if they did not already exist in the First Amendment, we would want to create some limitations on government intervention in order to protect robust political competition and the free exchange of ideas, especially from bad actors.

Think about a law giving the government the power to remove "misleading political speech" from social media sites, and now imagine that a Trump appointee (or an appointee of whichever president you think might not play fairly under the rules) has the power to decide what counts as "misleading speech" and to order such speech immediately removed from social media sites. That kind of system would ill serve voters even if courts could not block such a law on First Amendment grounds.

The same concern applies to a government body empowered to decide if social media companies were being "evenhanded" or "fair" in their coverage. There is no easy way for the government to define when coverage is evenhanded, and having the government police evenhandedness produces obvious dangers of viewpoint discrimination and manipulation. As we will see, there are better ways of dealing with platform bias than government mandates directed at content itself.

Again, we need look no further than Trump, who as president routinely called reporting he did not like "fake news," even when the reporting followed ordinary journalistic standards and reasonable observers believed it to contain only truthful information. (He used the "fake news" trick even when the journalists accurately quoted his recorded comments.) Any government agency that is under the control of a Trump-like leader and that is charged with separating true from false information would promote a very skewed idea of what coverage is misleading or biased. The regulation easily could do more harm than good. The general lesson is that solutions to cheap speech problems must be carefully crafted to avoid government overreach and unintended consequences.

On the other hand, we do not want a First Amendment so absolute in its speech protection that it blocks laws that would chill little speech but ameliorate social harms. Laws should aim for the sweet spot that helps voters make decisions that are consistent with their values and interests and that preserves democratic government but does not inhibit the free expression of valuable information and ideas.

In thinking about reaching that sweet spot, we must recognize the market failure of our current approach to speech. As Professor Nathaniel Persily puts it: "Perhaps to state the obvious, there simply is no support for the strong version of the marketplace of ideas when it comes to anonymous speech in the internet age. . . . The masking of identity built into the structure of internet communication brings with it inevitable risks of misrepresentation and manipulation." He adds: "The inability to identify the other person (if it is a person) at the other end of the computer conversation often leads that person to engage in certain types of speech that they would not engage in face-to-face. The norms of civility, the fears of retaliation and estrangement, as well as basic psychological dynamics of reciprocity that might deter some types of speech when the speaker and audience know each other—all are retarded when the speech is separated from the speaker, as it is online."[9]

Courts should resist the libertarian impulse that the cure for bad speech is always more speech in the social media age. Instead, while still being on the lookout for improper censorship, they should favor narrowly crafted laws that help voters make more competent election choices, understand the integrity of voting systems, avoid improper foreign influence, and avoid manipulation of opinion by those wielding troves of personal data. As we will see, law can be an important part of the answer, though it alone cannot save American elections.

Competent Election Administration

It may seem odd to begin a look at how law can deal with some of the pathologies for American democracy caused by cheap speech by calling for competent election administration, but the two ideas are connected. Legal requirements to run fair and transparent elections can combat disinformation about election integrity without raising any of the First Amendment problems discussed in the rest of this chapter.

One of the strongest refutations of Donald Trump's repeated false claims that hundreds of thousands of people in each state voted fraudulently in the 2020 U.S. presidential election was the evidence showing that election officials followed the rules, made their processes open for public view and inspection, and counted the ballots accurately. The Trump campaign and its allies filed sixty-two lawsuits in state and federal courts challenging aspects of the counting of ballots and certification of results, losing sixty-one and winning only one insignificant case. No case included credible evidence calling the election results in any state into serious question.[10]

These losses did not convince millions of Trump's most ardent followers, but they did assuage the concerns of millions of others who took the president's claims as serious until proven otherwise. The requirement that Trump bring his claims to official election proceedings such as recounts or to court to seek to overturn the election acted as a put-up-or-shut-up moment.

Georgia's Secretary of State Brad Raffensperger ordered a hand counting of all the presidential ballots cast in the state when the Trump campaign without evidence alleged fraud in the state of Georgia, won by Trump's opponent, Joe Biden; the audit revealed two counties that missed counting some votes, but otherwise affirmed the state's results. Trump later called Raffensperger in an effort to get him to "find" more than 11,000 votes to overturn the results of the election. The secretary refused and released a recording of the event, which eventually led Georgia officials to consider indicting Trump for election interference and related crimes.[11]

As one federal appeals court wrote in unanimously rejecting Trump's attempt to overturn Pennsylvania's election results on the basis of weak legal theories and no evidence of fraud: "Free, fair elections are the lifeblood of our democracy. Charges of unfairness are serious. But calling an election unfair does not make it so. Charges require specific allegations and then proof. We have neither here."[12]

A full exploration of how to run fair and transparent elections is a broad topic for another time; I have devoted two other books and many articles to these questions. Among other things, state and federal election laws should require maintenance of accurate and up-to-date lists of eligible voters; voting technology that relies on hand-marked paper ballots or at least produces a physical paper that may be subject to a full audit or recount after results are announced; regular audits of election results; reasonable procedures for verifying the identity of those submitting ballots by mail; adequate opportunity for party officials and nonpartisan watchdogs to observe every key aspect of ballot counting; and frequent communication from election officials about the status of ballot counting and recount procedures.[13]

The 2020 Trump campaign's manufactured claims of widespread

voter fraud and election irregularities would have been even worse with a more poorly run election system, and a good part of the reason the 2020 election did not end in a complete meltdown is that the results were not close enough in any state to prompt a serious recount or election contest. In the key states that were subject to Trump lawsuits and recounts, paper ballots proved essential in verifying vote totals. Accurate elections are a necessary but perhaps insufficient condition for the acceptance of election results by most American voters.[14]

Disclosure of Funders

Any discussion of how to deal with the general cheap speech problem in American elections should not neglect the low-hanging fruit: government-required disclosure of the funders of significant election-related online activity. Disclosure is no panacea, and it will not reach those who cannot be convinced by evidence; but it should be part of the overall solution. When done right, and especially when done alongside the messages themselves, mandated disclosure can aid voter competence amid a sea of disinformation and surreptitious influence campaigns. The Supreme Court has long supported the constitutionality of disclosure laws in campaign finance and related contexts, although there is ample reason to worry the Court's new conservative supermajority could change course.

Disclosure of truthful and relevant information can at least partially counteract false and misleading information, especially messages spread on social media. It also can serve other purposes, such as limiting corruption by restraining those who would seek to curry favor with politicians by supporting them without public disclosure, and help the enforcement of other laws, such as those barring foreign governments and other entities from participating in American elections.

The 2017 Alabama disinformation campaign mentioned in chapter 2 illustrates the importance of enhanced mandatory disclosure of significant online activity. Alabama voters looking at Facebook for information about whom to support in that year's special election to replace Jeff Sessions for the U.S. Senate may have come across the "Dry Alabama" website, which backed the Republican candidate, Roy Moore, against the Democrat Doug Jones. The *New York Times* explained that the page, "illustrated with stark images of car wrecks and videos of families ruined by drink, had a blunt message: Alcohol is the devil's work, and the state should ban it entirely." The Facebook and companion Twitter pages "appeared to be the work of Baptist teetotalers who supported the Republican, Roy S. Moore, in the 2017 Alabama Senate race. 'Pray for Roy Moore,' one tweet exhorted." The teetotalers, however, were not behind the Dry Alabama page on Facebook and they did not support Moore. Instead, according to the *Times,* those behind the page "thought associating Mr. Moore with calls for a statewide alcohol ban would hurt him with moderate, business-oriented Republicans and assist the Democrat, Doug Jones, who won the special election by a hair-thin margin."[15]

Nor were the scores of purportedly Russian bots with their Cyrillic names and symbols popping up on Twitter to support Roy Moore actually from Russia. Instead, a liberal group supporting Jones, working independently and apparently without his knowledge, engaged in a concentrated social media campaign to flip the votes of moderate Republicans, or at least get them to stay home and not vote at all in the normally deep red state. The faux Russian bots following Moore were a false flag planted by Moore's liberal opponents. This was a Democratic voter suppression effort aimed at white Republicans in a red state.[16]

The operation was funded by the billionaire LinkedIn cofounder Reid Hoffman, through an outfit called American Engagement Technologies (AET). The stated goal of the operation was to sway fifty thousand votes toward Jones by experimenting "with many of the tactics now understood to have influenced the 2016 elections." According to portions of a leaked postelection report on what was dubbed "Project Birmingham," the group aimed to "radicalize Democrats, suppress unpersuadable Republicans ('hard Rs'), and faction moderate Republicans by advocating for write-in candidates. . . . We aggressively targeted evangelical hard Rs with messaging meant to provoke disgust and depress turnout."[17]

Some of AET's activities disseminated disinformation, but others involved amplification of truthful information or nonfactual opinion, where the real chicanery was not in the content of the message but in lying about or obscuring the identity of the speaker. Alabama voters might well have cared that progressive Democrats, not teetotalers or Russians, were the ones trying to influence their votes.

But information about the source of the influence campaign was not available to voters. It came to light only well after the election, through leaks to the *New York Times* and *Washington Post*. Without those leaks, we still might not know of these efforts, just as we learned of some of the Russian activity aimed at sowing social discord and influencing the 2016 election only through the work of American intelligence agencies and the prosecutors who produced the Mueller Report.

Campaign finance disclosure law has long been about making sure voters have the information they need to make informed decisions. Social science demonstrates that voters use mental shortcuts to make decisions, and one piece of information they rely on is who is behind an election message aimed at them. For example, in 2010 California voters turned down a ballot proposition that would have benefited the utility Pacific Gas and Electric (PG&E). PG&E provided almost all of the $46 million spent on the "Yes on 16" campaign, compared with very little spent opposing the measure. Yet California's disclosure laws required PG&E's name to appear on every "Yes on 16" ad, and voters clearly considered the source. Voters defeated the measure.[18]

In its foundational decision in *Buckley v. Valeo* (1976), the Supreme Court recognized that campaign finance disclosure laws may serve this *information* interest, as well as interests in preventing the *corruption* of elected officials, by allowing voters to follow the money and look for special treatment given to campaign donors or those who spend to favor or oppose candidates, and the *enforcement* interest of ensuring that no other campaign finance laws are broken. For example, it is illegal for foreign governments, other foreign entities, and most noncitizens (except green card holders residing in the United States) to spend money advocating the election or defeat of candidates for office in the United States, and adequate disclosure allows regulators, the press, and the public to ensure that foreign sources are not secretly participating in our elections.[19]

But our current campaign finance disclosure laws are not up to the task of ferreting out the true sources of new social media campaigns aimed at influencing elections. Roughly speaking, the federal campaign finance disclosure law in effect since 1974 requires the disclosure of spending by and contributions to persons or entities who engage in express advocacy, such as an advertisement directly urging a vote for or against a candidate. The Bipartisan Campaign Reform Act of 2002, commonly known as the McCain-Feingold law, also requires disclosure of the funding behind so-called electioneering communications: advertising appearing on broadcast, cable, or satellite television or radio that mentions or features a federal candidate thirty days before primaries and sixty days before a general election. Candidates, political parties, and campaign committees must also disclose their election-related spending. Courts are split over whether political organizations that have as a major purpose the election or defeat of candidates may constitutionally be compelled to disclose their expenses as well.[20]

Unfortunately, these rules do not require disclosure for a great deal of important campaign activity, which makes it impossible for the law to fulfill its information, anticorruption, and enforcement purposes. Most of the paid social media advertising that Russia engaged in during the 2016 election did not contain express advocacy and was not electioneering communication because the ads were not on television or radio. It might surprise nonspecialists in the area, but placing an online ad saying, "Hillary Clinton is a Satan," as Russian operatives did in 2016, probably would not be considered express advocacy under federal campaign finance rules. And unless Dry Alabama registered as a political action committee, it probably was not legally required to disclose who paid for its activities if it avoided express advocacy. "Pray for Roy Moore" is not express advocacy. Even regular campaign ads broadcast on streaming services like Hulu are not covered by federal campaign disclosure rules, while the same ads would be subject to disclosure if run on broadcast, cable, or satellite television. Such a distinction, based on the technology that carries an advertisement to a viewer's television, makes no sense.[21]

Campaign finance disclosure laws should be updated to deal with the changing campaign and technology landscape. They especially need to grapple with the increasing use of streamed content, social media, and artificial intelligence to influence elections.

First, Congress should extend the same rules that apply to television and radio advertisements to advertising distributed online, including that on social media. This means disclosure of spending on ads placed close to the election that feature the name or likeness of candidates for office.

Back in the early 2000s, I was among those arguing that the Federal Election Commission's (FEC's) failure to extend the rules to the online space would leave one of the most important arenas for campaigning unregulated and without adequate disclosure. But libertarian opposition to any regulation related to campaigns and the Internet successfully beat back most efforts to extend the rules for almost two decades. Meanwhile, the use of new technologies for campaigning has exploded. Had those early efforts succeeded, those who spend significant sums seeking to support or oppose candidates for office and who mention candidates' names or feature their likenesses in online content would have had to disclose who they are.[22]

Today, with so much campaigning moving online, there is no good argument against extending generally applicable disclosure rules to online activity. The world is topsy-turvy when online political activity, which needs disclosure the most, gets it the least.

Proposed federal legislation called the Honest Ads Act would close this loophole for traditional campaign ads disseminated over the Internet. But the act would simply bring disclosure rules passed in the 2002 McCain-Feingold law to online political ads. This legislative fix will not be enough to deal with cutting-edge methods of influence.[23]

Disclosure laws must do much more than simply cover electioneering ads shared on social media. They should also cover funding behind organized efforts to influence election-related decision making, such as efforts to microtarget political ads or use programmable bots that send direct messages to users and engage them in political conversations in an effort to influence their votes.[24]

It is impossible to know precisely which technological innovations will next be harvested for campaign purposes, but legislatures should write laws to allow for technological change. They should require the timely disclosure of the identity of funders behind coordinated attempts to influence elections on social media, even if the persuasion comes in the form of bot-generated private messages, including encrypted apps like WhatsApp, that lack express advocacy but refer to candidates for office. Any person or entity that spends in the aggregate over a certain generous dollar threshold, such as $10,000 (indexed for inflation), on online activity to directly or indirectly influence voters for or against a particular candidate or ballot measure should be required to disclose the amount of their spending and their ultimate source of funding. To the extent it is technologically practicable, any message communicated to voters should provide an easy basis, such as clicking a link, to determine the sender's identity as well as how to obtain further information about funding.[25]

The spending threshold for mandated disclosure would count not only the funds paid to the platforms for services but also the hiring of software engineers, consultants, and others in an effort to influence elections on social media. Before they may use social media resources on the platform, those who fall within the reporting threshold would have to certify, under penalty of perjury, that they have made the required disclosures to the government. The law would not cover unpaid, nontargeted social media posts, such as those of an individual expressing support for or opposition to a candidate. It would leave unregulated great swaths of individual and group activity that does not involve substantial spending or resources. And like current campaign finance law, it would exempt from disclosure those who can credibly demonstrate that they would face a threat of harassment if their identities were disclosed and exempt media corporations when they are engaged in journalism.[26]

One of the stickiest points of such a disclosure law is figuring out what counts as an election-related activity subject to disclosure. For groups spending above a generous threshold with the major purpose of influencing elections—political parties, candidates, and other groups (like super PACs) organized primarily for political activity—disclosure of spending and contributions related to *any* content disseminated widely in the period close to the election would be mandated.

For everyone else, disclosure rules would kick in above a healthy dollar threshold only if a significant portion of the messages include the name or likeness of a candidate for federal office in the period close to the election. Individuals or groups primarily sending messages on issues such as climate change, abortion, Black Lives Matter, immigration, or gun rights would not be covered if the groups usually avoid mention of or reference to a candidate. A broader disclosure law covering all who spend significant resources sending online messages on issues without mentioning candidates would raise knottier First Amendment questions.

Even with these limitations, opponents no doubt would argue that an enhanced social media campaign disclosure law violates the First Amendment. This enhanced disclosure law would probably be constitutional under current Supreme Court doctrine, although there are signs that the Court's jurisprudence may soon move away from broad disclosure and toward a general right of anonymity in political speech and activity.

Since the 1976 case of *Buckley v. Valeo* and through the 2010 case of *Citizens United v. Federal Election Commission,* the Supreme Court has applied a midlevel "exacting scrutiny" in upholding most disclosure laws challenged under the First Amendment, reasoning that the federal government has anticorruption, information, and enforcement interests. These laws do not prohibit any speech but allow voters to know who is paying to influence their political decisions. Compared to limits or bans on spending, they are a more narrowly tailored approach to the issue of money in politics. When they exempt those demonstrating a threat of harassment, an important safety valve for those who must engage in important speech anonymously, disclosure laws generally pass constitutional muster.[27]

Federal election law requires disclosure of certain expenditures, and it defines an expenditure as "any purchase, payment, distribution, loan, advance, deposit, or gift of money or anything of value, made by any person *for the purpose of influencing any election for Federal office.*" Current FEC regulations exempt certain Internet-based activities from regulation. The federal statute, and these regulations, should be rewritten to require disclosure above a certain dollar threshold on Internet and social media efforts undertaken for the purpose of influencing federal elections. Disclosure should no longer be limited to those who spend money on express advocacy or who engage in electioneering communications on television and radio.[28]

A key question is how to write a law or regulation defining what counts as spending "for the purpose of influencing federal elections" without running afoul of vagueness and chilling problems that the Court has recognized under the First Amendment. Fortunately, the Supreme Court has held that the government may require disclosure of spending on political activity that goes well beyond express advocacy for elections. In the 1954 case *United States v. Harriss,* the Court upheld a law mandating the disclosure of certain lobbying activities. In the 1978 case *First National Bank of Boston v. Bellotti,* it upheld campaign finance disclosure requirements applicable to ballot measure campaigns, where there is no involvement of candidates.[29]

Further, in *Citizens United,* the Court rejected the plaintiffs' argument that the government could require disclosure of spending only on express advocacy and its functional equivalent. And in a portion of the 2003 *McConnell v. Federal Election Commission* case that was not overruled by *Citizens United,* the Court upheld the broad "issue request" requirement in Section 504 of the McCain-Feingold Act. It requires broadcasters to keep records of requests made by anyone to broadcast any "message" related to a "national legislative issue of public importance" or "otherwise relating to a political matter of national importance."[30]

Given these precedents, a law targeted at the disclosure of spending and contributions funding large social media, web, and app activities intended to influence federal elections should pass constitutional muster even if it reaches more broadly than express advocacy—if, for example, it covers large spending on electoral issues by groups aligned with the Tea Party or Black Lives Matter. The disclosure rule should rely on clear factors for determining what counts as election-related spending, tied to both content (most importantly the inclusion of the name or likeness of the candidate) and timing. Clear rules avoid the potential for administrative and prosecutorial discretion in their application. The high dollar threshold allows small, grassroots political speech and activity to proceed anonymously, preserving the privacy of those who are not major election players.[31]

Although I am confident of the constitutionality of such a measure under existing Supreme Court doctrine, the Court is beginning to turn hostile to disclosure. The conservative justices Anthony Kennedy and the late Antonin Scalia were great supporters of campaign disclosure laws, but they are no longer on the Court. Nor is the late Justice Ruth Bader Ginsburg, a liberal supporter of broad campaign finance laws.

Justice Clarence Thomas has long believed in a general right to anonymity when engaging in campaign activity, a view the Court flirted with in a 1995 case, *McIntyre v. Ohio Election Commission*, but later all but abandoned. In the 2010 case of *Doe v. Reed*, Justices Thomas and Samuel Alito both expressed concern about the potential for harassment of campaign donors given the ease with which information about contributors and spenders flows on the Internet. This issue seems to have broken along ideological lines; conservatives expressed greater concern about harassment. These justices hold these views about harassment even though the evidence shows that even hot-button ballot measures like those involving gay rights cause almost no unconstitutional harassment. Some justices have also suggested that the government interest in providing relevant information to voters is insufficient to justify a burden on political activity.[32]

Indeed, in the most recent disclosure case before the Supreme Court, the Court's conservative majority, including the newest justices, Neil Gorsuch, Brett Kavanaugh, and Amy Coney Barrett, signaled a more skeptical approach to the constitutionality of campaign disclosure laws, making a new majority on such issues. In the July 2021 case, *Americans for Prosperity Foundation v. Bonta*, the Supreme Court in an opinion written by Chief Justice Roberts, over a strong dissent by Justice Sonia Sotomayor for the Court's liberals, struck down a law requiring disclosure of information about charitable donors not to be released publicly, but released only to California law enforcement officials. Government officials did a poor job keeping the information secret, and the groups showed they faced a danger of harassment.

But rather than hold that the law could not be applied against just these groups, the Court decided the case broadly and struck it down for those not facing harassment. The Court's opinion signaled closer scrutiny of disclosure laws going forward, including campaign finance laws. The Court pointed to the "chilling" risk: "The petitioners here, for example, introduced evidence that they and their supporters have been subjected to bomb threats, protests, stalking, and physical violence. Such risks are heightened in the 21st century and seem to grow with each passing year, as anyone with access to a computer can compile a wealth of information about anyone else, including such sensitive details as a person's home address or the school attended by his children."[33]

On top of its concerns about harassment and donor privacy, the new Supreme Court majority could be concerned about the administrative toll such laws impose and their potential to burden those running advertising and influence campaigns about issues mentioning a candidate, even if they don't expressly advocate the election or defeat of any candidate. This is one of the reasons for having a high dollar threshold—ensuring that the administrative burdens and disclosure requirements do not fall on those engaged in organic, small-scale speech. The conservative orientation of these justices on First Amendment issues means that they could balk at multifactor tests to determine when a political group has a "major purpose" to influence an election outcome. Even if some of the justices would not overturn the bulk of disclosure laws, the justices could easily find ways to make disclosure laws ineffective by upholding only laws that do not cover some of the core political activity intended to be covered by such laws. In short, these enhanced disclosure laws are probably constitutional under current doctrine, but things are much less certain with the recent changes in justices.

Enhanced disclosure would help voters obtain valuable information about who is trying to influence their votes. It could also help with the enforcement interest by making sure prohibited foreign sources do not illegally try to influence our elections. And it is likely to be much more effective than private efforts to require disclosure.

Mandated disclosure, as I propose it here, would still leave much activity behind a veil of anonymity. Efforts to sow discord, for example, by organizing pro- and anti-Muslim rallies on opposite street corners, as Russian government operatives did in 2016, might be revealed only if a social media platform looked closely enough, flagged the spenders as engaging in these activities in order to influence U.S. elections, and excluded them for not filing a certification. The cost to organize Facebook Groups or to run ads is much lower than the $10,000 threshold, leaving much smaller-scale but potentially important political activity not subject to disclosure. But to the extent that political actors use considerable resources for online campaign purposes, the certification requirement will create the right legal incentives for the platforms to look for such activity and improve disclosure.

Labeling of Synthetic Media (Deep Fakes)

In the cheap speech era, mandated disclosure can do more than just provide information about who is financially backing efforts to influence voters. It can also let voters know whether they should believe their eyes and ears.

Federal and state governments should mandate truth-in-labeling laws requiring social media platforms and other websites with large numbers of users to deploy the best reasonably available technology to label synthetic media containing altered video and audio images of political candidates and elected officials as exactly that—altered. According to a recent Pew poll, Americans across the political spectrum broadly favor regulating these images. The technology to detect the most sophisticated deep fakes does not exist yet, but with the investment of significant resources—which it is in the country's national security interest to develop quickly—we could soon have adequate means to ferret out when someone has posted altered media. It will be a constant arms race between the makers of synthetic media and those who seek to detect it.[34]

As detection technology continues to develop, the government's interest in preventing consumer and voter deception should support a truth-in-labeling regime as the top way to deal with the deep fake problem. This labeling is a form of government intervention against the market's failure to solve the information lemons problem. Viewers would become more confident that the videos they see and the audio they hear are genuine when such media land in their feeds without a label indicating alteration.

Of course, regulation would have to specify what counts as an alteration of a video subject to labeling. The regulation would not require the "altered" label on those videos that used commercially ordinary cropping and color correction, for example, or that showed only portions of video. It would focus instead on digital "impersonations," what professors Danielle Citron and Robert Chesney describe as "hyper-realistic digital falsification of images, video, and audio." These are videos or audio clips that make people look or sound as if they are saying or doing something they are not.[35]

Such a truth-in-labeling requirement would be viewpoint-neutral, and it would not enmesh the government or websites in the difficult business of determining what is legitimate satire. Media altered for satirical purposes, for example, would be labeled the same way as media manipulated for malicious reasons.

A law requiring labeling of synthetic media faces a more uphill constitutional climb than one requiring disclosure of spending meant to influence voters, but it should be held constitutional by a Supreme Court that recognizes the government's compelling interest in promoting voter competency and access to truthful information. Whether the present Court would do so is uncertain, however, because it could view the requirement as a form of compelled speech.

Courts will subject any law purporting to regulate the content of political communications to heightened First Amendment scrutiny— either strict scrutiny, in which the government would have to show that any regulation satisfied a compelling interest and that the means adopted were narrowly tailored to that interest, or some intermediate level of scrutiny, like the "exacting scrutiny" the Court has applied to campaign disclosure laws.[36]

The government has a compelling interest in assuring that voters have access to truthful political information and to the tools to discover its truth or falsity. The Supreme Court has long recognized the value of an "active, alert" citizenry, and democracy's dependence on voters' ability to evaluate arguments in order to make political decisions. As the Supreme Court stated in *Citizens United*, quoting *Buckley*: "In a republic where the people are sovereign, the ability of the citizenry to make informed choices among candidates for office is essential."[37]

Requiring the labeling of deep fakes is a more narrowly tailored means of dealing with the voter competence problem than laws that would punish deep fakes or require their removal from websites and social media platforms. Compare my proposal to a recently enacted California law (in effect only until January 1, 2023) that makes it illegal for anyone "within 60 days of an election at which a candidate for elective office will appear on the ballot, [to] distribute, with actual malice, materially deceptive audio or visual media . . . of the candidate with the intent to injure the candidate's reputation or to deceive a voter into voting for or against the candidate" unless the video or audio was labeled as "manipulated." The law exempts news media and "satire or parody." It allows a candidate injured by a deep fake to obtain an injunction and, in appropriate cases, damages.[38]

The California law was inspired by a crudely altered 2019 video (sometimes referred to as a "cheap fake") making it appear that House Speaker Nancy Pelosi was drunk during an interview, but it presents constitutional problems because of its breadth and its pejorative labeling.[39]

To begin with, the California law bans some political speech, and bans, as we will see, face a high hurdle in light of the First Amendment's protection of robust political exchange. Further, a deep fakes ban raises vagueness and overbreadth problems by preventing the use of synthetic media when one is reckless about distributing "deceptive" video or audio about a candidate to a voter. Deceptiveness is undefined. It is not clear what counts as "parody or satire" under the law's safe harbor, and how to tell whether someone who is intending to influence an election using manipulated media is engaged in an act of deception. In addition, the label "manipulated" is more pejorative than "altered," and that too may raise a constitutional issue because the government would be requiring the disseminator of a video or audio file to add a negative label to political speech.[40]

Unlike the California law, which is probably unconstitutional, a truth-in-labeling requirement for political deep fakes is not government censorship. It stops no one from being able to create and post whatever altered video one likes, and it does not pejoratively label the material as "manipulated." It is not vague and it raises no issues of prior restraint of speech through the availability of an injunction to stop distribution of questionable content.[41]

The most serious constitutional argument against a labeling law for political deep fakes is that it would run afoul of First Amendment prohibitions on certain forms of "compelled speech." The Supreme Court's compelled speech doctrine is complex, but it makes it difficult for the government in certain circumstances to require someone to say or write something he or she otherwise would not. The principle is far from absolute, particularly in the election context, where the Court has upheld written "disclaimer" requirements on ads saying who is paying for them. A prominent example is the McCain-Feingold's "Stand by Your Ad" provision, which requires federal candidates to say that they "approved this message" as part of their television and radio ads. In 2003 the Supreme Court upheld that form of compelled speech with virtually no discussion.[42]

In the 2018 case *National Institute of Family and Life Advocates v. Becerra,* the Supreme Court struck down two California laws requiring certain "crisis pregnancy centers" to notify clients about the availability of publicly funded family planning services, including abortion and contraception. These centers are run by groups opposed to abortion who seek to attract women looking for an abortion provider so as to counsel them against the procedure. The Court held that such disclosures were a form of compelled speech on a controversial topic that were not justified under even intermediate scrutiny. It also held that the law was underinclusive because it provided only some information about state-sponsored services to low-income women, namely, that related to reproductive health and services. And it held that California could have provided the information to California women directly without burdening the centers.[43]

In holding California's laws unconstitutional, however, the Court reaffirmed that the government could mandate "purely factual and uncontroversial disclosures about commercial products." It pointed to its earlier decision in *Zauderer v. Office of Disciplinary Counsel of Supreme Court of Ohio*, upholding an Ohio law that required attorneys who advertised contingency fee arrangements for legal services to disclose that clients might have to pay certain fees and costs. The Court described *Zauderer* as an instance in which it applied a lower level of scrutiny in certain contexts to compelled disclosure, and it stressed the commercial and factual context of permissible disclosures. Lower courts have read *Zauderer* as applying to disclosures aimed at preventing consumer deception, and as allowing the government to mandate that certain individuals and entities provide other factual and uncontroversial disclosures.[44]

A requirement that websites and social media platforms with large numbers of users label altered videos as "altered" would mandate the disclosure of purely factual and uncontroversial information in a political context to protect voters from deception. Although the videos themselves may be quite controversial, whether they were digitally altered is not a controversial topic and requires no political judgment. Objective truth can be verified by a scientific comparison of original content with what is posted online. Websites would not be forced to make value judgments about the reasons for the alteration.

In short, the proposed deep fakes law is closer to the one upheld in *Zauderer* than the one struck down in *Becerra*, even though the disclosure I propose is in a more political than commercial context.[45]

It is not certain how the Supreme Court would handle a deep fake labeling law under the compelled speech doctrine, and a court with a strong libertarian view of the First Amendment could well reject it even though it could serve a compelling purpose in protecting consumers from deception in a viewpoint-neutral way.

Tightening the Foreign Campaign Spending Ban

Federal law prohibits foreign individuals (aside from permanent legal residents), governments, and other entities from spending or contributing money to elect candidates to federal, state, or local office. But Russian government interference in the 2016 and 2020 U.S. elections shows that the current laws need tightening. Once again, it is not clear that the new Supreme Court will allow the necessary fix.[46]

In a 2010 case called *Bluman v. Federal Election Commission,* Judge Brett Kavanaugh (now a Supreme Court justice) explained the sound basis for federal laws limiting foreign contributions and spending in candidate campaigns: "It is fundamental to the definition of our national political community that foreign citizens do not have a constitutional right to participate in, and thus may be excluded from, activities of democratic self-government. It follows, therefore, that the United States has a compelling interest for purposes of First Amendment analysis in limiting the participation of foreign citizens in activities of American democratic self-government, and in thereby preventing foreign influence over the U.S. political process."[47]

Bluman upheld a federal law barring foreign nationals—in this case, Benjamin Bluman, a foreign national working as a lawyer in New York on a temporary work visa—from spending even fifty cents to photocopy and distribute flyers advocating the reelection of President Obama in 2012. Justice Kavanaugh wrote the *Bluman* opinion for a unanimous three-judge federal district court, and the Supreme Court issued a "summary affirmance," meaning that it did not see a need for a full set of arguments in the case and simply agreed that the lower court's result was right.

Summary affirmance was all the more remarkable because Bluman's lawyers had argued, with some force, that barring noncitizens from spending even a penny in candidate elections was in tension with the Court's *Citizens United* decision. *Citizens United* held that the government violated the First Amendment in barring business corporations from independently spending money to support or oppose candidates because the identity of the speaker should not matter for purposes of promoting free speech. The Court's summary affirmance in *Bluman* suggested that foreign identity is different, and the government's compelling need to protect democratic self-government is stronger than the anticorruption and equality arguments it advanced, without success, in support of the corporate spending limits in *Citizens United*.[48]

Despite *Bluman*'s recognition that a complete ban on political speech is constitutionally permissible in some circumstances—and in some ways thanks to how Justice Kavanaugh crafted the court's opinion—much of the troublesome Russian campaign activity in the 2016 U.S. election did not violate federal law. Recall from chapter 2 that a key form of Russian interference in 2016 involved advertising on social media in an attempt to sow discord and build support for Donald Trump's presidential campaign. In the 2020 election, Russia sought to set up false news sites and pay U.S. journalists to write stories for those sites, again to foment discord and support Trump's reelection. Neither of these activities appears to violate current federal law as interpreted in *Bluman*.[49]

Federal law bars foreign nationals, including foreign governments, from making certain expenditures and electioneering communications in connection with a federal, state, or local election. But it is at best uncertain whether independent online ads such as those the Russians ran in 2016, or their faux 2020 news sites that did not expressly advocate the election or defeat of candidates, are covered by the foreign expenditure ban.[50]

Justice Kavanaugh in *Bluman* interpreted the foreign spending ban only to cover express advocacy and not even issue advocacy mentioning a candidate. "This statute, as we interpret it, does not bar foreign nationals from issue advocacy—that is, speech that does not expressly advocate the election or defeat of a specific candidate." While this interpretation is not free from doubt, the current Supreme Court seems likely to favor a narrow interpretation of laws implicating free speech rights under the First Amendment. Under this interpretation, neither online ads nor faux news sites mentioning candidates are covered by the foreign spending ban. Foreign entities violate the ban only when they expressly advocate the election or defeat of a candidate for federal office, or when they feature the candidate in television or radio advertisements broadcast close to the election (which makes them "electioneering communications" under the McCain-Feingold law).[51]

Suppose Congress wanted to write broader coverage to capture more foreign-funded activity by, for example, extending the definition of "electioneering communications" to online activities in the proposed Honest Ads Act. This proposed law would bar foreign individuals, governments, and entities from running online ads featuring candidates in the months before an election, just as they are now prohibited from running those ads on radio and television. Or perhaps Congress could proceed even more broadly and outlaw all the social media and Internet activity Russians engaged in to influence the 2016 and 2020 elections.

It is not clear how big an expansion of the foreign spending ban the Supreme Court would accept as consistent with the First Amendment, even if it continues to see democratic self-government as a compelling societal interest. Extending the current advertising rules from television and radio to online ads does not seem like a big leap, given how technological change has blurred the distinction between broadcast and online video. Extending the rules to online ads is something Congress should do and that the Court should uphold. The strong libertarian impulses of some justices on the Court, however, mean that their agreement on the constitutionality of such a law cannot be taken for granted. If the Court were to strike down disclosure rules related to the funding of such communications, for instance, then enforcing any foreign spending ban would be impossible.

Going further than the Honest Ads Act would almost certainly prompt Supreme Court resistance. For example, it could well strike down a law barring foreign entities from running paid ads that stir up unrest on contentious issues such as racial justice, immigration, or gay rights. The Court could rule that such a law is overbroad because it covers some speech that is not intended to influence elections, and because it unconstitutionally deprives Americans of potentially valuable information from foreign sources.[52]

This libertarian resistance to a broad reading of laws regulating foreign campaign activities was on display a few years ago in a controversy over whether President Trump's son Donald Trump Jr. could constitutionally be prosecuted for allegedly soliciting Russian government sources for "dirt" on Hillary Clinton during the 2016 campaign. Eugene Volokh, the leading libertarian First Amendment scholar who coined the term *cheap speech*, argued against a broad reading of the statute barring Americans from soliciting contributions, including in-kind contributions, from foreign sources.

Although I and others showed that the opposition research that

Trump Jr. hoped to get from Russian agents counts as a prohibited contribution under the statute (which defines these contributions capaciously to include "anything of value") as courts and the FEC had interpreted it, Volokh argued that foreign nationals (including perhaps foreign governments) should be allowed to share "information" such as "opposition research" with American campaigns because this information might help the public decide whom to vote for. He suggested that such an interpretation of the statute could be compelled by the First Amendment and pointed to a 1965 case, *Lamont v. Postmaster General,* in which the Supreme Court struck down a law that required Americans wishing to receive "Communist propaganda" from outside the United States to request it in writing.[53]

In its *Lamont* ruling, the Court did not discuss society's compelling interest in self-government specifically related to elections; it limited its consideration to the constitutionality of licensing schemes for receipt of foreign propaganda by mail. The Court has often allowed election-related speech to be more closely regulated than political speech more generally, and in *Bluman* it upheld the foreign campaign spending ban. Nonetheless, Volokh's reliance on cases like *Lamont* suggests that a conservative majority of Supreme Court justices may be attracted to arguments against broad limits on foreign campaign-related activities. The Court could focus less on the rights of foreign individuals to share the information and more on the rights of Americans to solicit it. And striking laws barring such speech is much more consistent with the Court's decisions about domestic speakers in the campaign finance context, such as the 2010 *Citizens United* case recognizing the right of domestic corporations to spend unlimited sums independently supporting or opposing candidates for office.

Limiting the reach of foreign campaign bans to express advocacy would make it child's play for foreign governments, entities, and individuals to get around the ban by avoiding words like "vote for" and "vote against."

As difficult as any dispute over an expanded general foreign campaign spending ban might be, any law specifically aimed at shutting down fake news sites run by foreign entities such as Russia's Peace Data site (described in the last chapter) promises to stir up a hornet's nest among the Court's conservatives because of the definition of who counts as the news media.

The Court weighed in on a related issue in its 2010 *Citizens United* case. There, the conservative majority held that barring corporations from expressly advocating the election or defeat of candidates, but exempting media corporations involved in producing news and commentary, violates the First Amendment. The Court held that "freedom of the press" protected explicitly in the First Amendment did not justify more favorable treatment for media corporations and that such discrimination among corporations violated the Constitution. As Justice Stevens put it in his partial dissent: "Under the majority's view, the legislature is thus damned if it does and damned if it doesn't. If the legislature gives media corporations an exemption from electioneering regulations that apply to other corporations, it violates the newly minted First Amendment rule against identity-based distinctions. If the legislature does not give media corporations an exemption, it violates the First Amendment rights of the press. The only way out of this invented bind: no regulations whatsoever."[54]

The approach of the *Citizens United* majority was the opposite of the one taken by the Court in a 1990 case overruled in *Citizens United: Austin v. Michigan Chamber of Commerce,* which held that it was constitutionally permissible to exempt media corporations engaged in producing news and commentary from a generally applicable law barring corporate campaign spending on express advocacy. The *Austin* Court, recognizing the important educational functions served by the media, held that the government could give special protections to news media when they are engaged in these functions.[55]

Current law still partially reflects the *Austin* sensibility. Despite *Citizens United,* the media exemption still applies to rules requiring disclosure of certain political spending. Corporate and individual news media are exempt from such disclosure even when their newspapers and other journalistic platforms publish editorials or other commentary expressly advocating the election or defeat of a candidate. The media exemption is consistent with other laws in which the government gives the institutional press access to trials or the benefits of a shield against revealing anonymous sources of information.

At some point, those media exemptions may be challenged as discriminatory, potentially leading the Court to strike more disclosure rules. Although that outcome seems unlikely given some justices' continued support for at least some disclosure laws, the debate over the treatment of news media demonstrates the danger of any congressional or state attempts to further regulate foreign fake news sites and the emerging domestic fake news sites I described in the last chapter. It will be up to private actors, such as websites controlling search functionality or associations of journalists (as I discuss in the next chapter), to determine how to treat these fake news sites.

Ultimately, as I explained in my 2016 book, *Plutocrats United,* any attempt to preserve the media exemption in campaign finance laws will depend on having a working definition of journalism that distinguishes between entities engaged in the regular business of fact gathering and analysis that is consistent with journalistic norms, and advocacy organizations masquerading as news media. I would embrace the functional definition of journalism put forward by Professor

Sonja West. She pointed to four factors that should be of the greatest importance in identifying "the press": "(1) recognition by others as the press; (2) holding oneself out as the press; (3) training, education, or experience in journalism; and (4) regularity of publication and established audience."[56]

The Court's conservatives may find Professor West's definitions too vague or subject to government officials' unconstitutionally broad administrative discretion. But eliminating the press exemption could have terrible consequences for both disclosure laws and the foreign ad ban as more malicious foreign actors shift to medialike activity.

Narrow Ban on Empirically
Verifiable False Election Speech

As we have seen, the government has the constitutional ability to ban some election-related speech, such as foreign government–sponsored advertising explicitly calling on Americans to vote for or against candidates for office.

Speech bans are serious matters, and they should require very strong justifications. The perjury prohibition is effectively a ban on false speech in sworn testimony, which we maintain because truth telling is essential for a fair legal process. Perjury prosecutions are hard for good reason, but people are punished for perjury when it is appropriate. The Supreme Court explained the permissibility of perjury prosecutions under the First Amendment in a 2012 case, *United States v. Alvarez:* "Perjury undermines the function and province of the law and threatens the integrity of judgments that are the basis of the legal system. . . . Unlike speech in other contexts, testimony under oath has the formality and gravity necessary to remind the witness that his or her statements will be the basis for official governmental action, action that often affects the rights and liberties of others."[57]

The Constitution similarly allows narrow bans on obscene material because of the social harms that such material can cause. But the narrowness of the definition of obscenity limits the reach of such laws to a relatively small amount of speech.[58]

In elections, the government should be able to ban what I term false *election* speech, which is false speech about the mechanics of voting. Such a law would apply wherever the statement is made: on television, in a newspaper, or on social media, a website, or a messaging app.

One should face appropriate punishment for lying about when, where, and how people may vote. Saying, "You can now vote by text," or "You need a photo ID to vote" in a state that does not require it, is demonstrably false speech that interferes with the franchise. So is speech that contains demonstrably false statements about an upcoming election's being rigged, such as a false claim that election officials do not count ballots submitted by mail. Government officials acting under a false election speech law could punish someone who spreads such information with actual malice (that is, knowing that it is false or acting in reckless disregard to its truth or falsity). They also could order social media platforms and websites to remove such false speech when detected.[59]

The federal government is even in the midst of prosecuting a Trump-supporting Twitter user under an existing federal law barring conspiracies "to injure, oppress, threaten, or intimidate any person . . . in the free exercise or enjoyment of any right or privilege secured to him by the Constitution." The user allegedly tricked 4,900 voters to "cast" their ballots by text during the 2016 election. The defendant may well argue both that current law does not cover the conduct and that he is protected by the First Amendment.[60]

There is nothing contestable in ordinary elections about the date of the election, how people may register to vote, and where they may cast their ballots. This makes a prohibition against such statements clear and easy to understand. Such a law would not cover general statements that an upcoming election will be stolen or rigged if the statement is unaccompanied by empirically falsifiable details about how this stealing purportedly would happen. This limitation means a lot of potentially damaging speech would remain legal and will require means other than this law to combat. Indeed, during the 2020 election season there was relatively little empirically verifiable false election speech and much more speech, uncovered by my proposed law, calling or suggesting the election was "stolen" or "rigged."

Given Trump's statements after the 2020 election, one can imagine an extension of this law to bar a candidate's false *postelection* statements that an election was rigged or stolen. But such statements about how an election *was* conducted, while damaging to American democracy, do not directly interfere with people's ability to exercise their franchise. Sometimes candidates' postelection speech will be about legitimately contested elections, and a broader speech ban could deter important debate about the conduct of an election. An extension to postelection false election speech is perhaps justified to preserve the integrity of *future* elections.

The law also would not ban false *campaign* speech about the positions, actions, and views of candidates, such as a charge that a candidate's opponent has voted to raise taxes. Such speech is often contested, and disputes over the veracity of campaign speech do not go to the core matter of exercising the franchise. We rely on counterspeech by candidates, the press, and others to ferret out the truth. That in large part is what a modern campaign is all about.[61]

It is likely that the Supreme Court would subject any election-related speech ban to strict scrutiny, as a content-based restriction on pure political speech. A tightly drawn ban on empirically falsifiable false speech about when, where, and how people may vote should have a good chance of being upheld by even a conservative Supreme

Court applying strict scrutiny, but the matter once again is far from certain.[62]

The Court has become much more skeptical about banning false political speech generally. Back in 1964, *New York Times Company v. Sullivan* famously held that the state could punish those who engage in false, defamatory speech made with actual malice, recognizing the harm that false speech can cause. In the 1982 case *Brown v. Hartlage,* the Court rejected an attempt to void an election result after the winner was accused of violating a Kentucky law barring candidates from certain corrupt practices. The candidate had promised not to take a salary if elected, and Kentucky courts had previously held that promises not to take a salary violated the statute and could be grounds for voiding the election. In holding the Kentucky law unconstitutional, the Court stated that "demonstrable falsehoods are not protected by the First Amendment in the same manner as truthful statements."[63]

By 2012, however, the Court appeared to have shifted its view. It strongly suggested in *Alvarez,* a case involving a person who lied about receiving a congressional Medal of Honor, that laws penalizing false political speech would violate the First Amendment. There was no majority opinion, but Justice Kennedy's plurality opinion for four justices rejected the argument that the First Amendment categorically does not protect false statements, just as it categorically does not protect other types of speech, such as obscenity and fighting words. He wrote that counterspeech is normally the constitutionally acceptable response to false political speech and that the Stolen Valor Act violated the First Amendment. Separate opinions by Justice Stephen Breyer for himself and Justice Elena Kagan, and by Justice Alito, similarly express great skepticism about laws regulating the truth or falsity of political content.[64]

While *Alvarez* and other cases suggest that a broad ban on false campaign speech would be unconstitutional, a more focused ban on empirically falsifiable election speech has a much greater chance of gaining Court approval. In the 2018 case *Minnesota Voters Alliance v. Mansky*, the Court acknowledged that the government could ban false speech about when and how to vote. It declared: "We do not doubt that the State may prohibit messages intended to mislead voters about voting requirements and procedures." Punishing such false speech does not raise the risk of the state's having to make judgment calls about truth or falsity. The location of a polling place is objectively verifiable.[65]

A law that goes further and prohibits merely misleading campaign speech is more problematic despite *Mansky*'s reference to "messages intended to mislead voters." Consider a flyer distributed some years ago in University of Wisconsin dormitories, telling voters to vote "at the polling place of your choice." A vote cast anywhere but in the voter's actual assigned polling place would be cast on provisional ballot, which would not have counted under state law. The statement is misleading, but arguably it does not contain a literal falsity, and it may be impossible to write a law that would prohibit misleading statements without raising a risk of arbitrary enforcement and political censorship.[66]

A law that went further and targeted speech aimed at suppressing the vote of certain groups of voters, but containing no empirically false information, would almost certainly be unconstitutional. Think of the Russian "Blacktivist" Facebook page in the 2016 election telling viewers that Hillary Clinton did not care enough about Black Lives Matters protesters, a message apparently intended to depress African American turnout for Clinton. Or consider messages intended to support Doug Jones in the 2017 U.S. Senate race in Alabama by suggesting that his Republican opponent, Roy Moore, would seek to ban the sale of alcohol in the state. Although there is no question these messages were aimed at suppressing votes in order to sway an election, there is no way to write a law against such messages that could be applied fairly and consistently without discretion by government officials. Even though they are a social ill, these messages can be handled legally only through adequate disclosure of the speakers' identities.

Although *Mansky* did not reach the issue, the government could probably require websites and platforms with large numbers of users, such as major social media companies, to remove demonstrably false election speech from their sites. Such regulation does not raise the risk of censoring controversial political ideas. If the law mandates that voting take place on Tuesday, a false social media post saying "Republicans vote on Wednesday" is demonstrably false, requires no value judgment by a government regulator, and raises no issues of ambiguity.

The alternative to such a law is sole reliance on counterspeech, but counterspeech may not be enough to defeat a flood of bot-driven fake news that makes it harder for voters, even those with civic competence, to separate truth from fiction about when, where, and how to vote. Professor Philip Napoli has neatly summarized the reasons that counterspeech generally may prove inadequate in the cheap speech era: "Technological changes have: 1) affected the relative prominence of the production of true versus false news; 2) diminished the gatekeeping barriers that have traditionally curtailed the production and dissemination of false news; 3) increased the ability of those producing false news to target those most likely to be receptive to/affected by the false news; 4) diminished news consumers' likelihood of being exposed to accurate news that counteracts false news; 5) diminished news consumers' ability to distinguish between true and false news; and 6) enhanced the speed at which false news can travel." The danger that counterspeech will be insufficient is especially great when it comes to false information about how to exercise the franchise itself, because a tricked voter may lose the opportunity to vote.[67]

For this reason, courts should not interpret the First Amendment to bar carefully drawn laws against false election speech. They are a form of consumer protection: outside the political arena, the government certainly has the power to protect the public by regulating against false advertising. False advertising in the political context is even more dangerous to voters.

A law requiring companies to remove false content about when, where, and how people vote would be supported by the same compelling interest the Court implicitly recognized in *Mansky:* protecting the integrity of the voting process. Though such a law would reach into the private property of websites, it is less intrusive than laws that prohibit other unprotected speech on private property, such as laws banning obscenity. And it is supported by a truly compelling state interest in assuring that voters have accurate information about how to participate in the voting process, one of the cornerstones of a democracy.[68]

Defamation Lawsuits

Defamation lawsuits also can help to promote truth telling and election integrity. False statements about elections being stolen that injure the reputation of the person or entity accused of rigging the election should create tort liability. The statements could be made in any venue, including television or radio, a newspaper, a website or social media post, or social messaging apps.

As I noted in chapter 1, voting machine manufacturers sued Sidney Powell and Rudy Giuliani as well as Fox News for making false statements about the integrity of the companies' voting machines used in the 2020 presidential election. Such lawsuits allow judges and juries to determine whether election-related statements were false, as well as the state of mind of those who made the statements. The Supreme Court has interpreted the First Amendment to require proof of "actual malice" to bring a defamation suit for statements about public figures or matters of public concern. Actual malice means that the defendant made the statement knowing it was false or with reckless disregard about its truth or falsity.[69]

Defamation verdicts by lay juries who heard evidence about people who knowingly lied about election integrity would not convince everyone to reject such lies, but they probably would convince some people who were uncertain what to make of such allegations. Even the threat of such lawsuits in 2020 had the salutary effect of shutting down a part of the false talk about the 2020 election being stolen.

The biggest limitation to defamation lawsuits is that they cover only false statements about elections that injure someone's reputation. Lots of false statements about elections being stolen or rigged would not injure anyone's reputation in particular, which makes such suits unavailable. In many cases involving false claims about stolen elections, no plaintiff has standing to bring a lawsuit.

Consider, for example, the faux audit of 2020 presidential election ballots cast in Maricopa County ordered by Arizona's Republican-dominated state senate in spring 2021. The state senate forced the audit despite the complete lack of evidence that election results from the county were in question, and over the protests of Republican elected and election officials from the county. The company hired to conduct the audit, Cyber Ninjas, had no experience running an election audit. The company did not follow ordinary audit guidelines, and the audit became the butt of jokes when news leaked that the organization was using ultraviolet light to hunt for bamboo strands in ballots (supposedly to show that some fraudulent ballots originated in Asia). Those running the show limited press access, giving some exclusive access to OANN, which raised undisclosed sums to pay for part of the audit. Not only did the threat of defamation suits not deter the Arizona faux audit; the conspiracy theories it spawned, and President Trump's enthusiasm for the Arizona chicanery, prompted calls for similar "audits" in other states won by Biden in 2020, including Georgia and Wisconsin. Even the fake Arizona "audit" confirmed Biden's victory, but did nothing to dampen false claims of a stolen 2020 election.[70]

It is possible that defamation lawsuits could become a more potent tool to police disinformation in the future. Two Supreme Court justices, Clarence Thomas and Neil Gorsuch, have suggested that the Supreme Court reconsider the line of cases beginning with the 1964 *New York Times v. Sullivan* case that established the "actual malice" standard and made bringing defamation cases quite difficult. Drawing on an important article by Professor David Logan, Justice Gorsuch tied the Supreme Court's actual malice standard to the rise of disinformation in the cheap speech era. Dissenting from the Court's refusal to reconsider the standard in a 2021 case, Gorsuch wrote: "No doubt, this new media world has many virtues—not least the access it affords those who seek information about and the opportunity to debate public affairs. At the same time, some reports suggest that our new media environment also facilitates the spread of disinformation. . . . All of which means that the distribution of disinformation—which costs almost nothing to generate—has become a profitable business while the economic model that supported reporters, fact-checking, and editorial oversight has deeply eroded."[71]

Easing the actual malice standard will do little to counter disinformation, given that much of it does not defame anyone in particular and lawsuits are cumbersome things. And the danger of "opening up" libel laws, as former President Trump had urged, is that people will be chilled from criticizing government officials for fear of a lawsuit. The openness of these conservative justices to rethinking First Amendment law in light of the rise of cheap speech is encouraging, but lowering the bar for libel suits is a dangerous way of attacking the disinformation problem.[72]

Banning Data-Driven Microtargeting
of Election-Related Advertising

The last chapter explained what happens when campaigns and others use intricately detailed personal demographic data to target political ads in order to manipulate public opinion. In their influential book, *Network Propaganda,* Yochai Benkler, Robert Faris, and Hal Roberts write that microtargeting, by getting users to "want, believe, or do things," "threatens to undermine the very possibility of a democratic polity."[73]

The concern here is that microtargeted advertising is different in kind from normal advertising measures because it relies on deeply personal information that people do not realize they are giving up, bit by bit, each time they pick up and use their smartphone or computer. A ban on the microtargeting of political advertising on websites, social media platforms, and apps would protect consumer privacy and autonomy. Such a ban would simply stop campaigns and others from relying on intimately personal data collected by the platforms to serve ads; it would not prevent campaigns or others from targeting ads to anyone using other means of identifying recipients. Nor would it prevent the use of social media data to target ads geographically at all voters who are eligible to vote in a given race.

A ban on the use of such intimate social media data to target voters would be especially protective against disinformation likely to resonate with a finely targeted recipient. Allowing normal targeting of voters but not microtargeting is similar to allowing people to use cameras to take pictures of others as a means of deciding which goods to offer them for sale but barring the use of mind-reading machines for the same purpose. As the law and technology expert Julie Cohen argues, limiting the ability to harness platform data for election-related purposes serves society's compelling interests in limiting further factionalization of our politics, preventing manipulation of our choices through platform architecture, and deterring authoritarianism.[74]

Anyone wishing to use platform data to target a political ad to some voters in a congressional district who are on a social media platform, for example, would have to target all the identified voters in the district on that platform. Platforms could not use data supplied by the campaign to target more ads to "look-alike" voters (as Facebook currently allows) as identified by the platform algorithm. Campaigns would remain free to use their own means to target voters; they would simply not be able to continue piggybacking on data collected by the platforms.

Political disinformation overall should decrease when campaigns cannot use platform data to send messages to a particular demographic such as young Latinas or retired, white, blue-collar workers. Lies and misleading or incendiary statements that would resonate with one group might backfire with many others.[75]

Such a ban sounds paternalistic. Just as consumers can avoid the intrusive ads popping up in their Facebook feeds, voters can reject emotional and false political information meant to gain their votes or at least dissuade them from voting for an opponent. But the paternalism charge misses the key point: social media companies and others harness huge amounts of personal data as a source of profits, often without consumers fully understanding the extent to which they have made themselves vulnerable to targeting through perfectly normal online behavior. Voters formally consent to the use of their data when they sign up for these sites or apps, but they do not (and probably cannot) recognize the scale of what they have given up. A little paternalism is justified in the face of this huge informational asymmetry.

Counterspeech is not an effective tool for combating microtargeted misinformation. If candidates and campaigns do not know who has received campaign messages and what messages voters have received, they cannot target counterspeech. At the least, a law could require the opportunity for opposing candidates to know about the targeted ads and use the platforms to target counter-ads to the same group of voters.[76]

Like the proposed ban on empirically verifiable false election speech, a ban on using platform data for microtargeting political messages would be a content-based speech restriction subject to strict scrutiny. If one could use platform data to direct a message to someone on social media to buy a chair or take a trip somewhere but could not use data to direct a message to that same person to vote for a political candidate, then the law is discriminating on the basis of the type of message. As the Court explained in *Reed v. Town of Gilbert*, "A law banning the use of sound trucks for political speech—and only political speech—would be a content-based regulation, even if it imposed no limits on the political viewpoints that could be expressed."[77]

It is uncertain whether a ban on election-related microtargeting could survive the strict scrutiny triggered by a content-based law. If the Supreme Court views it as aimed primarily at protecting consumer privacy, such a law would probably fail for its underinclusiveness in targeting only political speech. In the 2020 case *Barr v. American Association of Political Consultants,* the Court considered the constitutionality of a law that banned automated telephone calls ("robocalls") to cell phones but that made an exception for messages about the collection of government debt. Political consultants argued that the partial ban was an unconstitutional content-based restriction on speech that favored speech about debt collection, and therefore the entire robocall ban had to be struck down under the First Amendment. The Court agreed that favoring debt collectors was an unconstitutional content-based speech restriction, but it held that the appropriate remedy was to strike the debt collector exception and leave the full robocall ban standing.[78]

Under *Barr*, it is likely that an election-only microtargeting ban would be unconstitutional if it was based on a consumer privacy rationale because it is a content-based restriction on a particular type of speech. But Congress still might enact a ban on microtargeting of all messages across the board. This broader ban would solve the content discrimination problem, but only through the kind of law that would draw existential opposition from social media and tech companies whose business models depend on the data mining that allows targeting of consumer ads. Even then, it is not clear that a blanket ban on microtargeting could survive a Supreme Court skeptical of any burden on those who wish to locate people with whom to share political or other speech. I return to this possibility later in this chapter.

Perhaps a narrower law could survive, like the proposed ban on empirically verifiable false election speech, on the basis of the unique need to protect a healthy democracy by shielding voters from political disinformation and promoting democratic legitimacy. The question is if the Court would recognize the inevitable trade-offs and allow the ban under the First Amendment even though it is driven by concerns about the content of messages themselves. Julie Cohen rightfully asked, even before the events of January 6, 2021, if "we should agree to trade reduced scope for the viral spread of grass-roots political dissent against reduced scope for the viral spread of messaging about the need for armed insurrection in response to purported racial 'replacement' or purportedly 'rigged' elections."[79]

Although I find the argument for the constitutionality of a narrower microtargeting ban persuasive, the conservative Supreme Court is more likely to view it as paternalistic and content-driven and to embrace the oversimplified marketplace-of-ideas notion that counterspeech and opting out from data disclosure are effective antidotes to microtargeting.

How to Limit Platform Power

I conclude this discussion of legal remedies with perhaps the most difficult issue: how to best—and constitutionally—deal with the potential for platform bias and election-distorting data-driven platform power.

Platforms are private entities, not subject to the types of First Amendment restrictions that apply to the government. In 2019 the Supreme Court reaffirmed in *Manhattan Community Access Corporation v. Halleck* that even regulated private television broadcasters are private actors, not state actors bound by the First Amendment. New York law required cable operators to set up public access channels for content, and the Court held that Time Warner, which controlled access in New York City, could prohibit content critical of its coverage from being included on the channel. If TV stations and platforms can decide whom to include or exclude, Twitter and Facebook also had the right during the 2020 election to label some of Donald Trump's election fraud tweets and later to deplatform him after the Capitol insurrection on January 6. Still, both liberals and conservatives have called for greater regulation of platform conduct.[80]

From the right have come charges that the platforms are biased against conservative voices and that Congress should therefore change a federal law, Section 230 of the 1996 Communications Decency Act, to allow platforms to be held liable for hosting content from users that is libelous or might otherwise subject publishers to liability. Trump vetoed a must-pass defense bill because Congress did not include a provision repealing Section 230; Congress overrode Trump's veto.[81]

As we saw in the last chapter, claims of bias against conservatives are overstated. At least on Facebook, conservatives have received especially favorable treatment under the rules for suspending and removing accounts. If conservatives are sharing more false stories about election fraud, for example, they are more likely to have their content labeled as disputed or incorrect under a fair process for policing such conduct. (We will see in the next chapter that some conservative claims of bias have merit, such as an ill-conceived decision of Facebook and Twitter to limit access to a sketchy *New York Post* story on the contents of Hunter Biden's laptop.)

Eliminating Section 230 immunity from libel claims would do nothing to prevent anti-conservative bias. If anything, eliminating such immunity could lead to the removal of more conservative content than before, to the extent that conservatives are more likely to raise potentially libelous claims about elections, as Trump's lawyers Sidney Powell and Rudy Giuliani did in falsely accusing voting machine manufacturers of election fraud.[82]

Without Section 230 immunity for claims based on platform content, platforms would have to engage in a great deal of content moderation to avoid potential liability, and platforms might have trouble doing so at scale. The potential for lawsuits based on claims that platforms did not do enough to stop harms, such as the January 6, 2021, insurrection, could lead platforms to shut down their forums and deprive many people of opportunities for self-expression. It seems this would be a very unpopular solution.

The deplatforming of Trump on Facebook and Twitter (and the subsequent decision of Facebook's Oversight Board to affirm Trump's deplatforming on that platform) has led to a remarkable turn by some conservative and libertarian lawyers and commentators in favor of regulation and against the free-market view of the First Amendment that they embrace in other contexts.

Justice Thomas, for example, has famously argued that virtually

← **Thread**

Donald J. Trump ✓ @realDonaldTrump · Dec 1   ○○○
Section 230, which is a liability shielding gift from the U.S. to "Big Tech"
(the only companies in America that have it - corporate welfare!), is a
serious threat to our National Security & Election Integrity. Our Country
can never be safe & secure if we allow it to stand.....

💬 28.5K   ↻ 65.8K   ♡ 248.3K   ⬆

Donald J. Trump ✓ @realDonaldTrump · Dec 1   ○○○
.....Therefore, if the very dangerous & unfair Section 230 is not completely
terminated as part of the National Defense Authorization Act (NDAA), I will
be forced to unequivocally VETO the Bill when sent to the very beautiful
Resolute desk. Take back America NOW. Thank you!

💬 21.1K   ↻ 46.4K   ♡ 195.8K   ⬆

*Screenshot of now-deleted Donald J. Trump tweets, Dec. 1, 2020
(archived at https://web.archive.org/web/20210104010052/https://
twitter.com/realDonaldTrump/status/1333965375839621120)*

all campaign finance regulation, even disclosure, is unconstitutional,
and that corporations and individuals have a constitutional right to
spend as much money as they would like to support or oppose candidates for office. He also argued against the constitutionality of the
Federal Communications Commission's now-defunct Fairness Doctrine, which required television and radio broadcasters to give fair
coverage of opposing viewpoints on public issues, seeing it as a violation of the First Amendment rights of broadcasters. That doctrine
was based on the supposed scarcity of the broadcast spectrum, which
does not apply to other media.[83]

Yet following Trump's deplatforming from Twitter, Thomas wrote
an unusual concurring opinion in *Biden v. Knight First Amendment
Institute,* a case raising the question whether Trump had the right to
block followers of his account on Twitter. The Court sent the case
back to the lower court to dismiss it as moot because Trump was no
longer president. Thomas agreed with that procedural decision but

wrote a concurring opinion for himself only addressing an issue that was not presented at all in the case. In it he suggested that platforms such as Facebook and Twitter could be compelled to carry speech from politicians that they do not wish to carry, much as private telephone companies are required to carry phone calls from everyone regardless of viewpoint, or private shopping mall owners must make their areas open to petition carriers. He even suggested that the portion of Section 230 granting immunity to platforms for decisions to block content could be unconstitutional if it prevented states from enacting laws—as Florida recently did—that require platforms to grant access to all candidates for public office regardless of what they might say. On that last point, Thomas relied on a blog post raising this possibility written by Eugene Volokh, the law professor who coined the phrase *cheap speech*.[84]

That Thomas of all people suggested regulating the content that private companies can include or exclude on their own websites is breathtaking. In Justice Thomas's world, the Koch Brothers or General Motors or George Soros could spend whatever they want, undisclosed, to support or oppose candidates to office, and Fox News or MSNBC could be as biased as they want in broadcasting political content to millions of viewers each day, excluding whomever the companies do not like from their stations. But Twitter, a private company, could not decide to exclude a candidate who had called for violence or perpetuated lies about election integrity on their branded website. Justice Thomas would uphold a law preventing Facebook, a private company, from deciding that it would rather not have its website associated with Trump's glorification of the violence of January 6.

There are many problems with Thomas's analysis. To begin with, as Eric Goldman has pointed out, the platforms are not neutral carriers such as telephone companies. They curate content all the time, as when they remove hate speech or pornography or when they promote certain content over others. And the platforms are hardly natural monopolies—Twitter and Facebook compete with one another or others—the usual defense of common carrier regulation.

Richard Epstein, another leading libertarian thinker, similarly raised the common carrier argument to force Twitter to carry Trump's content but conceded that whether the platforms are monopolies is a not "an easy question." And as Professor Genevieve Lakier noted, Thomas did not even try to reconcile his newfound love of content regulation with his earlier laissez-faire stance in some First Amendment cases or with decades of First Amendment jurisprudence to the contrary, such as the famous *Tornillo* case, in which the Court rejected a Florida law requiring that newspapers give a right to reply to those who disagreed with the newspaper's editorials, or with the requirement in *Reed* that content-based regulation of speech be subject to strict scrutiny.

Nor did Thomas explain why such a candidate's right of access would apply to Twitter and not to Fox News, the *New York Times,* or other media outlets with substantial market power. Twitter, like Fox News or the operators of the cable system in *Halleck,* creates a brand where people go to find certain content they want to see; that desire to create a holistic product is simply not true of telephone companies and other traditional common carriers. And while Thomas may support the idea of some private entities, such as shopping centers, being required to host speech on their properties that they do not want, he would not extend that access requirement to news organizations. The same logic should apply to the platforms: like a newspaper, a social media website is a curated space with an overall message.[85]

Justice Thomas's arguments are already causing a rethinking of broad First Amendment rights in some conservative circles. The *Washington Post* columnist and noted conservative Henry Olsen relied on Justice Thomas's concurrence in *Knight First Amendment Institute* to argue that Facebook and Twitter should not have a right to decide to remove content even from a politician who advocates violence or undermines election integrity. Olsen argued in support of Florida's new law and believes it is constitutional for states to mandate that social media companies be allowed to remove content only if it meets the Supreme Court's *Brandenburg* test, mentioned in chapter 1, for the exclusion of speech that calls for imminent lawless action that could lead to violence. "The alternative is that social media companies could bar speech regarding legal rallies and peaceful protests because the company's employees think—or, more ominously, hide behind the claim—that the rally could lead to violence. That's not consistent with widespread political discussion in the Internet age." What a deep intrusion on the decisions of private companies who are cultivating their own brand about what speech to include or exclude, especially about speech that could (and did) foment violence. A federal court unsurprisingly issued a preliminary injunction against the new Florida law.[86]

The district court preliminarily enjoining Florida's social media law specifically considered and rejected the common carrier argument put forward by Justice Thomas and others, and it held Florida's law unconstitutional because of its viewpoint discrimination and compelled speech. The court held that *Tornillo* was on point: "The activities of social media platforms that are the focus of the statutes now at issue are not the routine posting of material without incident or the routine exclusion without incident of plainly unacceptable content. These statutes are concerned instead primarily with the ideologically sensitive cases. Those are the very cases on which the platforms are most likely to exercise editorial judgment. Indeed, the targets of the statutes at issue are the editorial judgments themselves. The State's announced purpose of balancing the discussion—reining in the ideology of the large social-media providers—is precisely the kind of state action held unconstitutional in *Tornillo*" and other cases.[87]

It is not just those on the right who want to see more regulation of platforms to promote evenhandedness. The leading liberal constitutional scholar Erwin Chemerinsky has called for applying something akin to the Fairness Doctrine to the platforms. Writing with Prasad Krishnamurthy, Chemerinsky argues that "Congress . . . can regulate social media platforms by federal law and has the power to pass legislation that prohibits designated social media platforms from discriminating against users and content on the basis of their political views. Platforms would still be free to remove unprotected speech such as libel, slander, threats and the intentional dissemination of untruth. They would also be permitted to remove posts that do not conform to their community standards of decency and mutual respect. But platforms would not be permitted to censor speech based on its political content."[88]

Chemerinsky and Krishnamurthy presumably would allow platforms to remove some of Trump's statements that could promote violence or undermine confidence in elections on grounds that they violate "community standards of decency and mutual respect" or in some cases are provably intentional dissemination of "untruths," but giving government officials the ability to make judgment calls about decency seems dangerous. What if a Trump flunky could remove posts criticizing Trump on grounds that they did not show sufficient "decency" or "respect"? If these decisions are to be made in real time, are courts going to get involved litigating over which tweets can and cannot be removed?

More generally, evenhandedness requirements run the risk of arbitrary government enforcement, which itself could run afoul of the First Amendment. Surely if a Donald Trump–appointed bureaucrat were in charge of determining how fairly the platforms had handled Trump's tweets during and after the 2020 election, the bureaucrat could find bias even where none existed. And of course a left-leaning bureaucrat could determine that a platform's treatment of comments about the Biden administration's crime or immigration policy was not evenhanded.[89]

Some others on the left argue that with or without the immunity provisions for the inclusion of content in Section 230, the platforms need to remove more content, including content that is aimed at suppressing the vote or encouraging political violence. There are strong arguments that the platforms should remove some of this content voluntarily, as I discuss in the next chapter. But it is not clear that Congress or states could or should use *law* to mandate that they do so, at least not beyond the reforms suggested earlier in this chapter, such as the ban on empirically verifiable false speech about when, where, and how people vote.

All this criticism of evenhandedness requirements is not meant to understate the potential for platform bias. The real question is how to deal with that potential without making things worse through direct government control of content.

Recall how during the 2020 election, Instagram for some months returned links to pro-Trump messages on searches for Joe Biden but not pro-Biden messages on Donald Trump searches. Facebook, which owns Instagram, called the mistake inadvertent. But suppose one of the social media platforms, or Google—currently the dominant search firm—intentionally tweaked its algorithm to help one candidate and hurt another. That could have a big effect on election outcomes. What, if anything, could law do about it?

First, Congress could draft disclosure rules that would require the platforms to reveal deliberate algorithmic tweaking to favor one candidate over another. The platform would be said to "favor" a candidate when we see something like the Instagram glitch: prioritizing the display of positive stories about one candidate or unevenly serving negative stories about another. The question would be whether major candidates are treated symmetrically.

Congress could require platforms to provide a sworn statement about whether they were engaging in such tweaking. In the face of credible evidence (for example, that from biased search results) that the sworn statement is false, government inspectors would have the power to examine relevant coding. A government office would publicly disclose the platform's statements as well as the results of any investigations into biased search results. The platforms would face no penalty for the bias itself, only for providing any false sworn evidence about bias.[90]

Second, and more severely, evidence of platform bias could give the federal government a reason to apply antitrust law to break up platforms with too much market power. Given Google's dominance in search, a Google algorithm favoring one candidate or party over another could provide a major boost to one side of a campaign. Google would not have such power if it were no longer the dominant player in search; a more competitive search market would make bias less important. Instead, the world would look more like that of cable news, where some networks have a more liberal bias and others a more conservative bias, without a single network dominating coverage.

As Jack Balkin has put it, in some ways the United States has missed the boat because it has not already used this tool to deal with dominant speech and bias. "With stronger enforcement of antitrust and procompetition laws, innovations might have proliferated more widely, and we might have a healthier competition among social media companies and their sorting algorithms. Although we cannot be certain that this would have made it harder for foreign propaganda and fake news to proliferate and disrupt our democracy, it is generally harder to attack and compromise twelve targets than to attack and compromise one."[91]

If the platforms indeed have too much market power, antitrust law seems a better solution than laws compelling private platforms to carry speech they do not like, as Justice Thomas has suggested. Unfortunately, the use of antitrust law to break up the platforms in the name of protecting democracy could have unintended negative consequences for American democracy. A spun-off Instagram, for example, might not have the resources to detect deep fakes, ferret out attempts at foreign interference, or otherwise deal with issues of election security. The question requires more study.

Finally, and no doubt more dramatically, Congress could adopt super-strong privacy protections that would ban the use of private data in targeting online messages overall and prevent targeting ads based on the content with which users engage on the platform. Such a broader microtargeting ban would apply to all aspect of platforms' business and make political targeting much more difficult, which would potentially lower hyperpolarization and the spread of electoral misinformation. It could also put some of these companies out of business unless they drastically reworked their business models.

This recommendation may look more like one aimed at privacy law than election law, but, as Julie Cohen has argued, enhanced privacy protections also can be democracy-enhancing. Or as Shoshana Zuboff puts it: "Unequal knowledge about us produces unequal power over us, and so epistemic inequality widens to include the distance between what we can do and what can be done to us." Limiting commercialized deep data collection can deter all sorts of manipulation, including election manipulation by political actors. If, as Zuboff says, "we thought that we search Google, but now we understand that Google searches us," limitations on data use help preserve a sphere of democratic self-governance.[92]

Strict privacy regulation limiting the use of data for serving up advertising should avoid many of the knotty First Amendment problems that come with regulating content directly. Such a law stops no speech from any actor. But even a non-content-based law could raise First Amendment issues. Neil Richards argues that limiting data collection by platforms does not raise First Amendment concerns, but some others read a 2011 Supreme Court case, *Sorrell v. IMS Health Inc.,* as recognizing the First Amendment right to collect data and use it for targeting messages to people. Certainly, the platforms would push a First Amendment argument heavily should such regulation ever pass.[93]

The Limits of Law

"Governmental intervention," suggested by the economist George Akerlof as a means of combating the market-for-lemons problem, shows promise in dealing with some of the biggest problems plaguing fair elections and democracy in the United States, if Congress and states can enact these rules and if courts would uphold them.

There is good reason to doubt that Congress can soon come together to pass these proposed laws. Large numbers of Republican members of Congress still profess, despite all reliable evidence, that voter fraud swayed the 2020 election and that the problem was liberal media bias. And the Supreme Court may cling to an outmoded marketplace-of-ideas approach to the First Amendment that does not recognize the new challenges posed by technological advances and the rise of cheap speech. Given that the legal changes I have proposed here may not be adopted and, if adopted, may not be upheld by the courts, we must think about how the cheap speech problem may be addressed by private actors without reliance on law.

Law also has its limits. Even if Congress passed every proposal and the Court upheld them all, American democracy would face significant dangers absent further private action. Law alone is not going to stop millions of people from believing the election was stolen when a president popular within his party repeatedly uses social media to advance the false claim that it was. The violence of January 6, 2021, could have stopped a peaceful transition of power in the United States and threatened to end or limit democratic governance. The rise of cheap speech made it possible, and constitutionally permissible government regulation alone could not have stopped it.

Beyond Law

In early December 2020, about a month after the presidential election in which Joe Biden beat Donald Trump, the upstart right-wing cable television station Newsmax topped conservative stalwart Fox News in television ratings for the first time. According to CNN's Brian Stelter, Newsmax's anchor Greg Kelly's 7:00 P.M. show, which averaged about 100,000 viewers per night before the election, shot up to nearly one million viewers per night after the election. Many of those new viewers probably could not have found Newsmax on their cable boxes in October.[1]

Newsmax's meteoric, albeit temporary, rise was no mystery. Fox News had called the 2020 presidential race for Biden a few days after the election, once enough states had counted enough votes that Fox's decision desk, which operated independently from its news and opinion departments, had data to confidently predict a Biden win. Fox had created controversy by calling Arizona for Biden earlier than other news networks. It recognized Biden on its website and news programs as the "president-elect." A few days later, other networks and news agencies called Arizona and the presidency for Biden as well.[2]

Newsmax, however, perpetuated the false story that President Trump had actually won the election, but Biden stole it through voter fraud. Another upstart, One America News Network (OANN), followed a similar playbook. On Twitter, Trump repeatedly denounced Fox and urged viewers to watch its two small competitors, even as

Fox commentators and guests repeatedly raised spurious and dangerous voter fraud claims despite Fox's having called the race.[3]

Christopher Ruddy, a Trump friend and the head of Newsmax, gave an extraordinary interview in the midst of the 2020 election controversy to Ben Smith, a media columnist for the *New York Times,* in which Ruddy admitted Trump had lost the election but claimed Newsmax was just feeding audience demand. "In this day and age, people want something that tends to affirm their views and opinions," he told Smith. Smith saw Ruddy as cynically motivated to keep viewers around long enough to sell the network for a hefty profit, and he remarked that he had never seen anyone in the media treat an audience with the "blithe disdain" Ruddy showed Newsmax viewers. "When I pressed Mr. Ruddy on why he was stringing along his audience with a story he can't, really, himself believe—that Mr. Trump won the election—he didn't really defend it," Smith wrote. "Instead, he countered that he wasn't the only one. 'For two years, the liberal media pushed this Russian hoax theory, and there didn't seem to be any substantiation at the end of the day and it was a pretty compelling, gripping story—controversial personalities, things happened, sparks were flying,'" Ruddy told Smith.[4]

Ruddy was not the only one to benefit financially from Trump's disinformation campaign about voter fraud in the 2020 election. Trump himself raised over $200 million from willing donors in the weeks after the election. Although those donors thought they were funding the litigation efforts, the fine print revealed that up to 75 percent of donations went to a new postelection political committee known as a "leadership PAC," controlled by Trump, that he could use for his personal expenses. As Facebook and Twitter labeled or removed social media messages from the president and his allies falsely claiming fraud, some ardent Trump supporters fled to Twitter's upstart competitor Parler, where fraud claims could flourish without a fact check.

Parler was a top download in Apple's app store right after the election, showing that conservative donor Rebekah Mercer's investment in it was beginning to pay off. (Following the January 2021 insurrection, Parler was removed from Apple's and Google's app stores, and it had to scrounge around for new web hosting after being dropped by Amazon.)[5]

Trump was benefiting politically as well as financially. Leading Republican election officials signaled allegiance to Trump by declining to recognize Biden as president-elect. Soon after Republican state legislators resisted Trump's incessant entreaties to throw out the legitimate election results in their states and declare Trump the winner, they prepared new rollbacks of voting rights in the name of preventing phantom fraud.[6]

By the 2020 election, Donald Trump and his allies had weaponized cheap speech in a dangerous and destabilizing way. The anti-elitist, neopopulist rhetoric against the free press, the media, the courts, the FBI, the "deep state," higher education, and of course the main opposition political party fueled a hyperpolarized demand for more content fitting the worldview being sold to them. Ruddy was exactly right that some people wanted affirmance, not truth. And there were ample reasons to give it to them.

If Trump in 2016 had tapped into the secret formula for a new rural, older, mostly white coalition of voters, winning again in 2020 required boosting the turnout of his supporters while suppressing the turnout of others. When Trump lost but refused to concede in the days after the 2020 election, threats of violence against election officials and elected secretaries of state from his supporters grew as the dangerous rhetoric escalated on social media platforms, which led to some in-person confrontations.[7]

Nothing better illustrates the craziness of the weeks after the 2020 election than the actions of former Houston Police Department

Captain Mark Aguirre, who, according to a local television station, "was arrested and charged for running a man off the road and pointing a gun at his head in an attempt to prove claims of a massive voter fraud scheme in Harris County. . . . According to court documents, Aguirre told police that he was part of a group of private citizens called the 'Liberty Center,' who were conducting a civilian investigation into the alleged ballot scheme." Aguirre said he had been doing surveillance for four days of a supposed "mastermind" of a giant voter fraud scheme involving hiding 750,000 fraudulent ballots. The mastermind "turned out to be an innocent air conditioner repairman."[8]

Of course, as we saw in chapter 1, the craziness only escalated from there, as the January 6, 2021, insurrection at the U.S. Capitol was brought on by Trump's relentless circulating on social media of false election fraud claims.

A hyperpolarized era in which disinformation looms asymmetrically on one side of the political aisle and sometimes spills from the online world into the real world makes solving the problems of cheap speech, already a difficult task, that much harder. Steps to bolster truth that would gain cross-ideological support in ordinary times, such as legal measures ensuring that voters know who is trying to influence their votes or calls for more fact checking, themselves became part of the culture war.

It is hard to know, in the moment right after the Trump presidency, how much Trump himself drove the sea of disinformation on the right, or whether a Trumpist disinformation environment will persist among a core group of his supporters. Russell Muirhead and Nancy Rosenblum argue that "presidential conspiracism has unique power" but recognize that "the demonstrated capacity of conspiracist claims to activate followers, and the temptation to answer fire with fire, means that this aberrant mode of politics is likely to spread."[9]

Passing the Honest Ads Act and extending the definition of "electioneering communications" to online ads is hardly going to kill the conspiracy theories and restore us to the days of Walter Cronkite and trust in news. No one would want to go back to that era in any case: the information revolution of the last few decades has made life better in many ways and opened up new expanses of communication, collaboration, and consciousness.

More generally, the risks of cheap speech are deadly serious, and legal change can go only so far in taming broader cultural phenomena such as the current wave of conspiracism unmoored to any factual basis. There is much that private individuals and companies, nongovernmental organizations, and civic institutions can and should do to try to save American elections and democracy in this disruptive era, especially given the risk that the laws I proposed in the last chapter do not pass or get blocked by the Supreme Court.

Private action must include pressure aimed at social media and search companies to deal with disinformation and other cheap speech problems in ways that do not fundamentally squelch robust political debate. It also requires subsidizing local investigative media and creating means for identifying and bolstering organizations engaged in bona fide journalism. More ambitiously but even more urgently, private action must strengthen reliable political and informational intermediaries and launch education campaigns focused on digital literacy, respect for science, and the rule of law. Given the inchoate nature of these interventions, it will be hard to know if enough is being done.

Our democratic process for running fair elections depends on strengthening legitimate institutions and inculcating the value of truth. Private antidisinformation efforts will not reach everyone, but they can help limit the contagion that undermines election legitimacy, and they can encourage voters to make well-informed choices that are consistent with their interests and values.

Pressure on the Platforms

The 2020 election season demonstrated both that public pressure can get social media companies and other platforms to respond to the serious democracy problems caused by cheap speech, and that some of the voluntary measures the companies took may have done more harm than good. At the very least, 2020 showed that the platforms can be pressured, but they face a serious learning curve in dealing with the effects of cheap speech on American elections.

Russian interference in the 2016 election cast a shadow over the 2020 race, even if the foreign influence efforts we know of paled beside the work of the campaign organizations, parties, outside groups, and other domestic actors. Perhaps Russian interference was relatively minor in 2020 because one of the presidential candidates was far more effective at disinformation than Russian hackers operating out of a St. Petersburg boiler room could ever hope to be. Perhaps the Russians were so concerned with their 2020 "Solar Winds" hack into U.S. government computers that they did not want to draw more attention to themselves with a disinformation campaign.[10]

The platforms engaged in a great deal of self-regulation before 2020, including the removal of pornography, threats, hate speech, and more. Even with the protection of Section 230, the major companies recognized that certain steps are necessary to prevent their sites from becoming unpleasant and even dangerous.[11]

But 2020 brought a new level of self-regulation, as the platforms responded to criticism from the left and right. Facebook and Twitter restricted "coordinated inauthentic behavior" from foreign and domestic actors, revealing and removing accounts when they found a central actor coordinating groups of individuals or bots to create the appearance of organic grassroots activity. That summer, for example, Facebook, Twitter, and Reddit took steps to remove clusters of accounts pushing the QAnon conspiracy theory.[12]

The platforms dealt with political ads and disclosure differently. Facebook set up its own private disclosure rules. They proved both overinclusive, including journalists who should be exempt from disclosure, and underinclusive, allowing people to hide their true identities behind other persons or entities, such as Vice News's successful efforts to pretend to be all one hundred U.S. senators and to post ads falsely in their names. Facebook also refused to remove even obvious lies from political ads, as Senator Elizabeth Warren, then a presidential candidate, neatly demonstrated when she bought a Facebook ad falsely claiming that Facebook's head, Mark Zuckerberg, had endorsed Donald Trump. It is no wonder, given its failed efforts at self-regulating disclosure and its dominant market position, that Facebook has vaguely supported calls for government regulation.[13]

Twitter would not run Senator Warren's ad because it was not accepting political ads, and Google did not run it because it contained an unsubstantiated claim. Twitter banned all political ads during the 2020 election season, but its ban did not apply to unpaid statements made by politicians on their own pages. This left Trump free to make false claims about election fraud and to make other political statements directly to tens of millions of his followers while depriving his opponents of the ability to counter his speech with political ads. And by including broad subjects such as "climate change" within its even more broad definition of "political" for purposes of its advertising ban, Twitter regulated much more political speech than federal law would or could ever do.[14]

The biggest visible change some of the platforms made during the 2020 election season was adding warning labels to false election-related social media posts coming from Trump, and in some cases requiring users who wished to share that content to click through an additional warning or direction to see links to fact checks or more information. The labeling and fact checks certainly rankled Trump,

Elizabeth Warren ✓
@ewarren

Replying to @ewarren

We intentionally made a Facebook ad with false claims and submitted it to Facebook's ad platform to see if it'd be approved. It got approved quickly and the ad is now running on Facebook. Take a look:

Elizabeth Warren
Sponsored · Paid for by **Warren for President**

Breaking news: Mark Zuckerberg and Facebook just endorsed Donald Trump for re-election.

You're probably shocked, and you might be thinking, "how could this possibly be true?"

Well, it's not. (Sorry.) But what Zuckerberg *has* done is given Donald Trump free rein to lie on his platform — and then to pay Facebook gobs of money to push out their lies to American voters.

If Trump tries to lie in a TV ad, most networks will refuse to air it. But Facebook just cashes Trump's checks.

Facebook already helped elect Donald Trump once. Now, they're deliberately allowing a candidate to intentionally lie to the American people. It's time to hold Mark Zuckerberg accountable—add your name if you agree.

Mark Zuckerberg just endorsed Donald Trump
It's time to break up our biggest tech companies like Amazon, Google, and Facebook.
MY.ELIZABETHWARREN.COM

[Sign Up]

Elizabeth Warren tweet, Oct. 12, 2019 (available at https://twitter.com /ewarren/status/1183019897804197888, archived at https://web.archive.org /web/20191026235234/https://twitter.com/ewarren/status/1183019897804197888)

who complained about getting "Pinocchio" ratings from fact checkers. He also unsuccessfully pushed Congress to end Section 230 immunity because he did not like social media's labeling of his posts.[15]

Despite Trump's protests, it is hard to call the labeling effort successful. As we saw in chapter 1, the labels had little effect in deterring
the spread of false information. Some labels did not even suggest that
Trump's false posts contained misinformation. Early studies of the labels showed they were not particularly effective at convincing those in-
clined to believe the disinformation that it was false or stop the spread
of false claims; labeling might have reinforced the false beliefs of Trump
supporters, who saw the labels as a biased attack on the president. One
study found that labeled posts earned more than twice the interaction
of unlabeled posts (though that does not prove that the labels themselves spurred additional sharing). Another study found that blocked
Trump tweets about the election were posted more often and garnered
more visibility on other platforms than those labeled or left alone.[16]

About a month after the 2020 election, Trump posted a forty-
six-minute video filled with lies about how the election was stolen
through voter fraud. As CNN reported: "Within minutes of Trump's
posts going up on Facebook and Twitter, the social media platforms
sprang into action. Beneath the video, Facebook reminded users that
Joe Biden 'is the projected winner' of the election, citing Reuters and
other reporting agencies. Twitter applied a warning label beneath
the tweet containing the video clip, saying 'This claim about election
fraud is disputed.' Google's YouTube informed users in a label that the
Associated Press had called the race for Biden." Despite the labels,
the video racked up 14 million Facebook views within days, and a
shorter excerpt on Twitter had been viewed 3.5 million times.[17]

Facebook did make strides in improving its 2020 activities, when
compared to those in 2016, such as new efforts to stop foreign disinformation attempts and creating an ad library to let the public see

ads run on Facebook. It noted in a report on the 2020 election: "In the immediate pre- and post-Election Day periods, we took additional steps to maximize transparency and reduce opportunities for confusion and misinformation. We announced we would not allow ads that prematurely claim victory or attempt to delegitimize the election." The platform also took such steps as verifying the identity of those who manage large Pages, and it imposed new limits on data used by third-party apps.[18]

But the platform could have done much more. For example, Facebook could have tweaked its news algorithm to limit the flow of false information during the 2020 election. Despite protests from within the company and from the public, Facebook continued to feature Breitbart as a "trusted" news source. As we saw in chapter 1, after the 2020 election it briefly switched its algorithm so that users received more reliable news, such as that from NPR, instead of their normal diet, which, depending on a user's earlier choices, could have contained a great deal of misinformation. According to the *New York Times*, after the election "some Facebook employees asked at a company meeting whether the 'nicer news feed' could stay," but they were rebuffed. Facebook could have made these changes permanent or used other promising models, such as algorithms tied to the political diversity of a website's audience as a signal of quality. Instead, it reverted to its old, lousy algorithm.[19]

Facebook had the capacity to remove false and harmful content too, or at least to remove the financial incentive for posting it. We know from leaked documents that Facebook knew hate speech and disinformation were much more likely to flow on right-wing sites, but that Facebook's Mark Zuckerberg shut down internal efforts to rein in the groups. According to a BuzzFeed report, "Using data from a Facebook tool called the 'Hate Bait dashboard,' which can track content from groups and pages that leads to hateful interactions, [a

Facebook data scientist who quit in protest] listed the 10 US pages with the 'largest concentrated volume of likely violating Hate Speech comments' in the past 14 days. All were pages associated with conservative outlets or personalities, including Breitbart News, Fox News, the Daily Caller, Donald Trump's campaign and main account, and Ben Shapiro." "'I can't overemphasize that this is a completely average run-of-the-mill post for Breitbart or any of the other top Hate Bait producers,'" the data scientist wrote, according to Buzzfeed. "'They all create dozens or hundreds of posts like this [a] day, each eliciting endless volumes of hateful vile comments—*and we reward them fantastically for it.*"[20]

In addition to voluntarily reining in false election speech and related hate speech that nourishes polarization, the platforms could do much more to help American elections and democracy. If some of the legal changes proposed in the last chapter do not make it into law or survive court challenges, the companies could adopt them voluntarily. They could, on their own, ban microtargeting of political ads, label synthetic media as "altered," and set up improved disclosure requirements that would give voters more information about who was mounting large-scale efforts to influence them. That disclosure would help block the foreign ads that are already illegal under current law. The platforms could pledge not to favor candidates or parties secretly through their algorithms and even set up a voluntary inspection system that could protect their intellectual property. Facebook's experience with trying to regulate political advertising shows that these voluntary measures are unlikely to succeed as well as government regulations, but if done right and fairly, they would be an important step in the right direction.

The platforms could also go further in combating disinformation coming from politicians and public figures. For example, when Trump began incessantly tweeting about voter fraud in 2020 and then, after the election, falsely claimed that the election was stolen and that he had actually won, the platforms could have removed his account or deplatformed him. Although Twitter confirmed that Trump's tweets would have caused him to be removed under Twitter policies if he had not been president, the company gave him a pass through the 2020 election because of his office. A president has no special right of access to a private platform, and if a president's tweets violate election-related rules (or any other rules), there is no reason to give an exemption just because of the office. One could argue that because officeholders have greater power and visibility than average citizens, they also should have greater responsibility to tell the truth, not less, and the platforms have greater responsibility to remove false content from influential leaders.[21]

As we saw in chapter 1, Facebook and Twitter finally decided to deplatform Trump only following the January 6, 2021, U.S. Capitol insurrection, out of fear that Trump's actions could spur further violence. This was the right call, although it came too late.[22]

Removal of a political leader from the platforms should be strongly disfavored, and it should be a last resort given the great benefits of robust political debate and protection for political and election-related speech. But Trump's actions justified the step of indefinitely deplatforming him. Over many months, Trump consistently undermined public confidence in the fairness of the election results on the basis of false and discredited theories of voter fraud, and he encouraged violent insurrection as Congress engaged in the formal process of counting the Electoral College votes and declaring Joe Biden the winner over Trump. Had the platforms granted Trump continued broad, unmediated access, he could have provoked additional violence and further undermined the peaceful transition of power that is essential to a working democracy.

As responsible corporate citizens, platforms including Facebook and Twitter should ensure that their forums allow robust, political debate. They should have general policies of nondiscrimination across candidates and political views, and those policies should be applied evenhandedly. The platforms should not be in the business of favoring one candidate or party over another and instead should allow readers and viewers access to a variety of political viewpoints and expressions of political speech. They should be especially wary of removing the speech of political candidates and leaders, whose comments are both newsworthy and probably helpful to voters as they decide which candidates and parties to support or oppose.

Thus, platform rules should begin with the strong presumption to include political speech, especially from political candidates and leaders, that can inform debate, share information, and allow voters to make decisions that are consistent with their interests and values. Allowing a platform for political speech generally promotes free speech and democratic governance and merits inclusion on the platforms.

The strong presumption in favor of inclusive political speech should be overcome only upon a clear showing that the speech actually threatens to undermine, rather than support, democratic governance. Political speech that raises a serious and imminent danger of undermining democratic governance should be removed from the platforms. Serial offenders, even political leaders, should be deplatformed, at least temporarily. Platforms should have clear rules embodying these principles, and they should not be abused given the considerable power put in the hands of corporate entities.

The easiest case justifying removal of posts and potential deplatforming is political speech that calls for or justifies political violence against a democratically elected government or against people. Such speech has no place in democratic discourse, and platforms have a moral obligation not to spread it. Such speech need not rise to the level of incitement by calling for imminent lawless action (under the

First Amendment *Brandenburg* standard applicable to government suppression of speech) to merit removal from a private platform; instead, speech that consistently justifies or supports violence deserves no amplification over social media. Such posts should be removed whether or not they lead to eventual deplatforming. A repeated pattern of such conduct justifies more severe repercussions.

In addition, speech that consistently spreads misinformation about the democratic process—speech about when, where, and how people vote, and speech that makes demonstrably false claims about elections being "stolen," "rigged," or "fraudulent"—is similarly dangerous to democratic governance and justifies sanctions from the platforms. Again, repetition of such statements is more blameworthy.

Under these standards, President Trump's statements and course of conduct culminating on January 6, 2021, justified his deplatforming from social media. As we saw in chapter 1, before January 6 the president had made hundreds of comments falsely calling the election's integrity into question. He encouraged his supporters to come to the Capitol on January 6 for "wild" protests. He gave a speech shared on social media that encouraged his supporters to march to the Capitol and interfere with the vote counting, and in the post that led to his deplatforming, he praised those engaged in insurrection with "love" and repeated false claims of a "fraudulent" and "stolen" election as the violence in the Capitol was ongoing.

Not only did such speech lead to the deaths of four people and injuries to countless others, including police officers guarding the vice president of the United States and members of Congress; those political leaders came within moments of being kidnapped or killed but for the bravery of law enforcement. Without social media's spreading Trump's statements, it seems extremely unlikely these events would have occurred. The eventual deplatforming of Trump's accounts helped defuse a dangerous and antidemocratic situation.

Facebook eventually referred its deplatforming decision to its Oversight Board that it had created to deal with issues such as content moderation. The board issued its decision in May 2021, determining that Facebook was correct in deplatforming Trump: "In maintaining an unfounded narrative of electoral fraud and persistent calls to action, Mr. Trump created an environment where a serious risk of violence was possible." But the board also found that Facebook's "indefinite" suspension of Trump was not supported by Facebook's own rules. It required Facebook within six months to explain its rules for indefinite suspension and apply them to Trump. It also suggested more broadly a set of criteria rooted in international human rights principles that will both protect freedom of expression and require the platform to take action against threats of political violence by political leaders. Facebook's subsequent decision to impose at least a two-year ban on Trump conditioned his return on whether the risk to public safety caused by Trump's tweets had receded. Facebook's vice president of Global Affairs, Nick Clegg, explained that the company "will evaluate external factors, including instances of violence, restrictions on peaceful assembly and other markers of civil unrest. If we determine that there is still a serious risk to public safety, we will extend the restriction for a set period of time and continue to re-evaluate until that risk has receded."[23]

Deplatforming of Trump helped slow down the spread of false claims about election integrity on social media. Trump unsuccessfully tried to reclaim his social media relevance through his *From the Desk of Donald J. Trump* blog, shutting it down after only twenty-nine days because it gained no traction. A *New York Times* analysis of Trump's messages indirectly shared on social media after deplatforming found that though many of his messages were still amplified by his followers, false election claims were not: "Before the ban, Mr.

Trump's posts [with election misinformation] garnered 22.1 million likes and shares; after the ban, his posts earned 1.3 million likes and shares across Twitter and Facebook."[24]

Beyond deplatforming, the platforms could adopt much broader rules against speech that is meant to suppress voter turnout. If these rules are clearly written and fairly applied, they could improve political discourse. But steps to deal with voter suppression statements would have to be measured and rolled out slowly, and evaluated for their effects on political discourse. As someone who has long been concerned with large corporate power in elections, and who has opposed the Supreme Court's 2010 *Citizens United* decision giving corporations the right to spend unlimited sums supporting or opposing candidates for office, I worry about the broad private power of large platforms to shape political speech. At the least, this constitutionally recognized vast corporate power to influence elections should be exercised responsibly.

The danger of limiting speech that may suppress votes is that the effort will not be evenhanded, and it could make things worse by removing important political speech from major sites of discussion. As Professor David Kaye, a human rights lawyer, has written more generally about platforms moderating content, "Who will decide what is bogus and garbage? Who decides what is true and what is propaganda? Do we want a company with the profit-motive of expanding users to make those kinds of decisions? Will they set up administrative tribunals for those who challenge take-downs of content? And even if we are comfortable handing over that kind of censorship—for that's what it is—to a private company, how will this magic algorithm tell the difference between the awful garbage of Breitbart and the hilarious garbage of The Onion? Who creates the software that distinguishes purposeful lies from public interest satire?" Platform decisions to remove speech flagged as "voter suppression" is a much harder question than removing demonstrably false information about whether the 2020 election was stolen.[25]

Indeed, in at least one prominent instance during the 2020 election, the platforms overcompensated by blocking speech on a bona fide campaign controversy. The *New York Post* reported about the alleged contents of emails taken from the laptop of Hunter Biden, Joe Biden's son, which supposedly showed the son's connection to corruption at a Ukrainian gas company. Most reputable journalistic outfits did not extensively cover the Hunter Biden story, which remains under investigation, but the *Post* did. Facebook reduced the visibility of the article, and Twitter went further, removing tweets that linked to the *Post* story. It should not have done so.

Twitter said it blocked the content because it contained hacked and private information. But Twitter applied this rule selectively and in a politically charged context. Twitter certainly allowed tweets to link to lots of other reporting that relied on hacked and private information. Under pressure from Republicans, Twitter reversed itself, saying it would label some material based on hacked content and that, given the circulation of the Hunter Biden emails elsewhere, privacy was no longer a concern.[26]

Blocking tweets linking to the *Post* story undermined conservatives' faith that the platforms can be fair arbiters of what should or should not be shared. Twitter probably overreacted to the Hunter Biden story in light of the view held strongly by those on the left that hacked, truthful emails from the DNC in 2016 cost Hillary Clinton the presidential election to Donald Trump. But blocking potentially truthful, damaging information, particularly in a biased way, disserves the cause of providing voters with the information they need to make informed decisions. Just as platforms were right not to block stories about the alleged contents of the DNC emails in 2016 once they determined they were genuine documents and nor forgeries, they should not have blocked stories about the alleged content of the Hunter Biden emails in 2020. If the Hunter Biden emails were proven false at the time the *Post* published its story, there would have been a stronger case for demoting or blocking posts linking to stories about them.

More generally, aggressive private speech regulation could lead conservative readers to flee to other platforms, like Parler, where disinformation is apparently more prevalent. Platform fragmentation could then create deeper echo chambers and reinforce alternative realities. In this way, driving users away from larger platforms could impoverish not only the potential for dialogue but also the ability of voters to find truthful information.

Fragmentation does have the benefit of sealing off some of the worst behavior. As Professors Benkler, Faris, and Roberts showed in research described in chapter 2, disinformation came to dominate discussions of American elections in 2016 not when it first appeared from fringe right-wing sources but when it was amplified by mainstream journalistic sources applying objective journalistic criteria to cover outrageous claims. Traditional journalists got sucked in and played by these efforts, and they are less likely to do so when false and damaging election-related claims are not common on popular platforms. The 2020 Hunter Biden controversy showed an overcorrection.[27]

The lesson of 2020 was not that the platforms successfully dealt with disinformation and other problems of cheap speech—they did not—but that even these powerful companies felt compelled to respond to pressure. To be sure, the platforms did not want to alienate customers and wanted to stave off the threat of new regulation. Perhaps surprisingly, some of the pressure came from the companies' own employees, who pushed back—often through media leaks—against what they saw as the platforms' (especially Facebook's) complicity or cooperation with those spreading disinformation. The threat of losing talented engineers and others posed a competitive risk.

Pressuring a platform as big as Facebook is very tough, especially given Mark Zuckerberg's dominance over the company and Facebook's overwhelming presence in the social media market. Facebook refused to meaningfully respond to the Oversight Board's recommendation in its decision deplatforming Trump that the company should examine how its own policies and algorithms helped lay the groundwork for the January 6 insurrection. Forcing sufficient change may require antitrust remedies and other legal changes described in the last chapter. Direct regulation of most corporate political speech in a post–*Citizens United* world, even of big corporations, appears to be off the table. But 2020 proved that public pressure can be at least partially yet meaningfully effective.[28]

Getting the platforms to act will not fully solve the disinformation or polarization problems. Much of the 2020 disinformation appeared in other venues, most importantly cable news networks like Fox, Newsmax, and OANN. As Benkler writes: "The fact that 'fake news' located online is overwhelmingly shared by conservatives older than sixty-five, who also make up the core demographic of Fox News, and that only about 8 percent of voters on both sides of the aisle identified Facebook as their primary source of political news in the 2016 election, support[s] the conclusion that something other than social media, or the Internet, is driving the 'post-truth' moment."[29]

Bolstering Real, Especially Local, Journalism

Limiting the spread of disinformation that is relevant to voters on the platforms, on cable news, and elsewhere solves only part of the cheap speech problem. Equally worrisome is the declining supply of quality information produced by ethical journalists, and especially the loss of local investigative journalism. This kind of journalism may limit corruption and helps people make informed voting choices. The problem of producing quality journalism is compounded by the emerging phenomenon of foreign and domestic partisan actors mimicking the look of journalism to produce low-quality, biased information that can confuse voters about its authenticity and reliability.

As we saw in earlier chapters, over the last decade the shift of advertising to social media and search platforms has created a financial crisis for traditional newspapers and other news media. Quality journalism on the national level continues to find a market under a subscription-based model (think of the *New York Times, Wall Street Journal,* and the *Atlantic*) and under a donor-based model, sometimes with limited government subsidies (think of NPR and PBS). As the journalist Margaret Sullivan has shown, bona fide news production is in much worse shape on the local level, where advertising losses have been steeper and subscription models less successful.[30]

The market has not yet found a way to solve the local news problem, which leaves many localities without a local newspaper or with a newspaper whose coverage has been drastically curtailed by investors who are more interested in these legacy media organizations' real estate holdings than in their journalistic missions. Economists would describe this as a classic market failure, where local journalism is a "public good," something to which individuals do not necessarily have an incentive to contribute but which benefits the public overall. Christopher Ali argues that we should think of local journalism as a "merit good" that should be publicly available regardless of consumption habits. One typical solution to the public goods problem is funding through taxation, but public subsidies become difficult when one of journalists' key functions is to investigate those in power. Such subsidies no doubt would also face resistance from those who are distrustful of both media and government and believe that the media show a left-wing bias. Private philanthropy and donor models may be the only realistic solutions.[31]

Breaking up the platforms could decrease their market power, allowing local news organizations to cut better deals on website advertising profits. Alternatively, one could tax advertising on the platforms and transfer the money to local news organizations, but taxation raises similar concerns about public funding as well as potential unequal-treatment claims.

The donor-based model is beginning to have some success on the local level. High-quality journalism from nonprofit outlets such as the *Texas Tribune* and the *Nevada Independent,* as well as partnerships with the donor-driven national nonprofit news organization ProPublica, provide some hope. Such organizations increasingly partner with legacy newspapers and other media to assure broader dissemination of their stories. In 2020 ProPublica's Local Reporting Network included twenty newsrooms across the United States. One could even consider billionaire acquisitions of legacy newspapers in the United States as part of the donor model. Amazon's Jeff Bezos probably did not buy the *Washington Post*—nor did the surgeon and inventor Patrick Soon-Shiong buy the *Los Angeles Times*—with the expectation of making a profit.[32]

But the donor model is precarious: it depends on the beneficence of billionaires and other rich donors to keep things afloat. Aside from potential conflicts of interest—think, for example, of the *Washington Post* investigating Amazon—funding can always dry up, and a lack of ready resources to take their place can be a constant financial stress.[33]

Further, the donor model may not be easily replicated. Poorer urban and rural areas, which most need investigative, muckraking journalism to expose public corruption and other issues relevant to these voters, appear least likely to get quality journalistic coverage through the donor-based or any other model. Rural areas containing more Trumpist voters and fewer sources of reputable news for this reason may become even more susceptible to disinformation campaigns.

The rise of fraudulent websites masquerading as local news presents additional challenges. Voters can easily mistake cheap competitors created to spread disinformation, political propaganda, or slanted news for bona fide news sources. Private action can help solve this real "fake news" problem by providing reliability signals to voters. For example, bona fide news organizations can form (or use existing) voluntary journalism associations to certify quality among members who agree to abide by certain principles of journalistic fairness and integrity, such as not taking payment for running particular stories or promoting certain views. Legitimate news organizations should set up mechanisms to police complaints that members have violated the principles and to require corrective action. Social media companies and search platforms can promote those media organizations with a seal of approval and demote or block access to the content of news organizations that lack it.

The matter will be tricky: with the return of the partisan press, there will be fights over whether provocative sites such as Breitbart, which mix real stories with disinformation, qualify as bona fide news sources. But these debates themselves can make viewers aware of the journalistic values news organizations must embrace if they are to fulfill their important role in promoting democracy and ameliorating the dangers of cheap speech.

Strengthening and Building Reliable Intermediaries and Institutions

The first two sets of recommendations in this chapter, for platform self-regulation and for bolstering (especially local) journalism, include actionable, discrete steps to militate against the democracy-reducing effects of cheap speech and the rise of disinformation. A platform can ban microtargeting, for example, or philanthropists can endow funds to support enhanced investigative journalism in underserved rural areas. The next two sets of recommendations, for building and strengthening institutions and for inculcating truth and other values, present longer-term, less definable goals. It will be hard to point to specific changes in these areas and measure if and how they have helped. But they are among the most important private steps we can take to restore the health of American democracy.

In their introduction to a recently edited volume titled *The Disinformation Age,* W. Lance Bennett and Steven Livingston conclude that "stemming the flood of contemporary disinformation is unlikely to be aided by regulating social media, fact-checking, or improving media literacy. Our analysis suggests that solutions lie in *repairing the basic functioning of democratic institutions themselves.*" Yochai Benkler repeatedly cautions against assuming that social media reform will cure problems with disinformation, especially given the asymmetry in power and resources between those producing disinformation and those consuming it. He nonetheless notes that social media exacerbates the problem: "There is no question that by shifting the power to produce information, knowledge, and culture, the Internet and social media have allowed marginal groups and loosely connected individuals to get together, to share ideas that are very far from the mainstream, and try to shape debates in the general media ecosystem or organize for action in ways that were extremely difficult, if not impossible, even in the multichannel environment of cable and talk radio."[34]

It is important not to overstate claims about the utility of social media reform or see the cheap speech problem as only about social media. The bile and election disinformation that spread on messaging apps such as WhatsApp or on cable networks such as Fox News, Newsmax, or OANN are not driven by social media algorithms (though cable networks amplify their messages on social media). Given that the problem of disinformation and polarization extends well beyond social media, Bennett and Livingston's key point is even more urgent: strong democratic institutions and intermediaries matter for controlling the spread of disinformation and assuring that citizens are well-equipped to vote in elections.

Take, for example, the importance of respect for courts and the truth-telling function that courts serve in society. As we have seen, in the wake of the 2020 election results, Donald Trump, the Republican Party, and their allies filed sixty-two lawsuits in different states in an attempt to overturn his loss to Joe Biden that were based primarily on false claims of voter fraud. Only one of the lawsuits succeeded, on a minor issue in Pennsylvania. Twice in the same week, the U.S. Supreme Court, dominated by conservative justices, refused to take up Trump's cases.[35]

Although the main message that Trump and his leading spokespersons, Rudy Giuliani and Jenna Ellis, sent in press conferences and social media posts about these lawsuits was the false claim that the election was rife with fraud or "rigged," Trump's lawyers were more circumspect in their court filings and appearances. The courts utterly rejected the few claims of fraud the lawyers brought. Eighty-six judges across the country, Republican-appointed, Democratic-appointed, and elected alike, found no merit in the legal claims, whether based in fraud or raising other issues.[36]

Rules of evidence and codes of conduct that prevent lawyers from lying in court and filing frivolous actions, along with judicial power to punish lies under oath and other misconduct, helped discipline Trump's lawyers. Although conservative and liberal judges often divide in cases on contentious issues, they were united against turning vague and unsupported allegations into successful legal claims that could have overturned election results.

The courts' public function as truth-telling bodies can go a long way toward combatting disinformation about stolen elections. Anyone who paid attention to the lawsuits and trusted in the courts would be assured that forums were available in which Trump and his allies could fully air their claims of fraud or other irregularities and receive a fair hearing.

The scores of virtually unanimous court rulings, however, did not stop a sizable core of Trump's supporters from continuing to believe Trump's false claims of a rigged election. Media fact checkers were not alone in failing to siphon away Trump's flood of disinformation. Nor did the courts' emphatic and unequivocal rejection of his claims disabuse the Trumpists of their belief, sustained until his very last moments in office, that the election would be overturned.

Bolstering the courts and making sure they continue to serve their truth-telling function fairly and honestly is a key to preventing the uncontrolled spread of disinformation and other bad effects of cheap speech. And the point applies more broadly. We want the FBI, local law enforcement, state and local election officials, elected officials involved in certifying vote totals, and the press to be committed to both truth telling and accuracy. We want the public to then accept these institutions as acting competently and in good faith (and to call them out when they do not do so). The more these institutions can be trusted to do the right thing, the fewer people are likely to have their views of American elections swayed by disinformation and misinformation.

To put a finer point on it: in the cheap speech era, credible institutions serve as bulwarks against the spread of viral disinformation. Without courts and other authorities swatting down unsupported claims of fraud, such claims only grow in stature and gain more adherents.

Ensuring these institutions' credibility requires that their members continue to abide by social and professional norms and that they have professional and psychic incentives to do so. That means not only self-policing, such as when courts write opinions calling out bad conduct even among other courts or their colleagues, but also mutual reinforcement of norms, as when the press writes stories about how judicial norms of truth telling held against political pressure. Nongovernmental civic institutions, including law schools, legal organizations such as bar associations (that have begun investigating Trump lawyers lying about fraud), and private foundations also can play a key role in bolstering institutions that promote the values of truth and a free society.

An example of the breakdown of institutional norms toward responsible conduct came in one of the Trump-related 2020 election lawsuits. Texas Attorney General Ken Paxton, who was under indictment by state authorities for securities fraud and under federal investigation for separate potential bribery charges related to a campaign donor and perhaps angling for a presidential pardon, filed a highly unusual lawsuit on behalf of Texas directly in the U.S. Supreme Court. The suit sought to throw out the presidential Electoral College votes of Georgia, Michigan, Pennsylvania, and Wisconsin—all of which went to Biden—on the basis of false and debunked claims of voter fraud.[37]

The lawsuit was frivolous. Texas lacked standing to bring the case: the Constitution does not give one state the ability to complain about how another state chooses its presidential electors. Texas's factual allegations were based on a ludicrous statistical analysis showing supposed voting anomalies in select states voting for Biden. The bill of complaint audaciously moved for the Supreme Court to nullify the votes of millions of voters in these states and to allow Republican legislatures to choose electors directly, a remedy not allowed by any of these states' election rules. The Supreme Court rejected Texas's lawsuit without even giving it a hearing.[38]

None of the leading Supreme Court advocates who usually argue cases on behalf of the Republican Party filed briefs supporting Texas in the Supreme Court, which shows the continued value of institutional norms among elite lawyers. Leading legal academics and bar associations condemned the attempt to convince the Court to overturn the election on the flimsiest possible basis. But 17 Republican state attorneys general signed a brief supporting Paxton's petition, as did 126 Republican members of Congress. Even some members of Congress and legislators from states that Texas sued signed onto briefs or expressed support for the argument that their own voters should be disenfranchised, leaving the choice of the states' electors to the state legislatures.[39]

In this instance, neither professional norms nor oaths to uphold the Constitution deterred these Republican elected officials from joining the effort to overturn the results of an election on the basis of false and debunked fraud claims. It was uncertain whether the signers feared a Trumpist primary opponent in a future election, supported the false claims in order to delegitimize a Biden presidency, or actually believed the claims. But no matter the reason, by joining in the Texas lawsuit these officials signaled a dangerous failure of institutions and intermediaries to resist election-related disinformation.

It was difficult to shame these officials, given the polarized atmosphere in which appeals to truthful information were viewed as yet more partisan warfare. Never mind that former President George W. Bush and the 2012 Republican presidential nominee (and current U.S. senator from Utah), Mitt Romney, quickly recognized Biden's victory. Republican leaders such as Senate Majority Leader Mitch McConnell and House Minority Leader Kevin McCarthy, who did not embrace the fraud claims but still refused to recognize Biden as president-elect for weeks after the election, created the opening for other elected officials to spread election lies. As Trumpists held sway over primary voters, any hope for the emergence of a more responsible Republican leadership appeared to dim.[40]

This split between Bush and Romney on the one hand and Mc-Connell on the other suggests a potential focus on election reform efforts that could produce more moderate candidates. These candidates could help bolster institutions that promote truth telling and resist the spread of election disinformation. It is far from certain that reforms such as top-two primaries or campaign finance measures to strengthen political parties could produce more moderate candidates in the polarized cheap speech era—topics well beyond the scope of this book. Indeed, empowering the parties seems like a dangerous strategy when the parties themselves could be subject to a hostile takeover by a Trumpist actor. But efforts to bolster moderates who accept truth and the rule of law seem indispensable.[41]

The early responses by Republican leaders to the January 6, 2021, insurrection have not been encouraging. They blocked legislation to create an independent bipartisan congressional commission to investigate the causes of the insurrection. Responsible Republican election officials, such as Georgia's Secretary of State Brad Raffensperger, have been censured for affirming Biden's victory and have faced primary challenges from others parroting the Big Lie about the 2020 election being stolen from Trump. Some of these officials will be running the 2024 elections or certifying or counting Electoral College votes in 2024. Republicans in state legislatures began passing legislation that would make it easier to subvert the will of the voters in counting ballots in future elections. In short, the failures of the Republican Party to contain false election information have put incredible stress on other institutions of American society to pick up the slack and to help preserve American democracy.[42]

Inculcating Values of Truth, Respect for Science, and the Rule of Law

The essential need to bolster institutions that serve a truth-telling function and help voters make informed decisions depends even more fundamentally on inculcating respect for truth, science, and the rule of law. Without a general respect for these values among the public, these institutions can go only so far in battling disinformation.

The problem is how to inculcate these values when the Big Lie and disinformation run rampant online and in corners of cable news, and hyperpolarization threatens to swamp even what should seem like apolitical information, such as the benefits of wearing a mask to limit the spread of COVID-19. Socialization and education are needed to instill respect for truth and science, although they may be insufficient.

Digital literacy efforts to help voters identify and reject false information surely can help voters avoid some deception, but the 2020 election showed that such efforts face an uphill battle amid a torrent of deliberate disinformation. There was no shortage of truthful information about the election coming from reliable sources, and yet most of Trump's supporters embraced false notions about a stolen election.

Moreover, younger Americans are the ones most likely to get instruction in digital literacy, but older ones seem more likely to fall prey to online disinformation. As we saw in the first chapter, younger voters face a different information problem: they are more likely to reject even truthful information as false as the lemon problem grows on social media and they become conditioned to reject even truthful information as dubious. For both younger and older voters, education efforts may be swamped by political effects and motivated reasoning; politically aware and knowledgeable voters tend to be swayed more by disinformation that comports with their ideological views than less-aware voters. Emotion, rather than lack of knowledge, is sometimes the best predictor of susceptibility to disinformation.[43]

Overemphasis on formal fact checking and efforts to quickly reject controversial information as false also can backfire and deter the search for truth. Social science evidence shows that the repetition of false statements, even in the context of fact checks, can reinforce rather than undermine belief in the false statements. Social science can help point the way toward methods to better combat disinformation rather than amplify it and polarize society further through debunking efforts.

We must acknowledge that science is an iterative process and not every scientific study definitively resolves empirical questions. Indeed, belief that scientific findings themselves are immune from further examination and correction is itself dangerous. As Cailin O'Connor and James Weatherall remind us, "Temporary diversity of beliefs is crucial for a scientific community. If everyone starts out believing the same thing, they can fail to try out better options." Respect should be for the scientific method rather than for some incorrect belief in the infallibility of scientists themselves.[44]

Further, no silver bullet exists to slay election disinformation through education. The battle against such false information cannot be won or lost decisively at one moment. Instead, fighting disinformation demands constant work from civic institutions that reject falsehoods by offering specific evidence and explaining how and why it is reliable. The need to promote the truth is not new, but it is more challenging as new technology allows disinformation to spread more quickly and deeply than in earlier eras and as technological change overlaps with a particular American period of hyperpolarization. The unfortunate confluence of the two phenomena vastly complicates truth-telling efforts.

The Way Forward

The survival of American democracy depends on the success of free and fair periodic elections in which voters have access to reliable information to make ballot decisions that are consistent with their preferences and interests, and where the losers accept the results as legitimate and agree to fight another day. In our time of rapid, disruptive technological change, this democratic model can no longer be taken for granted. The ability of malicious actors to spread disinformation is the biggest threat to democracy's survival, but it is hardly the only threat from cheap speech. Demagoguery, corruption, and our increasing inability to rely on the veracity of what we see, read, and hear present new challenges for voter competence and therefore successful elections.

George Akerlof describes two paths to overcoming market failure in a lemons market: governmental intervention and private action. When it comes to the challenges of the information market in the era of cheap speech, both legal and private paths are urgently needed. One alone will not be enough.

Hyperpartisanship makes many of the laws proposed in chapter 3, such as improved disclosure rules and bans on false election speech, unlikely to be passed soon. And even if the laws pass, many will need Supreme Court approval. If the Court blocks the necessary legal changes, civil society will have to work even harder to strengthen institutions that promote truth telling.

The Supreme Court should recognize that First Amendment balancing must be recalibrated. Of course, the risk of censorship and of stifling robust debate still must figure heavily in constitutional analysis. But at least as serious as the risk of censorship is the risk of citizens' exposure to disinformation that undermines not only their ability to act as competent voters but their faith in the mechanics of democracy itself.

Perhaps the conservative justices will resist their impulses against election regulation because they understand that we are experiencing a flood of disinformation harming American democracy. It is more likely, however, that they will believe, despite the evidence, that the problem of potential harassment and the advantages of unfettered and even false speech in a political context are so great as to swamp the democracy benefits of new regulation to combat the political ills of cheap speech. They may continue to embrace the false construct of a working marketplace of ideas in which counterspeech is enough to combat the social ills from election disinformation. And, despite their otherwise libertarian impulses, they could even uphold state laws that force social media companies to share election disinformation and posts glorifying violence from Trump-like politicians.

In an ideal world, sound new laws would be coupled with private action by platforms, philanthropists, nongovernmental organizations, bona fide media organizations, government actors, and educators to strengthen American democracy against disinformation and other threats to vibrant elections decided by competent voters. But private actors may have to go it alone.

In the cheap speech era, it is wrong to assume that the marketplace of ideas is self-correcting. We cannot make lemonade from lemons amid a disinformation crisis. As the 2020 election, marked by relentless presidential disinformation about voter fraud, demonstrated, the dangers our democracy faces are deep, perhaps existential. Next time, the norms may not hold, and disinformation easily could provide a path to stealing an election under the guise of election integrity. It almost did on January 6, 2021.

American democracy faces its most difficult period since the Civil War of the 1860s. It is uncertain whether the Supreme Court will accept as consistent with the First Amendment my proposed cures for the disinformation poisoning our politics, but now is not the time to surrender. The urgency of the democracy crisis precipitated by the rise of cheap speech demands immediate, decisive, and courageous action from all of us.

Notes

1. Clear and Present Danger

1. Peter Baker & Sabrina Tavernise, *One Legacy of Impeachment: The Most Complete Account So Far of Jan. 6*, N.Y. Times, Feb. 13, 2021 (updated Mar. 19, 2021), https://www.nytimes.com/2021/02/13/us/politics/capitol-riots-impeachment-trial.html [https://perma.cc/VBE5-UYSY]; Jack Healy, *These Are the 5 People Who Died in the Capitol Riot*, N.Y. Times, Jan. 11, 2021 (updated Feb. 22, 2021), https://www.nytimes.com/2021/01/11/us/who-died-in-capitol-building-attack.html [https://perma.cc/8SDU-95NB]. Although it was initially reported that five people died in the January 6 insurrection, Capitol Police officer Brian Sicknick, listed as one of the five, was later found to have died of natural causes and two strokes a day after rioters attacked him with chemical irritants. Peter Hermann & Spencer S. Hsu, *Capitol Police Officer Brian Sicknick, Who Engaged Rioters, Suffered Two Strokes and Died of Natural Causes, Officials Say*, Wash. Post, Apr. 19, 2021, https://www.washingtonpost.com/local/public-safety/brian-sicknick-death-strokes/2021/04/19/36d2d310-617e-11eb-afbe-9a11a127d146_story.html [https://perma.cc/226L-LWUF]. On the suicides, see Peter Hermann, *Two Officers Who Helped Fight the Capitol Mob Died by Suicide. Many More Are Hurting*, Wash. Post, Feb. 21, 2021, https://www.washingtonpost.com/local/public-safety/police-officer-suicides-capitol-riot/2021/02/11/94804ee2-665c-11eb-886d-5264d4ceb46d_story.html [https://perma.cc/5E22-XZPA]; Jan Wolfe, *Four Officers Who Responded to U.S. Capitol Attack Have Died by Suicide*, Reuters, Aug. 2, 2021, https://www.reuters.com/world/us/officer-who-responded-us-capitol-attack-is-third-die-by-suicide-2021-08-02/.

For my earlier writing on January 6, 2021, see Richard L. Hasen, *Op-Ed: Election Law Can't Protect Democracy If Our Representatives Are Lawless*, L.A. Times, Jan. 20, 2021, https://www.latimes.com/opinion/story/2021-01-20/election-2020-election-lawlessness [https://perma.cc/9DKS-YV6D]; Richard L. Hasen, *The Only Way to Save American Democracy Now*, Slate, Jan. 11, 2021, https://slate.com/news-and-politics

/2021/01/biden-pelosi-schumer-john-lewis-save-democracy.html [https://perma.cc/L6GB-6HPR]; Richard L. Hasen, *We Can't Let Our Elections Be This Vulnerable Again*, Atlantic, Jan. 4, 2021, https://www.theatlantic.com/ideas/archive/2021/01/we-cant-let-our-elections-be-vulnerable-again/617542/ [https://perma.cc/S7ME-SNNQ].

2. Luke Broadwater, Emily Cochrane, & Matt Stevens, *Lawmakers End Republicans' Effort to Subvert the Election in an Early Morning Vote*, N.Y. Times, Jan. 6, 2021, https://www.nytimes.com/2021/01/06/us/politics/lawmakers-end-republicans-effort-to-subvert-the-election-in-an-early-morning-vote.html [https://perma.cc/GQW2-3G8D]; Jessica Calefati, *Fact-Checking False Claims about Pennsylvania's Presidential Election by Trump and His Allies*, Phila. Inquirer, Dec. 6, 2020 (updated Dec. 7, 2020), https://www.inquirer.com/politics/election/pennsylvania-election-results-trump-fraud-fact-check-20201206.html [https://perma.cc/AN58-XV2A]; Dylan Byers, *How Facebook and Twitter Decided to Take Down Trump's Accounts*, NBC News, Jan. 14, 2021, https://www.nbcnews.com/tech/tech-news/how-facebook-twitter-decided-take-down-trump-s-accounts-n1254317 [https://perma.cc/E2YX-K5JK]; Nicholas Fandos, *Trump Acquitted of Inciting Insurrection, Even as Bipartisan Majority Votes "Guilty,"* N.Y. Times, Feb. 13, 2021, https://www.nytimes.com/2021/02/13/us/politics/trump-impeachment.html [https://perma.cc/3P7B-GZHX]. Had Trump been convicted on a two-thirds vote in the Senate, he could have been disqualified from holding further office by a simple majority vote. Jan Wolfe, *Explainer: Impeachment or the 14th Amendment—Can Trump Be Barred from Future Office?*, Reuters, Jan. 14, 2021, https://www.reuters.com/article/us-usa-trump-impeachment-explainer/impeachment-or-the-14th-amendment-can-trump-be-barred-from-future-office-idUSKBN29I356 [https://perma.cc/8MG4-DFCC].

3. Emily Bazelon, *Democracy Worked This Year. But It Is Fragile and Under Threat*, N.Y. Times Mag., Nov. 7, 2020, https://www.nytimes.com/interactive/2020/11/07/magazine/election-voting-democracy.html [https://perma.cc/7X4A-5RA5]; Tom Scheck, Geoff Hing, Sabby Robinson, & Gracie Stockton, *How Private Money from Facebook's CEO Saved the 2020 Election*, NPR, Dec. 8, 2020, https://www.npr.org/2020/12/08/943242106/how-private-money-from-facebooks-ceo-saved-the-2020-election [https://perma.cc/47U3-DMQN].

4. "In Georgia, more than 1.2 million people have requested absentee ballots for the state's June 9 primary—compared to just 36,200 requests for the 2016 presidential primary." Reid J. Epstein, *Democrats' Vote-by-Mail Effort Won in Wisconsin: Will It Work Elsewhere?*, N.Y. Times, May 10, 2020 (updated Sept. 14, 2020), https://www.nytimes.com/2020/05/10/us/politics/Wisconsin-election-vote-by-mail-.html

[https://perma.cc/A4FJ-3K7K]. As of August 2020, President Trump's @realDonald Trump account had 84.6 million followers, per Twitter [https://perma.cc/X5TE -433M], and he had 30 million followers of @DonaldTrump on Facebook [https:// perma.cc/H85Z-468T]. On COVID-19 deaths, see Alana Wise & Bill Chappell, *More Than 150,000 People Have Died from Coronavirus in the U.S.*, NPR, July 29, 2020, https://www.npr.org/sections/coronavirus-live-updates/2020/07/29/896491060 /more-than-150-000-people-have-died-from-coronavirus-in-the-u-s [https://perma .cc/SKC6-W7Z3]; Miles Parks, *Trump, While Attacking Mail Voting, Casts Mail Ballot Again*, NPR, Aug. 19, 2020, https://www.npr.org/2020/08/19/903886567/trump -while-attacking-mail-voting-casts-mail-ballot-again [https://perma.cc/U462-VVSX].

5. Elizabeth Dwoskin, *A Quarter of Trump's 6,081 Facebook Posts Last Year Featured Misinformation or Extreme Rhetoric*, Wash. Post, Feb. 18, 2021, https://www .washingtonpost.com/technology/2021/02/18/trump-facebook-misinformation/ [https://perma.cc/43YG-DVWL]; Susan B. Glasser, *Trump Is the Election Crisis He Is Warning About*, New Yorker, July 30, 2020, https://www.newyorker.com/news /letter-from-trumps-washington/trump-is-the-election-crisis-he-is-warning-about [https://perma.cc/9PAE-NNBX].

6. On election fraud allegations in the United States, see Richard L. Hasen, *Election Meltdown: Dirty Tricks, Distrust, and the Threat to American Democracy* ch. 1 (2020). The Harvard study is Yochai Benkler et al., *Mail-in Voter Fraud: Anatomy of a Disinformation Campaign*, Berkman Ctr. Rsch. Publ'n 2020-6, Oct. 2, 2020, https:// papers.ssrn.com/sol3/papers.cfm?abstract_id=3703701. The Election Integrity Partnership is made up of the Digital Forensic Research Lab, Graphika, the Stanford Internet Observatory, and the University of Washington Center for an Informed Public. The report is Election Integrity Partnership, *The Long Fuse: Misinformation and the 2020 Election* 183–92 (2021), https://stacks.stanford.edu/file/druid:tr171zs0069 /EIP-Final-Report-v2.pdf [https://perma.cc/WGC6-KDTC].

7. Jonathan Lai, *The "Blue Shift" in Pennsylvania Meant a 14-Point Swing from Trump to Biden—For Now*, Phila. Inquirer, Nov. 6, 2020, https://www.inquirer .com/politics/election/biden-trump-pennsylvania-blue-shift-20201106.html [https://perma.cc/72RC-JM6Y]; Jonathan Lai & Jeremy Roebuck, *Pennsylvania Certifies Its Presidential Election Results, Officially Declaring Joe Biden the Winner*, Phila. Inquirer, Nov. 24, 2020, https://fusion.inquirer.com/politics/election/pennsylvania -certification-2020-presidential-election-vote-20201124.html [https://perma.cc/GU7N -FQ3R] (Biden with an official 80,555 vote lead over Trump). On the blue shift phenomenon, see Edward B. Foley & Charles Stewart III, *Explaining the Blue Shift*

in Election Canvassing (draft of Mar. 1, 2020), https://papers.ssrn.com/sol3/papers
.cfm?abstract_id=3547734.

8. Michael D. Shear, *Trump, Trying to Cling to Power, Fans Unrest and Conspiracy Theories,* N.Y. Times, Nov. 15, 2020 (updated Nov. 21, 2020), https://www.ny
times.com/2020/11/15/us/politics/trump-biden-election.html [https://perma.cc/JZ5E
-TSJ6].

9. Katie Benner, *Former Acting Attorney General Testifies About Trump's Effort to Subvert Election,* N.Y. Times, Aug. 7, 2021, https://www.nytimes.com/2021/08/07
/us/politics/jeffrey-rosen-trump-election.html [https://perma.cc/993B-AF7X]; William Cummings, Joey Garrison, & Jim Sergent, *By the Numbers: President Donald Trump's Failed Efforts to Overturn the Election,* USA Today News, Jan. 6, 2021,
https://www.usatoday.com/in-depth/news/politics/elections/2021/01/06/trumps
-failed-efforts-overturn-election-numbers/4130307001/ [https://perma.cc/3B72-DDR8];
Amy Gardner, *"I Just Want to Find 11,780 Votes": In Extraordinary Hour-Long Call, Trump Pressures Georgia Secretary of State to Recalculate the Vote in His Favor,* Wash.
Post, Jan. 3, 2021, https://www.washingtonpost.com/politics/trump-raffensperger
-call-georgia-vote/2021/01/03/d45acb92-4dc4-11eb-bda4-615aaefd0555
_story.html [https://perma.cc/ZF8M-9JS6]; Maria Polletta, *Trump Lashes Out at Gov. Doug Ducey Following Certification of Arizona Election Results,* Ariz. Cent., Nov.
30, 2020 (updated Dec. 1, 2020), https://www.azcentral.com/story/news/politics
/elections/2020/11/30/president-trump-slams-arizona-gov-ducey-after-election
-certification/6472784002/ [https://perma.cc/39NC-LMGE]; Kyle Cheney, *Trump Calls on GOP State Legislatures to Overturn Election Results,* Politico, Nov. 21, 2020,
https://www.politico.com/news/2020/11/21/trump-state-legislatures-overturn
-election-results-439031 [https://perma.cc/UNT9-K3RV]; Brent Kendall & Deanna
Paul, *Trump's Legal Path to Challenge Election Is Closing,* Wall St. J., Nov. 22, 2020,
https://www.wsj.com/articles/trumps-legal-path-to-challenge-election-is
-closing-11606074745 [https://perma.cc/ZC6N-57RP]; Michael D. Shear, Maggie
Haberman, Nick Corasaniti, & Jim Rutenberg, *Trump Administration Approves Start of Formal Transition to Biden,* N.Y. Times, Nov. 23, 2020 (updated Nov. 24,
2020), https://www.nytimes.com/2020/11/23/us/politics/trump-transition-biden.html
[https://perma.cc/64N7-QA97].

10. Karen Yourish & Larry Buchanan, *Since Election Day, a Lot of Tweeting and Not Much Else for Trump,* N.Y. Times, Nov. 24, 2020, https://www.nytimes.com
/interactive/2020/11/24/us/politics/trump-twitter-tweets-election-results.html
[https://perma.cc/LZN4-RUV2]; Maggie Haberman & Alan Feuer, *Trump Lawyers*

Disavow Sidney Powell, Another Member of His Legal Team, over Spurious Voter Fraud Accusations, N.Y. Times, Nov. 23, 2020 (updated Dec. 8, 2020), https://www.nytimes .com/2020/11/23/us/trump-lawyers-disavow-sidney-powell-another-member-of-his -legal-team-over-spurious-fraud-accusations.html [https://perma.cc/UZ8E-MF2A]; Aaron Morrison, Kat Stafford, & Christine Fernando, *Pres. Trump Election Challenges Sound Alarm among Voters of Color,* Associated Press, Nov. 22, 2020, https:// apnews.com/article/joe-biden-donald-trump-race-and-ethnicity-georgia-wisconsin -a2f5155019a0c5aa09a7a6a82fb7d14b [https://perma.cc/L739-HBA2]. On the origins of the #StopTheSteal phrase, and its use through the Jan. 6, 2021, insurrection, see Atlantic Council's DFR Lab, *#StopTheSteal: Timeline of Social Media and Extremist Activities Leading to 1/6 Insurrection,* Just Security, Feb. 10, 2021, https://www.just security.org/74622/stopthesteal-timeline-of-social-media-and-extremist-activities -leading-to-1-6-insurrection/ [https://perma.cc/37NG-W6YS]. The Election Integ rity Partnership report, *supra* note 6, at 78–84, provides a detailed examination of the #StopTheSteal social media campaign in the 2020 election. On Giuliani's poor lawyering, see Daniel E. Slotnik, *Prominent Lawyers Want Giuliani's Law License Suspended over Trump Work,* N.Y. Times, Jan. 21, 2021 (updated Feb. 10, 2021), https:// www.nytimes.com/2021/01/21/nyregion/giuliani-trump-law-license.html [https://perma .cc/PWE7-DQLF]; Dareh Gregorian, *"Beyond an Embarrassment," Legal Experts Say of Trump and Giuliani's Floundering Efforts in Court,* NBC News, Nov. 24, 2020, https:// www.nbcnews.com/politics/2020-election/beyond-embarrassment-legal-experts -say-trump-giuliani-s-floundering-efforts-n1248667 [https://perma.cc/GG7B-6Q66].

11. Sheera Frenkel, *How Misinformation "Superspreaders" Seed False Election Theories,* N.Y. Times, Nov. 23, 2020 (updated Nov. 24, 2020), https://www.nytimes .com/2020/11/23/technology/election-misinformation-facebook-twitter.html [https://perma.cc/W3QD-STQG]; Chris Williams, *Senate Majority Leader McConnell Staying Silent on President Trump's Claims of Election Fraud,* WHAS, Nov. 6, 2020, https://www.whas11.com/article/news/politics/mcconnell-appears-frustrated -by-questions-of-election-fraud/417-b14d026c-b022-4fcd-8c7a-4a4653d16e08 [https://perma.cc/Y2HW-QE4Y]; Donie O'Sullivan (@donie), Twitter, Nov. 18, 2020, 9:10 P.M., https://twitter.com/donie/status/1329290911717711872; Election Integrity Partnership, *supra* note 6, at 48.

12. Kate Conger & Davey Alba, *Twitter Refutes Inaccuracies in Trump's Tweets about Mail-In Voting,* N.Y. Times, May 26, 2020 (updated May 28, 2020), https:// www.nytimes.com/2020/05/26/technology/twitter-trump-mail-in-ballots.html [https://perma.cc/5ABC-6AJN]. The Twitter Safety warning appears at Twitter Safety

(@Twitter Safety), Twitter, May 27, 2020, 10:54 P.M., https://twitter.com/Twitter Safety/status/1265838823663075341 [https://perma.cc/UE58-F2AA].

13. Craig Silverman & Ryan Mac, *Facebook Knows That Adding Labels to Trump's False Claims Does Little to Stop Their Spread*, BuzzFeed News, Nov. 16, 2020, https://www.buzzfeednews.com/article/craigsilverman/facebook-labels-trump-lies -do-not-stop-spread [https://perma.cc/3L2B-YHFG]; Donie O'Sullivan & Marshall Cohen, *Facebook Begins Labeling, but Not Fact-Checking, Posts from Trump and Biden*, CNN Business, July 21, 2020, https://www.cnn.com/2020/07/21/tech/face book-label-trump-biden/index.html [https://perma.cc/3GD6-HAU4]; Ryan Mc-Carthy, *"Outright Lies": Voting Misinformation Flourishes on Facebook*, ProPublica: Electionland, July 16, 2020, https://www.propublica.org/article/outright-lies-voting -misinformation-flourishes-on-facebook [https://perma.cc/YUC2-U36V]. Trump's Facebook post and Facebook's original label are pictured in Sonam Sheth, *Facebook Added a Label to Trump's Post Claiming That Voting by Mail Will Lead to a "CORRUPT ELECTION,"* Bus. Insider, July 21, 2020, https://www.businessinsider.com/facebook -adds-label-trump-post-about-mail-in-voting-2020-7 [https://perma.cc/6QSE-3QW5]; image of Facebook post at https://perma.cc/8ZHM-KPBY.

14. Kevin Roose, Mike Isaac, & Sheera Frenkel, *Facebook Struggles to Balance Civility and Growth*, N.Y. Times, Nov. 24, 2020 (updated Jan. 7, 2021), https://www .nytimes.com/2020/11/24/technology/facebook-election-misinformation.html [https://perma.cc/9U7L-KY6A].

15. On Fox News calling Biden "president-elect" once its decision desk reached the conclusion that Biden had won, see Richard L. Hasen, *What Happens If Trump Won't Concede?*, Slate, Nov. 8, 2020, https://slate.com/news-and-politics/2020/11 /trump-concede-threat-legitimacy-biden.html [https://perma.cc/5FTV-BLZE]. On Tucker Carlson, see Jeremy W. Peters, *Tucker Carlson Dared Question a Trump Law-yer. The Backlash Was Quick*, N.Y. Times, Nov. 20, 2020 (updated Nov. 23, 2020), https://www.nytimes.com/2020/11/20/us/politics/Tucker-Carlson-trump.html [https://perma.cc/8SC8-DVRK]. On the move to Fox News alternatives, see chap-ter 4. The video of Trump's November 26, 2020, Thanksgiving address is posted on C-Span at https://www.c-span.org/video/?478850-1/president-trump-mistake-electoral -college-votes-joe-biden; see also Rick Hasen, *During Thanksgiving Press Availability, Trump Engaged in Repeated, Despicable Lies about Hundreds of Thousands of Fraudu-lent Votes Cast in Each State, Trying to Explain His Election Loss; FOX News Broadcast It in Full without Fact Checking*, Election L. Blog, Nov. 27, 2020, 7:22 A.M., PST,

https://electionlawblog.org/?p=119093 [https://perma.cc/A5ZT-KACU]. On the defamation lawsuits, see Kevin Collier, *Newsmax, OANN Sued by Makers of Voting Machines*, NBC News, Aug. 10, 2021, https://www.nbcnews.com/tech/security/newsmax -oann-sued-maker-voting-machines-rcna1636 [https://perma.cc/TT7K-664A].

16. Trial Memorandum of the United States House of Representatives in the Impeachment Trial of President Donald J. Trump, Jan. 28, 2021, at 12–13, https:// judiciary.house.gov/uploadedfiles/house_trial_brief_final.pdf?utm_campaign =5706-519 [https://perma.cc/6SWZ-TEST] (cleaned up) [hereafter cited as Trial Memorandum].

17. *Id.* at 13–14.

18. Maggie Haberman & Annie Karni, *Pence Said to Have Told Trump He Lacks Power to Change Election Result*, N.Y. Times, Jan. 5, 2021 (updated Jan. 15, 2021), https://www.nytimes.com/2021/01/05/us/politics/pence-trump-election-results .html [https://perma.cc/QZY9-PJY5].

19. Press release, U.S. Dep't of Just., *Six Individuals Affiliated with the Oath Keepers Indicted by a Federal Grand Jury for Conspiracy to Obstruct Congress on Jan. 6, 2021*, Feb. 19, 2021, https://www.justice.gov/usao-dc/pr/six-individuals-affiliated-oath -keepers-indicted-federal-grand-jury-conspiracy-obstruct [https://perma.cc/YLV8 -QMNV]; David Mack, Ryan Mac, & Ken Bensinger, *"If They Won't Hear Us, They Will Fear Us": How the Capitol Assault Was Planned on Facebook*, BuzzFeed News, Jan. 19, 2021, https://www.buzzfeednews.com/article/davidmack/how-us-capitol -insurrection-organized-facebook [https://perma.cc/LMT3-RFM3]; Brian Naylor, *Read Trump's Jan. 6 Speech, a Key Part of Impeachment Trial*, NPR, Feb. 10, 2021, https://www.npr.org/2021/02/10/966396848/read-trumps-jan-6-speech-à-key-part -of-impeachment-trial [https://perma.cc/V38R-PUCN]. Trump posted a link to the rally on the Right Side Broadcasting Network in a tweet archived at https:// media-cdn.factba.se/realdonaldtrump-twitter/1346891760174329859.jpg [https://perma .cc/86L4-LY5X]. The linked video of the rally was still posted as of October 2021 at https://www.pscp.tv/w/1eaJbnwgERXJX?t=3h32m2s.

20. Election Integrity Partnership, *supra* note 6, at 149; Jeff Horwitz, *Facebook Knew Calls for Violence Plagued "Groups," Now Plans Overhaul*, Wall St. J., Jan. 31, 2021, https://www.wsj.com/articles/facebook-knew-calls-for-violence-plagued-groups -now-plans-overhaul-11612131374 [https://perma.cc/S8DC-H5JG].

21. Baker & Tavernise, *supra* note 1; Naylor, *supra* note 19; Ashley Parker, Carol D. Leonnig, Paul Kane, & Emma Brown, *How the Rioters Who Stormed the Capitol*

Came Dangerously Close to Pence, Wash. Post, Jan. 15, 2021, https://www.washington
post.com/politics/pence-rioters-capitol-attack/2021/01/15/ab62e434-567c-11eb
-a08b-f1381ef3d207_story.html [https://perma.cc/QZ8X-6D5F]; Adam Goldman,
John Ismay, & Hailey Fuchs, *Man Who Broke into Pelosi's Office and Others Are
Charged in Capitol Riot,* N.Y. Times, Jan. 8, 2021 (updated Jan. 10, 2021), https://
www.nytimes.com/2021/01/08/us/politics/capitol-riot-charges.html [https://perma
.cc/XT3K-RMLC]; *New Timeline Shows Just How Close Rioters Got to Pence and His
Family,* CNN, Jan. 15, 2021, https://www.cnn.com/videos/politics/2021/01/15/mike
-pence-close-call-capitol-riot-foreman-vpx.cnn [https://perma.cc/7R2D-KHCP] (video).
On the three deaths, see *supra* note 1.

22. Maggie Haberman & Jonathan Martin, *After the Speech: What Trump Did
as the Capitol Was Attacked,* N.Y. Times, Feb. 13, 2021, https://www.nytimes.com
/2021/02/13/us/politics/trump-capitol-riot.html [https://perma.cc/CXC2-82PV]; Trial
Memorandum, *supra* note 16, at 32 (cleaned up). The video of the speech was on
YouTube at https://www.youtube.com/watch?v=2AeI6MvoALg, but it has since
been removed as violating community standards.

23. On the uncertainty of Trump's resistance to deployment of the National
Guard, see Robert Farley, *Timeline of National Guard Deployment to Capitol,* Fact-
Check.org, Jan. 13, 2021 (updated Jan. 28, 2021), https://www.factcheck.org/2021/01
/timeline-of-national-guard-deployment-to-capitol/ [https://perma.cc/UD2X-HM3M].
On the timeline for restoration of government control of the Capitol, see Laurel
Wamsley, *What We Know So Far: A Timeline of Security Response at the Capitol on
Jan. 6,* NPR, Jan. 15, 2021 (updated Feb. 23, 2021), https://www.npr.org/2021/01/15
/956842958/what-we-know-so-far-a-timeline-of-security-at-the-capitol-on-january-6
[https://perma.cc/66W2-JXTK].

On Hawley continuing to object to Pennsylvania's vote count even after the
riot, see Associated Press, *Sen. Hawley Still Objects to the Election Results in Pa. after DC
Chaos,* NBC Phila., Jan. 6, 2021 (updated Jan. 7, 2021), https://www.nbcphiladelphia
.com/news/politics/sen-hawley-still-objects-the-election-results-in-pa-after-dc
-chaos/2657539/ [https://perma.cc/BP3D-63U9]. On Trump's potential liability for
election tampering in Georgia, see Richard Fausset & Danny Hakim, *Georgia Prosecutors Open Criminal Inquiry into Trump's Efforts to Subvert Election,* N.Y. Times,
Feb. 10, 2021 (updated Mar. 17, 2021), https://www.nytimes.com/2021/02/10/us
/politics/trump-georgia-investigation.html [https://perma.cc/L8ND-R675].

24. Nick Clegg, *In Response to Oversight Board, Trump Suspended for Two Years;
Will Only Be Reinstated If Conditions Permit,* Facebook Newsroom, June 4, 2021,

https://about.fb.com/news/2021/06/facebook-response-to-oversight-board-recom
mendations-trump/ [https://perma.cc/XH8X-WELQ]; Mike Isaac, *Facebook Oversight Board Upholds Social Network's Ban of Trump*, May 5, 2021, https://www.ny
times.com/2021/05/05/technology/facebook-trump-ban-upheld.html [https://perma
.cc/27PP-J37C]; Byers, *supra* note 2; Adi Robertson, *Parler Is Back Online after a Month
of Downtime*, Verge, Feb. 15, 2021, https://www.theverge.com/2021/2/15/22284036
/parler-social-network-relaunch-new-hosting [https://perma.cc/5S7G-JW7Z].

25. On the Russian activity during the 2016 election season, see Hasen, *Election
Meltdown, supra* note 6, ch. 3. According to Facebook's internal standards on "inauthentic behavior": "In line with our commitment to authenticity, we don't allow
people to misrepresent themselves on Facebook, use fake accounts, artificially boost
the popularity of content, or engage in behaviors designed to enable other violations
under our Community Standards. This policy is intended to . . . create a space where
people can trust the people and communities they interact with." The rules say that
a Facebook user may not "engage in, or claim to engage in Coordinated Inauthentic
Behavior, defined as the use of multiple Facebook or Instagram assets, working in
concert to engage in Inauthentic Behavior (as defined above), where the use of fake
accounts is central to the operation." *Community Standards: 20. Inauthentic Behavior*,
Facebook, https://www.facebook.com/communitystandards/inauthentic_behavior
[https://perma.cc/9LVJ-W53J] (last visited Dec. 17, 2020). Among Twitter's rules is
a "civic integrity policy," which states: "You may not use Twitter's services for the
purpose of manipulating or interfering in elections or other civic processes. This includes posting or sharing content that may suppress participation or mislead people
about when, where, or how to participate in a civic process." *Civic Integrity Policy:
Overview*, Twitter, https://help.twitter.com/en/rules-and-policies/election-integrity
-policy [https://perma.cc/9DC7-XK5Y] (last visited Dec. 17, 2020).

26. David E. Sanger & Julian E. Barnes, *U.S. Warns Russia, China and Iran Are
Trying to Interfere in the Election. Democrats Say It's Far Worse*, N.Y. Times, July 24,
2020 (updated Aug. 18, 2020), https://www.nytimes.com/2020/07/24/us/politics
/election-interference-russia-china-iran.html [https://perma.cc/VTS6-M2AD].

27. Ryan Mac, *Instagram Displayed Negative Related Hashtags for Biden, but Hid
Them for Trump*, BuzzFeed News, Aug. 5, 2020, https://www.buzzfeednews.com
/article/ryanmac/instagram-related-hashtags-favoring-trump-over-biden [https://perma
.cc/H7GM-EMTC].

28. Olivia Solon, *Sensitive to Claims of Bias, Facebook Relaxed Misinformation
Rules for Conservative Pages*, NBC News, Aug. 7, 2020, https://www.nbcnews.com

/tech/tech-news/sensitive-claims-bias-facebook-relaxed-misinformation-rules-con
servative-pages-n1236182 [https://perma.cc/JZ23-7U7L]; Maggie Haberman & Kate
Conger, *Trump Prepares Order to Limit Social Media Companies' Protections*, N.Y.
Times, May 28, 2020 (updated June 2, 2020), https://www.nytimes.com/2020/05
/28/us/politics/trump-executive-order-social-media.html [https://perma.cc/A5KE
-EV8T]; Craig Silverman & Ryan Mac, *Facebook Fired an Employee Who Collected
Evidence of Right-Wing Pages Getting Preferential Treatment*, BuzzFeed News, Aug. 6,
2020, https://www.buzzfeednews.com/article/craigsilverman/facebook-zuckerberg
-what-if-trump-disputes-election-results [https://perma.cc/5MMA-M4AP] ("Some
of Facebook's own employees gathered evidence they say shows Breitbart—along
with other right-wing outlets and figures including Turning Point USA founder
Charlie Kirk, Trump supporters Diamond and Silk, and conservative video production nonprofit Prager University—has received special treatment that helped it
avoid running afoul of company policy. They see it as part of a pattern of preferential
treatment for right-wing publishers and pages, many of which have alleged that the
social network is biased against conservatives").

29. Rachel Lerman, Katie Shepherd, & Taylor Telford, *Twitter Penalizes Donald
Trump Jr. for Posting Hydroxychloroquine Misinformation amid Coronavirus Pandemic*, Wash. Post, July 28, 2020, https://www.washingtonpost.com/nation/2020/07
/28/trump-coronavirus-misinformation-twitter/ [https://perma.cc/EP7J-U4FP].

30. Casey Newton, *How Another Video of COVID-19 Misinformation Went Viral
on Facebook*, Verge, July 29, 2020, https://www.theverge.com/interface/2020/7
/29/21345138/facebook-viral-hydroxychloroquine-video-removal-trump-junior-stella
-immanuel [https://perma.cc/G9U3-58VH]; Adi Robertson, *Mark Zuckerberg Is
Struggling to Explain Why Breitbart Belongs on Facebook News*, Verge, Oct. 25, 2019,
https://www.theverge.com/2019/10/25/20932653/facebook-news-breitbart-mark
-zuckerberg-statement-bias [https://perma.cc/S4Y3-LVUW]; Shannon Bond, *Twitter, Facebook Remove Trump Post over False Claim about Children and COVID-19*,
NPR, Aug. 5, 2020, https://www.npr.org/2020/08/05/899558311/facebook-removes
-trump-post-over-false-claim-about-children-and-covid-19 [https://perma.cc/G99P
-Y434].

As an example of false reporting by Breitbart, see Brianna Sacks & Talal Ansari,
*Breitbart Made Up False Story That Immigrant Started Deadly Sonoma Wildfires, Sher-
iff's Office Says*, BuzzFeed News, Oct. 18, 2017 (updated Oct. 19, 2017), https://www
.buzzfeednews.com/article/briannasacks/no-an-undocumented-immigrant-did
-not-start-the-deadly#.fhYVDKoOPn [https://perma.cc/2CWK-VAYX]. On Breit-

bart's spreading of false election information during the 2020 election, see Election Integrity Partnership, *supra* note 6, at 194.

31. Eugene Volokh, *Cheap Speech and What It Will Do*, 104 Yale L.J. 1805, 1808–18, 1831 (1995).

32. *Id.*, at 1823, 1841–42, 1848–49. Volokh recently wrote a retrospective on his essay in a U.C. Davis symposium on it. The retrospective does not consider the democracy and election issues discussed in this book. Eugene Volokh, *What Cheap Speech Has Done: (Greater) Equality and Its Discontents*, 54 U.C. Davis L. Rev. 2303 (2021).

33. Further, as Anupam Chander argues: "For groups marginalized by mainstream society, the Internet offers a way to find community. American indigenous peoples can discuss issues of interest to many tribes at NativeWeb.org. A gay youth growing up in a small town can find support through the Internet, despite a hostile local setting. Sikh Americans might find community in cyberspace. Cyberspace offers a respite from the median consumer perspective of mainstream media. Here is the world's diversity, in its full glory (and, at times, disgrace)." Anupam Chander, *Whose Republic?*, 69 U. Chi. L. Rev. 1479, 1488–89 (2002). Any suggestions for reforming social media practices must consider how reform could burden these multicultural benefits.

34. W. Lance Bennett & Steven Livingston, *A Brief History of the Disinformation Age*, in *The Disinformation Age: Politics, Technology, and Disruptive Communication in the United States* 3, 5 (W. Lance Bennett & Steven Livingston eds., 2020), https://www.cambridge.org/core/books/disinformation-age/1F4751119C7C4693E514 C249E0F0F997 [https://perma.cc/F63Z-5GPB] ("putting the spotlight on social media alone, misses deeper erosions of institutional authority which involve elected officials—traditionally among the most prominent sources of authoritative information—themselves becoming increasingly involved in the spread of disruptive communication").

35. Thomas Healy, *The Great Dissent: How Oliver Wendell Holmes Changed His Mind—and Changed the History of Free Speech in America* 249 (2013); Brandenburg v. Ohio, 395 U.S. 444 (1969); Abrams v. United States, 250 U.S. 616 (1919) (Holmes, J., dissenting).

36. On the 2016 Russian hacking into voter registration databases and related activities, see Hasen, *Election Meltdown, supra* note 6, at 91–92.

37. On the nonconsensual sharing of sexual images, see Danielle Keats Citron & Mary Anne Franks, *Criminalizing Revenge Porn*, 49 Wake Forest L. Rev. 345 (2014). On deep fakes and national security (among other issues), see Danielle K. Citron &

Robert Chesney, *Deep Fakes: A Looming Challenge for Privacy, Democracy, and National Security,* 107 Calif. L. Rev. 1753 (2019). On reform of Section 230 liability, see Danielle Keats Citron & Mary Anne Franks, *The Internet as a Speech Machine and Other Myths Confounding Section 230 Reform,* 2020 U. Chi. L. Forum 45.

2. More Speech, More Problems

1. George A. Akerlof, *The Market for "Lemons": Quality Uncertainty and the Market Mechanism,* 84 Q.J. Econ. 488 (1970); Nobel Prize, George A. Akerlof: Facts, 2001, https://www.nobelprize.org/prizes/economic-sciences/2001/akerlof/facts/ [https://perma.cc/22EX-GJHH].

2. Francis Fukuyama & Andrew Grotto, *Comparative Media Regulation in the United States and Europe,* in *Social Media and Democracy: The State of the Field, Prospects for Reform* 199, 200 (Nathaniel Persily & Joshua A. Tucker eds., 2020) [hereafter cited as Persily & Tucker] ("The explosion of bandwidth for communications of all sorts that has occurred since the 1980s has made state control vastly more difficult than in the days when citizens relied on a handful of local and national newspapers and two or three broadcasting channels operating over finite, government-allocated radio spectrum").

3. Margaret Sullivan, *Ghosting the News: Local Journalism and the Crisis of American Democracy* 25–29, 37–39 (2020); Jeffrey A. Trachtenberg, *New York Times Posts Record Uptick in Subscriptions, Expects Advertising to Drop by Over 50% Next Quarter,* Wall St. J., May 6, 2020, https://www.wsj.com/articles/new-york-times-posts -record-uptick-in-subscriptions-expects-advertising-to-drop-by-over-50-next-quarter -11588772725 [https://perma.cc/EG2K-42JZ]; Max Read, *Can Subscriptions Save All Media Companies, or Just the New York Times?,* N.Y. Mag.: Intelligencer, Feb. 8, 2019, https://nymag.com/intelligencer/2019/02/new-york-times-subscription-revenue-is -mixed-news-for-media.html [https://perma.cc/K9LN-JGQK]; Marc Tracy, *Chatham Hedge Fund Has the Winning Bid for McClatchy Newspapers,* N.Y. Times, July 12, 2020, https://www.nytimes.com/2020/07/12/business/media/hedge-fund-mcclatchy -newspapers.html [https://perma.cc/3A82-PTPM]; Joe Pompeo, *The Hedge Fund Vampire That Bleeds Newspapers Dry Now Has the* Chicago Tribune *by the Throat,* Vanity Fair, Feb. 5, 2020, https://www.vanityfair.com/news/2020/02/hedge-fund-vampire -alden-global-capital-that-bleeds-newspapers-dry-has-chicago-tribune-by-the -throat [https://perma.cc/CLG9-JWTP].

4. Benjamin Goggin, *7,800 People Lost Their Media Jobs in 2019 Landslide,* Bus. Insider, Dec. 10, 2019, https://www.businessinsider.com/2019-media-layoffs-job-cuts

-at-buzzfeed-huffpost-vice-details-2019-2# [https://perma.cc/AW5W-W4C4]; John Bonazzo, *Despite Trump Rhetoric, Journalists Are Losing Jobs at a Faster Rate Than Coal Miners,* Observer, Oct. 23, 2018, https://observer.com/2018/10/jobs-trump-coal -miners-journalism/ [https://perma.cc/J7SQ-A67S]. The Poynter Institute maintains a running list of journalism jobs lost during the COVID-19 pandemic. Kristen Hare, *Here Are the Newsroom Layoffs, Furloughs and Closures That Happened during the Coronavirus Pandemic,* Poynter, Aug. 11, 2020 (updated Mar. 2, 2021), https://www .poynter.org/business-work/2020/here-are-the-newsroom-layoffs-furloughs-and -closures-caused-by-the-coronavirus/ [https://perma.cc/QFV5-YDXY].

5. Ross Barkan, *The Biggest Threat to Journalism Isn't Donald Trump. It's Declining Revenues,* Guardian, July 17, 2017, https://www.theguardian.com/commentisfree /2017/jul/17/news-industry-revenue-declines-biggest-threat-to-journalism [https:// perma.cc/UAW2-3PZM]. Newspapers were declining even before the rise of the Internet, but the decline has been precipitous since 2000, especially with the loss of classified advertising. C. P. Chandrasekhar, *The Business of News in the Age of the Internet,* 41 Soc. Scientist 25 (2013); Matthew Gentzkow, *Trading Dollars for Dollars: The Price of Attention Online and Offline,* 104 Am. Econ. Rev. 481, 481 (2014); Robert H. Giles, *An Emergent Neo-Journalism: The Decline and Renewal of News Media,* 32 Harv. Int'l Rev. 36, 38 (2010); Mark J. Perry, *Creative Destruction: Newspaper Ad Revenue Continued Its Precipitous Free Fall in 2014, and It's Likely to Continue,* Am. Enter. Inst., Apr. 30, 2015, https://www.aei.org/carpe-diem/creative-destruction-newspaper-ad -revenue-continued-its-precipitous-free-fall-in-2014-and-its-likely-to-continue/ [https://perma.cc/KDV4-5656]; Derek Thompson, *The Print Apocalypse and How to Survive It,* Atlantic, Nov. 3, 2016, https://www.theatlantic.com/business/archive /2016/11/the-print-apocalypse-and-how-to-survive-it/506429/ [https://perma.cc/ L5JN-Q9Y2]; Kurt Wagner, *Digital Advertising in the US Is Finally Bigger Than Print and Television,* Vox: Recode, Feb. 20, 2019, https://www.vox.com/2019/2/20/18232433 /digital-advertising-facebook-google-growth-tv-print-emarketer-2019/ [https://perma .cc/4GA8-TZL6].

6. Sullivan, *supra* note 3, at 9. For more on the dangers for democracy of a collapsing news business, see Martha Minow, *Saving the News: Why the Constitution Calls for Government Action to Preserve Freedom of Speech* (2021).

7. Sullivan, *supra* note 3, at 34, 36; *id.* at 15 (citing Danny Hayes & Jennifer L. Lawless, *The Decline of Local News and Its Effects: New Evidence from Longitudinal Data,* 80 J. Pol. 332 (2018)); Gallup & Knight Foundation Survey, *American Views 2020: Trust, Media and Democracy; A Deepening Divide* 4 (2020), https://knightfoun

dation.org/wp-content/uploads/2020/08/American-Views-2020-Trust-Media-and
-Democracy.pdf [https://perma.cc/Y69W-54AV]; Leonard Downie Jr. & Michael
Schudson, *The Reconstruction of American Journalism,* Colum. Journalism Rev., Nov.–
Dec. 2009.

8. A good working definition of *disinformation* appears in W. Lance Bennett
& Steven Livingston, *A Brief History of the Disinformation Age,* in *The Disinformation Age: Politics, Technology, and Disruptive Communication in the United States* 3
(W. Lance Bennett & Steven Livingston eds., 2020), https://www.cambridge.org
/core/books/disinformation-age/1F4751119C7C4693E514C249E0F0F997 [https://
perma.cc/KM59-Q7K3] ("We define disinformation as intentional falsehoods or
distortions, often spread as news, to advance political goals such as discrediting opponents, disrupting policy debates, influencing voters, inflaming existing social conflicts, or creating a general backdrop of confusion and informational paralysis").

9. Alex Thompson, *Newsroom or PAC? Liberal Group Muddies Online Information Wars,* Politico, July 14, 2020, https://www.politico.com/news/2020/07/14/news
room-pac-liberal-info-wars-356800 [https://perma.cc/EYZ8-4NTS]; Richard L.
Hasen, *If Democrats Fight Right-Wing "Fake News" Fire with Fire, We All Lose,* Salon,
Feb. 23, 2020, https://www.salon.com/2020/02/23/if-democrats-fight-right-wing
-fake-news-fire-with-fire-we-all-lose/ [https://perma.cc/E7GB-JMRT]; Brian Flood,
*Liberal, Dark-Money-Funded Courier Newsroom Targets Battleground States' Voters
with Democratic Talking Points Billed as News,* Fox News, July 21, 2020, https://www
.foxnews.com/media/liberal-dark-money-funded-courier-newsroom-targets-voters
-democratic-talking-points-news [https://perma.cc/RN2R-YMVP]. The internal memo
posted by Vice News and dated June 20, 2019, is posted at https://www.document-
cloud.org/documents/6771809-Screenshot-PDF.html [https://perma.cc/F9Z2-APFW].

10. Anna Merlan & Tim Marchman, *Docs: Shadow Inc. Directly Tied to Left-
Wing Media Operation,* Vice News, Feb. 7, 2020, https://www.vice.com/en_ca/article
/dygyaq/docs-shadow-inc-directly-tied-to-left-wing-media-operation [https://perma
.cc/KA9F-CGXD].

11. Davey Alba & Jack Nicas, *As Local News Dies, a Pay-for-Play Network Rises
in Its Place,* N.Y. Times, Oct. 18, 2020 (updated Oct. 20, 2020), https://www.ny
times.com/2020/10/18/technology/timpone-local-news-metric-media.html [https://
perma.cc/2U5J-2987].

12. Elizabeth Dwoskin & Craig Timberg, *Facebook Takes Down Russian Operation That Recruited U.S. Journalists, amid Rising Concerns about Election Misinforma-*

tion, Wash. Post, Sept. 1, 2020, https://www.washingtonpost.com/technology/2020/09/01/facebook-disinformation-takedown/ [https://perma.cc/22EZ-Y7KN].

13. Gallup & Knight Foundation Survey, *supra* note 7, at 2–3.

14. *Id.* at 3–4; Andrew M. Guess et al., *"Fake News" May Have Limited Effects beyond Increasing Beliefs in False Claims,* 1 Harv. Kennedy Sch. Misinformation Rev. 1 (2020), https://doi.org/10.37016/mr-2020-004.

15. Hunt Allcott & Matthew Gentzkow, *Social Media and Fake News in the 2016 Election,* 31 J. Econ. Persp. 211, 219 (2017).

16. Alexander Bor et al., *"Fact-Checking" Videos Reduce Belief in, but Not the Sharing of Fake News on Twitter,* PsyArXiv Preprints, Jan. 20, 2021 (unpublished article), available at https://psyarxiv.com/a7huq/; Michael Thaler, *The "Fake News" Effect: Experimentally Identifying Motivated Reasoning Using Trust in News* 36, May 27, 2020 (unpublished article), available at https://scholar.harvard.edu/files/mthaler/files/mthaler_fake-news-effect_full.pdf ("Subjects significantly over-trust Pro-Party news and Fake News in an environment with uninformative signals, real monetary stakes, and little room for self-deception. This bias leads to other errors and biases such as underperformance, overconfidence, and overprecision"). But see Katherine Clayton, Jase Davis, Kristen Hinckley, & Yusaku Horiuchi, *Partisan Motivated Reasoning and Misinformation in the Media: Is News from Ideologically Uncongenial Sources More Suspicious?,* 20 Japanese J. Pol. Sci. 129 (2019), https://www.cambridge.org/core/journals/japanese-journal-of-political-science/article/partisan-motivated-reasoning-and-misinformation-in-the-media-is-news-from-ideologically-uncongenial-sources-more-suspicious/BCD0B8E0558FD72E8A3E0931FCB4E35A [https://permacc/85FH-MM3F] (finding that people tend to believe false information when they are exposed to it, regardless of whether it is from an ideologically compatible source); Reuters, *On Facebook, Health-Misinformation "Superspreaders" Rack Up Billions of Views,* NBC News, Aug. 19, 2020, https://www.nbcnews.com/tech/tech-news/facebook-health-misinformation-superspreaders-rack-billions-views-rcna88 [https://perma.cc/GZ42-GJMA] (citing report from Avaaz dated Aug. 19, 2020, and posted at https://secure.avaaz.org/campaign/en/facebook_threat_health/ [https://perma.cc/Y4V4-GNZJ]).

17. Melanie Freeze et al., *Fake Claims of Fake News: Political Misinformation, Warnings, and the Tainted Truth Effect,* Pol. Behav. (2020), https://doi.org/10.1007/s11109-020-09597-3.

18. Katherine Clayton et al., *Real Solutions for Fake News? Measuring the Effectiveness of General Warnings and Fact-Check Tags in Reducing Belief in False Stories on*

Social Media, 42 Pol. Behav. 1073, 1091 (2019), https://doi.org/10.1007/s11109-019
-09533-0 ("General warnings also reduce belief in real news"); see also Andrew M.
Guess et al., *A Digital Media Literacy Intervention Increases Discernment between
Mainstream and False News in the United States and India,* 117 PNAS 15536, July 7,
2020, https://doi.org/10.1073/pnas.1920498117 (exposure of social media users to
tips on how to spot false news stories "reduced the perceived accuracy of both mainstream and false news headlines, but effects on the latter were significantly larger").
For another note of caution, see Joseph Bernstein, *Bad News,* Harper's Magazine
(Sept. 2021), https://harpers.org/archive/2021/09/bad-news-selling-the-story-of-dis
information/ [https://perma.cc/FF3B-FVE9].

19. Professor Persily calls this phenomenon the "velocity" issue. Nathaniel Persily, *The Internet's Challenge to Democracy: Framing the Problem and Assessing Reforms*
10 (2019), https://perma.cc/A97Z-72PX. On lies spreading faster than the truth on
social media, see Soroush Vosoughi, Deb Roy, & Sinan Aral, *The Spread of True and
False News Online,* 359 Sci. 1146 (2018), https://doi.org/10.1126/science.aap9559.

20. The August 15, 2020, post by Bruce Mittlesteadt appeared on Facebook.
The post may be viewed at https://perma.cc/HBQ4-6UME?type=image. The photograph is reprinted with the permission of the author.

21. Eric Litke, *No, Wisconsin Mailbox Picture Isn't Proof of "Massive Voter Suppression,"* PolitiFact, Aug. 17, 2020, https://www.politifact.com/factchecks/2020/aug
/17/facebook-posts/no-wisconsin-mailbox-picture-isnt-proof-massive-vo/ [https://
perma.cc/D4LU-4ZQW]. The tweet appears at Thomas Kennedy (@tomaskenn),
Twitter, Aug. 14, 2020, https://twitter.com/tomaskenn/status/1294427812670124033
[https://perma.cc/DB3T-3H69].

22. Screenshots of the Twitter exchange on direct message are on file with the
author. Spelling and typographical errors corrected.

23. On President Trump's numerous unsupported statements about voter fraud
and election "rigging," see Richard L. Hasen, *Trump's Relentless Attacks on Mail-In
Ballots Are Part of a Larger Strategy,* N.Y. Times, Aug. 19, 2020, https://www.nytimes
.com/2020/08/19/opinion/trump-usps-mail-voting.html [https://perma.cc/C5YV
-3LUU]; see also Aaron Blake, *Trump Blurts Out His True Motive on Mail-In Voting,*
Wash. Post: The Fix, Aug. 13, 2020, https://www.washingtonpost.com/politics/2020
/08/13/trump-blurts-out-his-true-motive-blocking-post-office-funding-mail-in
-voting/ [https://perma.cc/342N-SNWJ].

24. Nathaniel Persily, *Can Democracy Survive the Internet?* 28 J. Democracy 63,
68 (2017); Andrew M. Guess & Benjamin A. Lyons, *Misinformation, Disinforma-*

tion, and Online Propaganda, in Persily & Tucker, *supra* note 2, at 11 ("We define disinformation as the subset of misinformation that is deliberately propagated"). Guess and Lyons note that one of the key reasons people share misinformation is its novelty. *Id.* at 22.

25. Cecilia Kang & Adam Goldman, *In Washington Pizzeria Attack, Fake News Brought Real Guns,* N.Y. Times, Dec. 5, 2016, https://www.nytimes.com/2016/12/05/business/media/comet-ping-pong-pizza-shooting-fake-news-consequences.html [https://perma.cc/S7U9-QR8X].

26. Cecilia Kang & Sheera Frenkel, *"PizzaGate" Conspiracy Theory Thrives Anew in the TikTok Era,* N.Y. Times, June 27, 2020 (updated July 14, 2020), https://www.nytimes.com/2020/06/27/technology/pizzagate-justin-bieber-qanon-tiktok.html [https://perma.cc/U4MW-QPWC].

27. Giovanni Russonello, *QAnon Now as Popular in U.S. as Some Major Religions, Poll Suggests,* N.Y. Times, May 27, 2021, https://www.nytimes.com/2021/05/27/us/politics/qanon-republicans-trump.html [https://perma.cc/ZQ44-GVU6]; Katie Rogers & Kevin Roose, *Trump Says QAnon Followers Are People Who "Love Our Country,"* N.Y. Times, Aug. 19, 2020, https://www.nytimes.com/2020/08/19/us/politics/trump-qanon-conspiracy-theories.html [https://perma.cc/NH9C-BTGK]; Annie Karni, *Trump Refrains from Disavowing QAnon Conspiracy,* N.Y. Times, Aug. 15, 2020 (updated Sept. 1, 2020), https://www.nytimes.com/2020/08/15/us/elections/trump-refrains-from-disavowing-qanon-conspiracy.html [https://perma.cc/7NHF-XWB9]; Ari Sen & Brandy Zadrozny, *QAnon Groups Have Millions of Members on Facebook, Documents Show,* NBC News, Aug. 10, 2020, https://www.nbcnews.com/tech/tech-news/qanon-groups-have-millions-members-facebook-documents-show-n1236317 [https://perma.cc/3NMP-566Z]; Isaac Stanley-Becker, *How the Trump Campaign Came to Court QAnon, the Online Conspiracy Movement Identified by the FBI as a Violent Threat,* Wash. Post, Aug. 2, 2020, https://www.washingtonpost.com/politics/how-the-trump-campaign-came-to-court-qanon-the-online-conspiracy-movement-identified-by-the-fbi-as-a-violent-threat/2020/08/01/ddoea9b4-d1d4-11ea-9038-af089b63ac21_story.html [https://perma.cc/ATY3-MHMR].

28. Laura Edelson et al., *Far-Right News Sources on Facebook More Engaging,* Medium, Mar. 3, 2021, https://medium.com/cybersecurity-for-democracy/far-right-news-sources-on-facebook-more-engaging-e04a01efae90 [https://perma.cc/F7QF-TCPT]; Karsten Müller & Carlo Schwarz, *Fanning the Flames of Hate: Social Media and Hate Crime,* J. European Econ. Ass'n (2020), https://doi.org/10.1093/jeea/jvaa045.

29. Nicolas Berlinski et al., *The Effects of Unsubstantiated Claims of Voter Fraud*

on Confidence in Elections, J. Experimental Pol. Sci. (2021), https://doi.org/10.1017 /XPS.2021.18; Katherine Clayton et al., *Does Elite Rhetoric Undermine Democratic Norms?,* Proceedings of the National Academy of Sciences of the United States of America, June 8, 2021, https://doi.org/10.1073/pnas.2024125118.

30. *53% of Republicans View Trump as True U.S. President — Reuters/Ipsos,* Reuters, May 24, 2021, https://www.reuters.com/world/us/53-republicans-view-trump -true-us-president-reutersipsos-2021-05-24/ [https://perma.cc/LS6H-PYEV]; Chris Kahn, *Half of Republicans Say Biden Won Because of a "Rigged" Election: Reuters/Ipsos Poll,* Yahoo News, Nov. 18, 2020, https://www.yahoo.com/news/half-republicans -biden-won-because-110417008.html [https://perma.cc/E693-D4ND]; Bright Line Watch, *A Democratic Stress Test—The 2020 Election and Its Aftermath,* Nov. 30, 2020, http://brightlinewatch.org/american-democracy-on-the-eve-of-the-2020 -election/a-democratic-stress-test-the-2020-election-and-its-aftermathbright-line -watch-november-2020-survey/ [https://perma.cc/QVN2-JNU8].

31. Nick Corasaniti, Jim Rutenberg, & Kathleen Gray, *Threats and Tensions Rise as Trump and Allies Attack Elections Process,* N.Y. Times, Nov. 18, 2020 (updated Feb. 1, 2021), https://www.nytimes.com/2020/11/18/us/politics/trump-election.html [https://perma.cc/6PTB-RCM2]; Renée DiResta, *Right-Wing Social Media Finalizes Its Divorce from Reality,* Atlantic, Nov. 23, 2020, https://www.theatlantic.com/ideas /archive/2020/11/right-wing-social-media-finalizes-its-divorce-reality/617177/ [https://perma.cc/QZJ6-M5BQ]: "Yet reducing the supply of misinformation doesn't eliminate the demand. Powerful online influencers and the right-wing demi-media— intensely partisan outlets, such as One America News and Newsmax, that amplify ideas that bubble up from internet message boards—have steadfastly reassured Trump's supporters that he will be reelected, and that the conspiracies against him will be exposed. No doubt seeing an opportunity to pull viewers from a more established rival, One America News Network ran a segment attacking Fox's Arizona call and declaring the network a 'Democrat Party hack.' The president himself, while tweeting about how the election was being stolen, amplified accounts that touted OANN and Newsmax as places to find accurate reporting on the truth about his election victory. And on Parler, the conspiracy-mongering has grown only more frenzied as Trump makes state-by-state fraud allegations: in addition to concerns about Sharpies, the social network abounds with rumors of CIA supercomputers with secret programs to change votes, allegations of massive numbers of dead people voting, claims of backdated ballots, and assorted other speculations that users attempt to coalesce into a grand unified theory of election theft."

32. Staff Report, *Examining the U.S. Capitol Attack: A Review of the Security, Planning, and Response Failures on January 6, United States Senate Committee on Homeland Security and Governmental Affairs and Committee on Rules and Administration,* June 8, 2021, at 34–36 and n. 187, https://www.rules.senate.gov/imo/media/doc/Jan%206%20HSGAC%20Rules%20Report.pdf [https://perma.cc/JH6W-F675] (citing *Examining the U.S. Capitol Attack—Part II: Joint Hearing Before the S. Comm. on Homeland Sec. & Governmental Affairs and the S. Comm. on Rules & Admin.,* 117th Cong. (2021) (written testimony of Melissa Smislova, Acting Under Secretary, Office of Intelligence and Analysis, Dep't of Homeland Sec.)). See also id. at 35 n. 189 (citing *Examining the U.S. Capitol Attack—Part II: Joint Hearing Before the S. Comm. on Homeland Sec. & Governmental Affairs and the S. Comm. on Rules & Admin.,* 117th Cong. (2021) (testimony of Jill Sanborn, Ass't Dir., Counterterrorism Div., Fed. Bureau of Investigation)); id. ("According to the Attorney General Guidelines for Domestic FBI Operations, the 'guidelines do not authorize investigating or collecting or maintaining information on United States persons *solely* for the purpose of monitoring activities protected by the First Amendment or the lawful exercise of other rights secured by the Constitution or laws of the United States.' However, the FBI does have existing authority to use open source information as part of its investigative efforts. Dep't. of Justice, *Attorney General's Guidelines for Domestic FBI Operations* 13 (2008) (emphasis added). The FBI informed the Committees that the FBI does have a guiding policy related to reviewing social media, which outlines available investigative methods to collect on social media or other online forums, and varies depending on the level of investigative activity authorized. The FBI stressed that it has safeguards in place to ensure the protection of Constitutional rights. Email from the FBI to the Committees (June 3, 2021)"); id. at 34 n. 187 ("DHS officials noted that I&A may have identified social media posts calling for violence, but may have been unable to discern them from 'bravado or constitutionally protected speech.' Email from DHS to the Committees (June 3, 2021)").

33. Gordon Pennycook, Tyrone D. Cannon, & David G. Rand, *Prior Exposure Increases Perceived Accuracy of Fake News,* 147 J. Experimental Psych. Gen. 1865 (2019), https://pubmed.ncbi.nlm.nih.gov/30247057/ [https://perma.cc/88ZZ-4ADR]; Danielle K. Citron & Robert Chesney, *Deep Fakes: A Looming Challenge for Privacy, Democracy, and National Security,* 107 Calif. L. Rev. 1753, 1758 (2019) ("[Deep fake technology] leverages machine-learning algorithms to insert faces and voices into video and audio recordings of actual people and enables the creation of realistic impersonations out of digital whole cloth. The end result is realistic-looking video

or audio making it appear that someone said or did something. Although deep fakes can be created with the consent of people being featured, more often they will be created without it"); see also Charlotte Stanton, Carnegie Endowment for Int'l Peace, June 2019 Convening on Defining Inappropriate Synthetic/Manipulated Media Ahead of the U.S. 2020 Election (July 2019), https://carnegieendowment.org/2019/06/19/june-2019-convening-on-defining-inappropriate-synthetic-manipulated-media-ahead-of-u.s.-2020-election-pub-79661 [https://perma.cc/PPJ4-85MX]; Rebecca Green, *Counterfeit Campaign Speech,* 70 Hastings L.J. 1445, 1447–48 (2019) (using label of "counterfeit" campaign speech for "a faked version of the real thing fabricated with the intent to deceive"); Melanie Mitchell, *Artificial Intelligence: A Guide for Thinking Humans* 279 (2019) ("One particular development that frightens me is the use of AI systems to generate fake media: text, sounds, images, and videos that depict with terrifying realism events that never actually happened").

34. Renée DiResta, *The Supply of Disinformation Will Soon Be Infinite,* Atlantic, Sept. 20, 2020, https://www.theatlantic.com/ideas/archive/2020/09/future-propaganda-will-be-computer-generated/616400/ [https://perma.cc/5V3F-8MWW].

35. Cristian Vaccari & Andrew Chadwick, *Deepfakes and Disinformation: Exploring the Impact of Synthetic Political Video on Deception, Uncertainty, and Trust in News,* 6 Soc. Media + Soc'y, Jan.–Mar. 2020, at 1–13, https://doi.org/10.1177/2056305120903408; Brendan Nyhan, *Why Fears of Fake News Are Overhyped,* Medium, Feb. 4, 2019, https://medium.com/s/reasonable-doubt/why-fears-of-fake-news-are-overhyped-2ed9ca0a52c9 [https://perma.cc/V877-RKCD]; see also Max Read, *Can You Spot a Deepfake? Does It Matter?,* N.Y. Mag.: Intelligencer, June 27, 2019, https://nymag.com/intelligencer/2019/06/how-do-you-spot-a-deepfake-it-might-not-matter.html [https://perma.cc/MT4P-539R] ("If you want a vision of the future, don't imagine an onslaught of fake video. Imagine an onslaught of commenters calling every video fake"); Jeffrey M. Jones, *U.S. Media Trust Continues to Recover from 2016 Low,* Gallup, Oct. 12, 2018, https://news.gallup.com/poll/243665/media-trust-continues-recover-2016-low.aspx [https://perma.cc/BJ45-PP7Q] ("53% of those aged 65 and older trust in the media, compared with just 33% of those under age 30. Younger adults have come of an age in an era marked by partisan media and fake news, while older Americans' trust may have been established long ago in an era of widely read daily newspapers and trusted television news anchors").

36. See Greg Miller, Ellen Nakashima, & Adam Entous, *Obama's Secret Struggle to Punish Russia for Putin's Election Assault,* Wash. Post, June 23, 2017, https://www

.washingtonpost.com/graphics/2017/world/national-security/obama-putin-election
-hacking/?utm_term=.6e02e087764a [https://perma.cc/ZNZ6-WMCZ] ("[Ameri-
can] intelligence captured Putin's specific instructions on the operation's audacious
objectives—defeat or at least damage the Democratic nominee, Hillary Clinton, and
help elect her opponent, Donald Trump"); Lauren Carroll, *Russia and Its Influence on
the Presidential Election,* PolitiFact, Dec. 1, 2016, https://www.politifact.com/article/2016
/dec/01/russia-and-its-influence-presidential-election/ [https://perma.cc/H889-K7N9].

37. Sheera Frenkel & Cecilia Kang, *An Ugly Truth* 130–32 (2021); Scott Shane
& Vindu Goel, *Fake Russian Facebook Accounts Bought $100,000 in Political Ads,* N.Y.
Times, Sept. 6, 2017, https://www.nytimes.com/2017/09/06/technology/facebook
-russian-political-ads.html [https://perma.cc/YM75-REJR]; Scott Shane, *The Fake
Americans Russia Created to Influence the Election,* N.Y. Times, Sept. 7, 2017, https://
www.nytimes.com/2017/09/07/us/politics/russia-facebook-twitter-election.html
[https://perma.cc/S77A-UYKF]; see Gwen Ifill's interview with Ken Goldstein and
Eitan Hersh, *How "Microtargeting" Works in Political Advertising,* PBS, Feb. 18, 2014,
https://www.pbs.org/newshour/show/microtargeting-works-political-advertising
[https://perma.cc/S37Y-B3AN] (explaining that microtargeting is not limited to the
spread of false reports; it aims information at particular voters on the basis of data
collected about them); Massimo Calabresi, *Inside Russia's Social Media War on America,* Time, May 18, 2017, https://time.com/4783932/inside-russia-social-media-war
-america/ [https://perma.cc/A2UJ-3XQ7]; Gabe O'Connor, *How Russian Twitter
Bots Pumped Out Fake News during the 2016 Election,* NPR, Apr. 3, 2017, https://
www.npr.org/sections/alltechconsidered/2017/04/03/522503844/how-russian-twitter
-bots-pumped-out-fake-news-during-the-2016-election [https://perma.cc/P99V-LZDZ].
Russia was not alone in 2016 in using bots to amplify microtargeting efforts. Professor Persily notes that "the advent of campaign bots represents the final breakdown
in established modes and categories of campaigning. . . . All the worry about shady
outsiders in the campaign-finance system running television ads seems quaint when
compared to networks of thousands of bots of uncertain geographic origin creating
automated messages designed to malign candidates and misinform voters." Persily,
supra note 24, at 70 ("During the 2016 campaign, the prevalence of bots in spreading
propaganda and fake news appears to have reached new heights. One study found
that between 16 September and 21 October 2016, bots produced about a fifth of all
tweets related to the upcoming election. Across all three presidential debates, pro-
Trump Twitter bots generated about four times as many tweets as pro-Clinton bots.

During the final debate in particular, that figure rose to seven times as many"). The next few paragraphs draw from Richard L. Hasen, *Election Meltdown: Dirty Tricks, Distrust, and the Threat to American Democracy* (2020).

38. Office of the Dir. of Nat'l Intelligence, ICA 2017-01D, *Assessing Russian Activities and Intentions in Recent US Elections,* at ii, 3, Jan. 6, 2017, https://www .dni.gov/files/documents/ICA_2017_01.pdf [https://perma.cc/DD8U-ZR5X]; *id.* at Annex A.

39. New Knowledge, *The Tactics & Tropes of the Internet Research Agency,* at 708, Dec. 17, 2018, https://cdn2.hubspot.net/hubfs/4326998/ira-report-rebrand_Final J14.pdf [https://perma.cc/9FGQ-TMGM]. Much of this ground is covered in vol. 1 of the report of Robert Mueller, the special counsel appointed to investigate Russian interference in the 2016 presidential election. See Special Counsel Robert S. Mueller III, *Report on the Investigation into Russian Interference in the 2016 Presidential Election,* Mar. 2019 [hereafter cited as Mueller Report]. The official version appears at https://www.justice.gov/storage/report.pdf, and a searchable version appears at https:// www.documentcloud.org/documents/5955379-Redacted-Mueller-Report.html #document/ [https://perma.cc/9TEW-JD3Z]. See also Philip N. Howard et al., *The IRA, Social Media and Political Polarization in the United States, 2012–2018,* Working Paper 2018.2, Oxford, U.K.: Project on Computational Propaganda, Oct. 2019, https:// demtech.oii.ox.ac.uk/wp-content/uploads/sites/93/2018/12/The-IRA-Social-Media -and-Political-Polarization.pdf [https://perma.cc/GW3J-L5A6]; Ryan Lucas, *How Russia Used Facebook to Organize 2 Sets of Protesters,* NPR, Nov. 1, 2017, https://www .npr.org/2017/11/01/561427876/how-russia-used-facebook-to-organize-two-sets-of -protesters [https://perma.cc/L5MZ-PD7D].

40. Mueller Report, *supra* note 39, at vol. 1, p. 29.

41. New Knowledge, *supra* note 39, at 8, 12, 13, 16, 45–46; Howard et al., *supra* note 38, at 9–10.

42. Howard et al., *supra* note 39, at 19, 34; Richard Engel, Kate Benyon-Tinker, & Kennett Werner, *Russian Documents Reveal Desire to Sow Racial Discord—and Violence—in the U.S.,* NBC News, May 20, 2019, https://www.nbcnews.com/news /world/russian-documentsreveal-desire-sow-racial-discord-violence-u-s-n1008051 [https://perma.cc/37SN-8VH8].

43. New Knowledge, *supra* note 39, at 24, 76–77. On the most shared Hillary Clinton post being the one about illegal voting, see p. 51 of the slide deck accompanying the New Knowledge report, posted at https://cdn2.hubspot.net/hubfs/4326998 /SSCI%20Presentation%20final.pdf [https://perma.cc/N8L4-S7AF].

44. Christopher Ingraham, *Somebody Just Put a Price Tag on the 2016 Election. It's a Doozy*, Wash. Post, Apr. 14, 2017, https://www.washingtonpost.com/news/wonk/wp/2017/04/14/somebody-just-put-a-price-tag-on-the-2016-election-its-a-doozy/ [https://perma.cc/FMD2-XF9N] ("The final price tag for the 2016 election is in: $6.5 billion for the presidential and congressional elections combined, according to campaign finance watchdog OpenSecrets.org. . . . Clinton's unsuccessful campaign ($768 million in spending) outspent Trump's successful one ($398 million) by nearly 2 to 1"); Roger Parloff, *Exclusive: Facebook Ex-Security Chief: How "Hypertargeting" Threatens Democracy*, Yahoo! Fin., Feb. 8, 2019, https://finance.yahoo.com/news/facebook-security-officer-alex-stamos-targeting-risk-142859539.html [https://perma.cc/G9MP-WWG8]; Andrew M. Guess, Brendan Nyhan, & Jason Reifler, *Exposure to Untrustworthy Websites in the 2016 US Election*, 4 Nature Hum. Behav. 472 (2020), https://www.nature.com/articles/s41562-020-0833-x [https://perma.cc/7KDJ-52W2] ("Survey and web-traffic data from the 2016 US presidential campaign show that supporters of Donald Trump were most likely to visit [untrustworthy] websites, which often spread through Facebook. However, these websites made up a small share of people's information diets on average and were largely consumed by a subset of Americans with strong preferences for pro-attitudinal information. These results suggest that the widespread speculation about the prevalence of exposure to untrustworthy websites has been overstated").

45. On the hacking of documents, as well as Russian probing of state voter registration databases in 2016, see Hasen, *Election Meltdown, supra* note 37, at 90–93. For one analysis of the effect of the leaked stolen emails, see Harry Enten, *How Much Did WikiLeaks Hurt Hillary Clinton?*, FiveThirtyEight, Dec. 23, 2016, https://fivethirtyeight.com/features/wikileaks-hillary-clinton/ [https://perma.cc/X5Q4-PUFJ].

46. Facebook commissioned a civil rights audit of its practices, and the audit found that the platform did not do enough to combat voter suppression. Charlie Osborne, *Civil Rights Auditors Slam Facebook Stance on Trump, Voter Suppression*, ZDNet, July 8, 2020, https://www.zdnet.com/article/civil-rights-auditors-slam-facebook-stance-on-trump-voter-suppression/ [https://perma.cc/4EQC-4XAK] ("With the US presidential election coming up, among the complaints are the 'narrow' focus of Facebook's voter suppression policies. The report says that Facebook's failure to tackle US President Trump's statements concerning potentially fraudulent mail-in ballot processes on the platform—as well as posts that could be classified as hate speech—shows that the company has been 'far too reluctant to adopt strong rules to limit misinformation and voter suppression'"). On Facebook's planning for a Trump

rejection of election results, see Mike Isaac & Sheera Frenkel, *Facebook Braces Itself for Trump to Cast Doubt on Election Results*, N.Y. Times, Aug. 21, 2020 (updated Nov. 3, 2020), https://www.nytimes.com/2020/08/21/technology/facebook-trump -election.html [https://perma.cc/J6QW-X2TH].

47. Julian E. Barnes, *Russia Continues Interfering in Election to Try to Help Trump, U.S. Intelligence Says*, N.Y. Times, Aug. 7, 2020 (updated Sept. 2, 2020), https:// www.nytimes.com/2020/08/07/us/politics/russia-china-trump-biden-election -interference.html [https://perma.cc/WMQ7-XZMM]; Natasha Bertrand & Daniel Lippman, *Ratcliffe Went Off Script with Iran Remarks, Officials Say*, Politico, Oct. 28, 2020, https://www.politico.com/news/2020/10/28/john-ratcliffe-iran-433375 [https://perma.cc/BS4B-DYAQ]; Julian E. Barnes, Nicole Perlroth, & David E. Sanger, *Russia Poses Greater Election Threat Than Iran, Many U.S. Officials Say*, N.Y. Times, Oct. 22, 2020, https://www.nytimes.com/2020/10/22/us/politics/russia -election-interference-hacks.html [https://perma.cc/W3UL-QPES]; Julian E. Barnes, *Russian Interference in 2020 Included Influencing Trump Associates, Report Says*, N.Y. Times, Mar. 16, 2021, https://www.nytimes.com/2021/03/16/us/politics/election -interference-russia-2020-assessment.html [https://perma.cc/SS4E-838Q]; Nat'l Intel. Council, *Foreign Threats to the US 2020 Federal Elections*, Mar. 10, 2021, https://int .nyt.com/data/documenttools/2021-intelligence-community-election-interference -assessment/abd0346ebdd93e1e/full.pdf [https://perma.cc/XT7P-DV4Y]; *Joint Report of the Department of Justice and the Department of Homeland Security on Foreign Interference Targeting Election Infrastructure or Political Organization, Campaign, or Candidate Infrastructure Related to the 2020 US Federal Elections*, Mar. 2021, https:// int.nyt.com/data/documenttools/2021-justice-department-and-homeland-security -election-interference-report/d7fd65924c984439/full.pdf [https://perma.cc/EK6T -3W3G].

48. For a closer examination of the Alabama social media campaign, see Hasen, *Election Meltdown, supra* note 37, at 75–80.

49. Isaac Stanley-Becker, *Facebook Removes Page Using Image of LeBron James over "Voter Suppression Tactics,"* Wash. Post, Aug. 22, 2020, https://www.washington post.com/politics/2020/08/21/facebook-removes-page-with-deceptive-lebron-james -ads-voter-suppression/ [https://perma.cc/UWG7-QDUE]; Isaac Stanley-Becker, *Disinformation Campaign Stokes Fears about Mail Voting, Using LeBron James Image and Boosted by Trump-Aligned Group*, Wash. Post, Aug. 20, 2020, https://www.wash ingtonpost.com/politics/disinformation-campaign-stokes-fears-about-mail-voting

-using-lebron-james-image-and-boosted-by-trump-aligned-group/2020/08/20
/fcadf382-e2e2-11ea-8181-606e603bb1c4_story.html [https://perma.cc/2JM9-RHGS].

50. Isaac Stanley-Becker, *Google Greenlights Ads with "Blatant Disinformation" about Voting by Mail,* Wash. Post, Aug. 28, 2020, https://www.washingtonpost.com/technology/2020/08/28/google-ads-mail-voting/ [https://perma.cc/WEM9-4WYQ].

51. Mark Bergen, *YouTube Election Loophole Lets Some False Trump-Win Videos Spread,* Bloomberg, Nov. 10, 2020, https://www.bloomberg.com/news/articles/2020-11-10/youtube-election-loophole-lets-some-false-trump-win-videos-spread [https://perma.cc/V2C6-75K9]; Drew Harwell, *How Viral Videos Helped Blast Voting Lies across the Web,* Wash. Post, Nov. 5, 2020, https://www.washingtonpost.com/technology/2020/11/05/trump-misleading-videos-youtube/ [https://perma.cc/VG85-MY84].

52. Joe Fitzgerald Rodriguez, Shannon Lin, & Jessica Huseman, *Misinformation Image on WeChat Attempts to Frighten Chinese Americans Out of Voting,* ProPublica, Nov. 2, 2020, https://www.propublica.org/article/misinformation-image-on-wechat-attempts-to-frighten-chinese-americans-out-of-voting [https://perma.cc/SKQ3-G2E3]; Ana Ceballos & Bianca Padró Ocasio, *"It's Getting Really Bad": Fake Threats Trigger Fear for Spanish-Speaking Trump Backers,* Miami Herald, Oct. 29, 2020 (updated Oct. 30, 2020), https://www.miamiherald.com/article246799572.html [https://perma.cc/CME4-Q4VE].

53. Yochai Benkler, Robert Faris, & Hal Roberts, *Network Propaganda* 73–74 (2018) ("The right wing of the media ecosystem behaves precisely as the echo-chamber models predict—exhibiting high insularity, susceptibility to information cascades, rumor and conspiracy theory, and drift toward more extreme versions of itself. The rest of the media ecosystem, however, operates as an interconnected network anchored by organizations, both for profit and nonprofit, that adhere to professional journalistic norms"). On the relative lack of echo chambers among the general public, but a greater echo-chamber effect among the more politically active and influential, see Andrew M. Guess, *(Almost) Everything in Moderation: New Evidence on Americans' Online Media Diets,* Am. J. Pol. Sci. (2021), https://doi.org/10.1111/ajps.12589; see also Gregory Eady et al., *How Many People Live in Political Bubbles on Social Media? Evidence from Linked Survey and Twitter Data,* 9 Sage: Special Collection—Soc. Media & Pol., Jan.–Mar. 2019, https://doi.org/10.1177%2F2158244019832705; Persily, *supra* note 19, at 19–20. Pablo Barberá offers a good review of the literature on echo chambers and political polarization. See generally Pablo Barberá, *Social Media, Echo Chambers, and Political Polarization,* in Persily & Tucker, *supra* note 2, at 34.

54. Benkler, Faris, & Roberts, *supra* note 53, at 8 (rejecting the view that "the internet polarizes" in favor of a view that "institutions, culture and politics" were the "prime movers" of increasing American polarization). The causes of American polarization have been analyzed extensively. For accessible and thoughtful introductions, see Ezra Klein, *Why We're Polarized* (2020), and Richard H. Pildes, *Why the Center Does Not Hold: The Causes of Hyperpolarized Democracy in America*, 99 Calif. L. Rev. 273 (2011). Klein is especially good in summarizing the literature on negative partisanship and the role of emotion over reason, especially among the most partisan.

On motivated reasoning and misperception in a polarized atmosphere, see D. J. Flynn, Brendan Nyhan, & Jason Reifler, *The Nature and Origins of Misperceptions: Understanding False and Unsupported Beliefs about Politics*, 38 Advances in Pol. Psych. 127 (2017), https://doi.org/10.1111/pops.12394. One of the early studies of the well-known tendency of people to be meaner and act out online is John Suler, *The Online Disinhibition Effect*, 7 CyberPsych. & Behav. 321 (2004), https://www.researchgate .net/publication/8451443_The_Online_Disinhibition_Effect [https://perma.cc/XCT5 -XGSM]. The causes for online disinhibition are complex; it stems not only from anonymity but also from social group norms of meanness or other behavior that develop in particular online environments. Leonie Rösner & Nicole C. Krämer, *Verbal Venting in the Social Web: Effects of Anonymity and Group Norms on Aggressive Language Use in Online Comments*, 2 Soc. Media + Soc'y (2016), https://doi.org /10.1177%2F2056305116664220. On the proliferation of online hate speech, see Alexandra A. Siegel, *Online Hate Speech*, in Persily & Tucker, *supra* note 2, at 56. On the nationalization of news caused by the closure of local newspapers, see Joshua P. Darr, Matthew P. Hitt, & Johanna L. Dunaway, *Newspaper Closures Polarize Voting Behavior*, 68 J. Commc'n 1007 (2018), https://doi.org/10.1093/joc/jqy051.

55. Allcott & Gentzkow, *supra* note 15, at 223; Andrew Guess, Brendan Nyhan, & Jason Reifler, *Selective Exposure to Misinformation: Evidence from the Consumption of Fake News during the 2016 U.S. Presidential Campaign*, Eur. Rsch. Council (Jan. 9, 2018), https://about.fb.com/wp-content/uploads/2018/01/fake-news-2016.pdf [https:// perma.cc/ZQ8D-2BWY] ("We estimate that approximately 1 in 4 Americans visited a fake news website from October 7–November 14, 2016. Trump supporters visited the most fake news websites, which were overwhelmingly pro-Trump. However, fake news consumption was heavily concentrated among a small group—almost 6 in 10 visits to fake news websites came from the 10% of people with the most conservative online information diets. We also find that Facebook was a key vector of exposure to fake news and that fact-checks of fake news almost never reached its

consumers"); Michele Cantarella, Nicolò Fraccaroli, & Roberto Volpe, *Does Fake News Affect Voting Behaviour?*, CEIS Working Paper No. 493 (last updated June 25, 2020), https://papers.ssrn.com/sol3/papers.cfm?abstract_id=3629666 (finding exposure to fake news correlated with support for Italian populist parties, but noting that less than half the correlation is causal; many supported populist parties before being attracted to fake news).

56. Benkler, Faris, & Roberts, *supra* note 53, at 13—14 ("We find that the influence in the right-wing media ecosystem, whether judged by hyperlinks, Twitter sharing, or Facebook sharing, is both highly skewed to the far right and highly insulated from other segments of the network, from center-right (which is nearly nonexistent) through the far left. . . . The behavior of the right-wing media ecosystem represents a radicalization of roughly a third of the American media system").

57. *Republicans, Democrats Move Even Further Apart in Coronavirus Concerns,* Pew Rsch. Ctr., June 25, 2020, https://www.pewresearch.org/politics/2020/06/25/republicans-democrats-move-even-further-apart-in-coronavirus-concerns/ [https://perma.cc/L8DP-SMTF] (35 percent of Republicans compared to 64 percent of Democrats "worry they will contract COVID-19 and need to be hospitalized"; "Democrats and Democratic-leaning independents are about twice as likely as Republicans and Republican leaners to say that masks should be worn always (63% vs. 29%). Republicans are much more likely than Democrats to say that masks should rarely or never be worn (23% vs. 4%)").

58. Saranac Hale Spencer & Angelo Fichera, *In Viral Video, Doctor Falsely Touts Hydroxychloroquine as COVID-19 "Cure,"* FactCheck.org, July 28, 2020, https://www.factcheck.org/2020/07/in-viral-video-doctor-falsely-touts-hydroxychloroquine-as-covid-19-cure/ [https://perma.cc/Q9RJ-7BZ6]; Brenda Major et al., *The Threat of Increasing Diversity: Why Many White Americans Support Trump in the 2016 Presidential Election,* Group Processes & Intergroup Relations, Oct. 20, 2016, https://doi.org/10.1177/1368430216677304. For a look at demand for far-right content on YouTube, see Kevin Munger & Joseph Phillips, *Right-Wing YouTube: A Supply and Demand Perspective,* Int'l J. Press & Pol. (2020), https://doi.org/10.1177%2F1940161220964767.

59. Benkler, Faris, & Roberts, *supra* note 53, at 367; Cailin O'Connor & James Owen Weatherall, *The Misinformation Age* 84 (2019); Dan M. Kahan, Ellen Peters, Erica Cantrell Dawson, & Paul Slovic, *Motivated Numeracy and Enlightened Self-Government,* 1 Behav. Pub. Pol'y 54 (2017), http://doi.org/10.1017/bpp.2016.2.

60. Persily, *supra* note 19, at 4.

61. Whitney Phillips & Ryan M. Milner, *You Are Here: A Field Guide for Navigating Polarized Speech, Conspiracy Theories, and Our Polluted Media Landscape* 144 (2021) (original emphasis); Klein, *supra* note 54, at 149.

62. David Enrich, *The Incestuous Relationship between Donald Trump and Fox News*, N.Y. Times, Aug. 23, 2020 (updated Sept. 16, 2020) (book review), https:// www.nytimes.com/2020/08/23/books/review/brian-stelter-hoax.html [https://perma .cc/7SQ2-BKES]; Michael M. Grynbaum, *Boycotted. Criticized. But Fox News Leads the Pack in Prime Time*, N.Y. Times, Aug. 9, 2020, https://www.nytimes.com/2020 /08/09/business/media/fox-news-ratings.html [https://perma.cc/GW3C-TBWH]; Joe Flint & Kimberly Chin, *Fox CEO Pins Hopes on Football Return, Fox News to Lift Profit*, Wall St. J., Aug. 4, 2020, https://www.wsj.com/articles/fox-posts-lower-quar terly-profit-on-decline-in-advertising-revenue-11596572454 [https://perma.cc/7TX4 -ZWSB].

63. Alan Cullison & David Gauthier-Villars, *Russian in Cyprus Was Behind Key Parts of Discredited Dossier on Trump*, Wall St. J., Oct. 28, 2020, https://www.wsj .com/articles/russian-in-cyprus-was-behind-key-parts-of-discredited-dossier-on -trump-11603901989 [https://perma.cc/KS2B-3E3H]; Eric Geller, *Collusion Aside, Mueller Found Abundant Evidence of Russian Election Plot*, Politico, Apr. 18, 2019, https://www.politico.com/story/2019/04/18/mueller-report-russian-election -plot-1365568 [https://perma.cc/6Z58-UUJ9] ("Although the investigation established that the Russian government perceived it would benefit from a Trump presidency and worked to secure that outcome, and that the Campaign expected it would benefit electorally from information stolen and released through Russian efforts, the investigation did not establish that members of the Trump Campaign conspired or coordinated with the Russian government in its election interference activities,' Mueller wrote").

64. Craig Silverman & Lawrence Alexander, *How Teens in the Balkans Are Duping Trump Supporters with Fake News*, BuzzFeed News, Nov. 3, 2016, https://www .buzzfeednews.com/article/craigsilverman/how-macedonia-became-a-global-hub -for-pro-trump-misinfo [https://perma.cc/T9GZ-7UGT]; Joshua Gillin, *Fake News Website Starts as Joke, Gains 1 Million Views within 2 Weeks*, PolitiFact: Punditfact, Mar. 9, 2017, https://www.politifact.com/article/2017/mar/09/fake-news-website -starts-joke-gains-1-million-view/ [https://perma.cc/QWP4-XG23].

65. Ben Smith, *The King of Trump TV Thinks You're Dumb Enough to Buy It*, N.Y. Times, Nov. 29, 2020, https://www.nytimes.com/2020/11/29/business/media /newsmax-chris-ruddy-trump.html [https://perma.cc/VM88-93WA].

66. Richard L. Hasen, *An Enriched Economic Model of Political Patronage and Campaign Contributions: Reformulating Supreme Court Jurisprudence,* 14 Cardozo L. Rev. 1311 (1993).

67. For an introduction, see Martin P. Wattenberg, *The Rise of Candidate-Centered Politics: Presidential Elections in the 1980s* (1991).

68. For an introduction, see Raymond J. La Raja & Jonathan Rauch, *Want to Reduce the Influence of Super PACs? Strengthen State Parties,* Brookings Institution: FixGov blog, Mar. 24, 2016, https://www.brookings.edu/blog/fixgov/2016/03/24/want-to-reduce-the-influence-of-super-pacs-strengthen-state-parties/ [https://perma.cc/L8J6-YY2A].

69. Richard H. Pildes, *Small-Donor-Based Campaign-Finance Reform and Political Polarization,* 129 Yale L.J. Forum 149 (2019), https://www.yalelawjournal.org/pdf/Pildes_SmallDonorBasedCampaignFinanceReformandPoliticalPolarization_1nbukg72.pdf [https://perma.cc/P3SS-D9DJ].

70. Gregory Svirnovskiy, *Marjorie Taylor Greene's Incredible Fundraising Haul Reveals What the GOP Is Really About,* Vox, Apr. 7, 2021, https://www.vox.com/22372051/marjorie-taylor-greene-campaign-donations-republican-primary-midterms [https://perma.cc/269Z-4S97]; Aaron Navarro, *Trump Makes It Complicated for Republicans Looking to Stay Away from QAnon,* CBS News, Aug. 27, 2020, https://www.cbsnews.com/news/qanon-trump-republicans-mainstream/ [https://perma.cc/8UT9-64WT]; Clare Foran, Daniella Diaz, & Annie Grayer, *House Votes to Remove Marjorie Taylor Greene from Committee Assignments,* CNN, Feb. 4, 2021, https://www.cnn.com/2021/02/04/politics/house-vote-marjorie-taylor-greene-committee-assignments/index.html [https://perma.cc/VFV7-TEW6].

71. Citron & Chesney, *supra* note 33, at 1758.

72. David A. Fahrenthold, *Trump Recorded Having Extremely Lewd Conversation about Women in 2005,* Wash. Post, Oct. 8, 2016, https://www.washingtonpost.com/politics/trump-recorded-having-extremely-lewd-conversation-about-women-in-2005/2016/10/07/3b9ce776-8cb4-11e6-bf8a-3d26847eeed4_story.html [https://perma.cc/W2RP-TQTQ]. The most salacious comments in the conversation between Trump and *Access Hollywood*'s host, Billy Bush, included: "And when you're a star, they let you do it," Trump says. "You can do anything." "Whatever you want," says another voice, apparently Bush's. "Grab them by the p—y," Trump says. "You can do anything."

73. Mueller Report, *supra* note 39, at vol. 1, p. 58.

74. *Id.* at vol. 1, p. 79 ("The President then told Sessions he should resign as

Attorney General. Sessions agreed to submit his resignation and left the Oval Office. Hicks saw the President shortly after Sessions departed and described the President as being extremely upset by the Special Counsel's appointment. Hicks said that she had only seen the President like that one other time, when the Access Hollywood tape came out during the campaign") (cleaned up); Chris Cillizza, *Here's What Donald Trump Really Meant When He Apologized Friday Night,* Wash. Post: The Fix, Oct. 8, 2016, https://www.washingtonpost.com/news/the-fix/wp/2016/10/08/donald -trump-finally-apologized-for-his-lewd-remarks-here-it-is/ [https://perma.cc/G8W2 -83D2] ("I've never said I'm a perfect person, nor pretended to be someone that I'm not. I've said and done things I regret, and the words released today on this more than a decade old video are one of them. Anyone who knows me knows these words don't reflect who I am. I said it, I was wrong, and I apologize"); Emily Stewart, *Trump Has Started Suggesting the Access Hollywood Tape Is Fake. It's Not,* Vox, Nov. 28, 2017, https://www.vox.com/policy-and-politics/2017/11/28/16710130/trump-says-access -hollywood-tape-fake [https://perma.cc/L5T4-26GN]; Jonathan Martin, Maggie Haberman, & Alexander Burns, *Why Trump Stands by Roy Moore, Even as It Fractures His Party,* N.Y. Times, Nov. 25, 2017, https://www.nytimes.com/2017/11/25/us /politics/trump-roy-moore-mcconnell-alabama-senate.html [https://perma.cc/UDS9 -RSC9].

75. Josh Delk, *Trump Voter on "Access Hollywood" Tape: "His Words Are Taken Out of Context,"* Hill, Jan. 19, 2018, https://thehill.com/blogs/blog-briefing-room /369715-trump-voter-on-access-hollywood-tape-his-words-are-taken-out-of [https:// perma.cc/AQ8Y-FXZY].

76. Stewart, *supra* note 74 (quoting Sarah Sanders: "Look, the president addressed this. This was litigated and certainly answered during the election by the overwhelming support for the president and the fact that he's sitting here in the Oval Office today"); Maya Oppenheim, *Donald Trump Says "You've Got to Deny" Accusations by Women, According to Bob Woodward Book,* Independent, Sept. 12, 2018, https://www.independent.co.uk/news/world/americas/us-politics/trump-women -bob-woodward-deny-sexual-assault-stormy-daniels-book-fear-a8534061.html [https:// perma.cc/G4TM-XEM7] ("'You've got to deny, deny, deny and push back on these women,' Mr. Trump said, according to Mr. Woodward. 'If you admit to anything and any culpability, then you're dead. That was a big mistake you made'").

77. Donald Trump (@realDonaldTrump), Twitter, June 13, 2017, 3:35 A.M., archived at https://web.archive.org/web/20170715152906/https://twitter.com/realdonald trump/status/874576057579565056. The 940-tweet figure comes from a search for

fake news on the Trump Twitter Archive, https://thetrumparchive.com, conducted March 4, 2021.

78. Richard L. Hasen, *Why Isn't Congress More Corrupt? A Preliminary Inquiry*, 84 Fordham L. Rev. 429, 436–37 (2015).

79. Filipe R. Campante & Quoc-Anh Do, *Isolated Capital Cities, Accountability, and Corruption: Evidence from US States*, 104 Am. Econ. Rev. 2456, 2459, 2460 (2014) ("Our preferred measure of isolation is the average of the log of the distance of the state's population to the capital city. . . . Our baseline measure of corruption across US states is the oft-used number of federal convictions for corruption-related crime (relative to the size of the population)").

80. *Id.* at 2478; Pengjie Gao, Chang Lee, & Dermot Murphy, *Financing Dies in Darkness? The Impact of Newspaper Closures on Public Finance*, 135 J. Fin. Econ. 445 (2020), https://doi.org/10.1016/j.jfineco.2019.06.003.

81. Benkler, Faris, & Roberts, *supra* note 53, at 72 (noting that voters continue to get much of their news through television and radio, but that online use is increasing; "television remains the primary source of news and will likely continue to occupy that spot for several more election cycles"); Rasmus Kleis Nielsen & Richard Fletcher, *Democratic Creative Destruction? The Effect of a Changing Media Landscape on Democracy*, in Persily & Tucker, *supra* note 2, at 139, 149; John Gramlich, *10 Facts about Americans and Facebook*, Pew Rsch. Ctr.: FactTank, May 26, 2019, https://www.pewresearch.org/fact-tank/2019/05/16/facts-about-americans-and-facebook/ [https://perma.cc/HCK7-9TKY].

82. Persily, *supra* note 19, at 15. For a review of the literature on the use of bots as a means of influencing opinion, see Samuel C. Woolley, *Bots and Computational Propaganda: Automation for Communication and Control*, in Persily & Tucker, *supra* note 2, at 89, 94. To this point, bots cannot fully substitute for humans in interacting online. "Even the most sophisticated machine learning or deep learning-enabled social bots have trouble parsing human emotion, humor, and sarcasm and as such can be identified more readily than bot-human hybrids that harness human intelligence." *Id.* at 92.

83. Young Mie Kim et al., *The Stealth Media Groups and Targets behind Divisive Issue Campaigns on Facebook*, 35 Pol. Commc'n, 515, 531 (2018), https://doi.org/10.1080/10584609.2018.1476425.

84. Kaili Lambe & Becca Ricks, *The Basics on Microtargeting and Political Ads on Facebook*, Mozilla Found., Jan. 14, 2020, https://foundation.mozilla.org/en/blog/basics-microtargeting-and-political-ads-facebook/ [https://perma.cc/G57A-TXL6].

85. Kim et al., *supra* note 83, at 531; Benkler, Faris, & Roberts, *supra* note 53, at 270, 271–72; Parloff, *supra* note 44; Ian Bogost & Alexis C. Madrigal, *How Facebook Works for Trump,* Atlantic, Apr. 17, 2020 (updated Apr. 18, 2020), https://www.the atlantic.com/technology/archive/2020/04/how-facebooks-ad-technology-helps -trump-win/606403/ [https://perma.cc/C23R-ZVQJ].

86. Benkler, Faris, & Roberts, *supra* note 53, at 274, 279; Report of the Select Committee on Intelligence, United States Senate, vol. 5, at 663, 689, https://www .intelligence.senate.gov/sites/default/files/documents/report_volume5.pdf [https:// perma.cc/9MXU-CA75]; Simona Weinglass, *Israel Ducks Blame for Firm with Ex-Intel Officers That Bid to "Shape" U.S. Vote,* Times of Israel, Aug. 25, 2020, https://www .timesofisrael.com/israel-ducks-blame-for-firm-with-ex-intel-officers-that-bid-to -meddle-in-us-vote/ [https://perma.cc/BG2G-CAPT]; press release, Fed. Trade Comm'n, *FTC Imposes $5 Billion Penalty and Sweeping New Privacy Restrictions on Facebook,* July 24, 2019, https://www.ftc.gov/news-events/press-releases/2019/07 /ftc-imposes-5-billion-penalty-sweeping-new-privacy-restrictions [https://perma.cc /748W-CG5U].

87. Sue Halpern, *How the Trump Campaign's Mobile App Is Collecting Huge Amounts of Voter Data,* New Yorker, Sept. 13, 2020, https://www.newyorker.com/news /campaign-chronicles/the-trump-campaigns-mobile-app-is-collecting-massive- amounts-of-voter-data [https://perma.cc/SZX8–67EL].

88. Anthony Nadler, Matthew Crain, & Joan Donovan, *Weaponizing the Digital Influence Machine: The Political Perils of Online Ad Tech,* Data & Soc'y, Oct. 17, 2018, https://datasociety.net/library/weaponizing-the-digital-influence-machine/ [https://perma.cc/6R3H-HC4A].

89. Will Oremus, *Why Facebook Can't Quash QAnon,* One Zero: Pattern Matching, Aug. 23, 2020, https://onezero.medium.com/why-facebook-cant-quash-qanon -abaf6671b376 [https://perma.cc/8MK8-8K89] (citing Phillips & Milner, *supra* note 61).

90. Persily, *supra* note 24, at 51–52; Sabrina Rodriguez & Mark Caputo, *"This Is F—ing Crazy": Florida Latinos Swamped by Wild Conspiracy Theories,* Politico, Sept. 14, 2020, https://www.politico.com/news/2020/09/14/florida-latinos-disinformation -413923 [https://perma.cc/L43E-G2YY].

91. Benkler, Faris, & Roberts, *supra* note 53, at 262–63 (noting the inability to determine the reach of voter suppression messages on Facebook because Facebook did not make such information available to researchers); *id.* at 333–34.

92. Persily, *supra* note 19, at 25; Robert M. Bond et al., *A 61-Million-Person*

Experiment in Social Influence and Political Mobilization, 489 Nature 295 (2012), https://doi.org/10.1038/nature11421.

93. Ryan Mac & Craig Silverman, *"Mark Changed the Rules": How Facebook Went Easy on Alex Jones and Other Right-Wing Figures,* BuzzFeed News, Feb. 21, 2021 (updated Feb. 22, 2021), https://www.buzzfeednews.com/article/ryanmac/mark-zuckerberg-joel-kaplan-facebook-alex-jones [https://perma.cc/M9W9-AGEG]; Kevin Roose, *What If Facebook Is the Real "Silent Majority"?,* N.Y. Times, Aug. 27, 2020 (updated Nov. 4, 2020), https://www.nytimes.com/2020/08/27/technology/what-if-facebook-is-the-real-silent-majority.html [https://perma.cc/ZFD3-9QDQ]; Olivia Solon, *Sensitive to Claims of Bias, Facebook Relaxed Misinformation Rules for Conservative Pages,* NBC News, Aug. 7, 2020, https://www.nbcnews.com/tech/tech-news/sensitive-claims-bias-facebook-relaxed-misinformation-rules-conservative-pages-n1236182 [https://perma.cc/JZ23-7U7L]; Craig Silverman & Ryan Mac, *Facebook Fired an Employee Who Collected Evidence of Right-Wing Pages Getting Preferential Treatment,* BuzzFeed News, Aug. 6, 2020, https://www.buzzfeednews.com/amphtml/craigsilverman/facebook-zuckerberg-what-if-trump-disputes-election-results [https://perma.cc/VG8D-G8S5].

94. Kate Conger, *Twitter Flags Trump Tweet for Dissuading Voting,* N.Y. Times, Aug. 23, 2020, https://www.nytimes.com/2020/08/23/technology/twitter-trump-tweet-warning.html [https://perma.cc/E8GZ-UPLF]. The Trump tweet is archived at https://web.archive.org/web/20201201224219/https:/twitter.com/realDonaldTrump/status/1297495295266357248. On Twitter's taking five hours to put up its warning label, see Donie O'Sullivan (@donie), Twitter, Aug. 23, 2020, 10:22 A.M., https://twitter.com/donie/status/1297585136058458118. On Facebook's taking no action in response to the identical post the day it appeared, see Donie O'Sullivan, Naomi Thomas, & Ali Zaslav, *Twitter Hits Trump for "Misleading Health Claims" That Could Dissuade People from Voting,* CNN, Aug. 23, 2020, https://www.cnn.com/2020/08/23/politics/trump-twitter-health-voting-claims-flagged/index.html [https://perma.cc/PWQ7-AR3D].

3. What Can Law Do?

1. George A. Akerlof, *The Market for "Lemons": Quality Uncertainty and the Market Mechanism,* 84 Q.J. Econ. 488, 488 (1970).

2. Gary Biglaiser, Fei Li, Charles Murry, & Yiyi Zhou, *Intermediaries and Product Quality in Used Car Markets,* 51 Rand J. Econ. 905, 906 (2020), https://onlinelibrary.wiley.com/doi/pdf/10.1111/1756-2171.12344 ("We document a dealer price

premium: for the same type of car, transaction prices of dealer sales are higher than transaction prices in the unmediated market"); Saul Levmore & Frank Fagan, *The End of Bargaining in the Digital Age,* 103 Cornell L. Rev. 1469, 1485 (2018) ("CarMax has become a major force at the high end of the used-car market. It also promises uniform prices, or no haggling, as well as fairly inclusive warranties to back up its promise that the automobiles in stock have been carefully inspected. The implication is that no duplicative inspection by buyers is necessary"). There is a rich literature on whether used car dealers obtain higher monopoly rents by using no-haggle set pricing, as CarMax does, or by haggling, as many car dealers do. See, for example, Guofang Huang, Hong Luo, & Jing Xia, *Invest in Information or Wing It? A Model of Dynamic Pricing with Seller Learning,* 65 Mgmt. Sci. 5556 (2019), https:// pubsonline.informs.org/doi/pdf/10.1287/mnsc.2018.3197; Guofang Huang, *When to Haggle, When to Hold Firm? Lessons from the Used-Car Retail Market,* 29 J. Econ. & Mgmt. Strategy 579 (2020), https://doi.org/10.1111/jems.12385. CarMax's current warranty is a thirty-day return policy (up to 1,500 miles), followed by a ninety-day/ 4,000-mile limited warranty (with the potential to buy a more extended warranty for a fee). *Car Buying Process,* CarMax, https://www.carmax.com/car-buying-process /maxcare-service-plans (last visited Mar. 20, 2021).

3. Ben Smith, *Why the Success of the New York Times May Be Bad News for Journalism,* N.Y. Times, Mar. 1, 2020, https://www.nytimes.com/2020/03/01/business /media/ben-smith-journalism-news-publishers-local.html [https://perma.cc/93F3 -BLK5].

4. On the demand for right-leaning content on YouTube, see Kevin Munger & Joseph Phillips, *Right-Wing YouTube: A Supply and Demand Perspective,* Int'l J. Press & Pol. (2020), https://doi.org/10.1177%2F1940161220964767.

5. Heather Kelly, *Why It's Easy to Hate Facebook but Hard to Leave,* Wash. Post, Nov. 19, 2020, https://www.washingtonpost.com/technology/2020/11/19/can-not -quit-facebook/ [https://perma.cc/5CJW-WSXQ]. On Facebook's profitability, see Mike Isaac, *Facebook Posts a 33 Percent Increase in Revenue and a 53 Percent Jump in Profit,* N.Y. Times, Jan. 27, 2021, https://www.nytimes.com/2021/01/27/business /facebook-earnings.html [https://perma.cc/5KMU-EX8C].

6. Akerlof, *supra* note 1, at 488.

7. N.Y. Gen. Bus. Law § 198-b (McKinney 2021).

8. U.S. Const., amend. I.

9. Nathaniel Persily, *The Internet's Challenge to Democracy: Framing the Problem and Assessing Reforms* 16 (2019), https://perma.cc/A97Z-72PX; see also Cass R. Sun-

stein, *Falsehoods and the First Amendment,* 33 Harv. J. L. & Tech. 387, 393 (2020) ("No one should doubt that for some falsehoods, the marketplace works exceedingly poorly; it can be the problem, not the solution, perhaps especially online. Far from being the best test of truth, the marketplace ensures that many people accept false-hoods or take mere fragments of lives or small events as representative of some alarming or despicable whole. Behavioral science makes this point entirely clear: scientific research has almost uniformly rejected the idea that the truth of a proposi-tion is the dominant factor in determining which propositions will be accepted") (cleaned up).

10. William Cummings, Joey Garrison, & Jim Sergent, *By the Numbers: Presi-dent Donald Trump's Failed Efforts to Overturn the Election,* USA Today News, Jan. 6, 2021, https://www.usatoday.com/in-depth/news/politics/elections/2021/01/06/trumps-failed-efforts-overturn-election-numbers/4130307001/ [https://perma.cc/3B72-DDR8].

11. Amy Gardner, *"I Just Want to Find 11,780 Votes": In Extraordinary Hour-Long Call, Trump Pressures Georgia Secretary of State to Recalculate the Vote in His Favor,* Wash. Post, Jan. 3, 2021, https://www.washingtonpost.com/politics/trump-raffensperger-call-georgia-vote/2021/01/03/d45acb92-4dc4-11eb-bda4-615aaefd0555_story.html [https://perma.cc/ZF8M-9JS6]; Richard Fausset & Danny Hakim, *Georgia Prosecutors Open Criminal Inquiry into Trump's Efforts to Subvert Election,* N.Y. Times, Feb. 10, 2021 (updated Mar. 17. 2021), https://www.nytimes.com/2021/02/10/us/politics/trump-georgia-investigation.html [https://perma.cc/HMM9-3ZCC]; Mark Niesse & Greg Bluestein, *Georgia Recount Shows "Verdict of the People" as Results Certified,* Atlanta J.-Const., Nov. 20, 2020, https://www.ajc.com/politics/georgia-recount-shows-verdict-of-the-people-says-elections-head/7ARKVPQM3VAXJOEFZYQTV477II/ [https://perma.cc/MVU6-2MMH].

12. Donald J. Trump for President, Inc. v. Sec'y of Pennsylvania, 830 F. App'x. 377, 381 (3d Cir. 2020).

13. The two books are Richard L. Hasen, *The Voting Wars: From Florida 2000 to the Next Election Meltdown* (2012) and *Election Meltdown: Dirty Tricks, Distrust, and the Threat to American Democracy* (2020).

14. Christopher Krebs, *Trump Fired Me for Saying This, but I'll Say It Again: The Election Wasn't Rigged,* Wash. Post, Dec. 1, 2020, https://www.washingtonpost.com/opinions/christopher-krebs-trump-election-wasnt-hacked/2020/12/01/88da94a0-340f-11eb-8d38-6aea1adb3839_story.html [https://perma.cc/8NRS-LJN3] ("The com-bined efforts over the past three years moved the total number of expected votes cast with a paper ballot above 90 percent, including the traditional battleground states").

15. The description of Dry Alabama's activities is drawn primarily from Hasen, *Election Meltdown, supra* note 13, at 75–80. See Scott Shane & Alan Blinder, *Democrats Faked Online Push to Outlaw Alcohol in Alabama Race,* N.Y. Times, Jan. 7, 2019, https://www.nytimes.com/2019/01/07/us/politics/alabama-senate-facebook -roy-moore.html [https://perma.cc/LAV4-7DND].

16. Brian Lyman, *Russian Invasion? Roy Moore Sees Spike in Twitter Followers from Land of Putin,* Montgomery Advertiser, Oct. 16, 2017 (updated Oct. 17, 2017), https://www.montgomeryadvertiser.com/story/news/politics/southunionstreet /2017/10/16/roy-moores-twitter-account-gets-influx-russian-language-followers /768758001/ [https://perma.cc/7JVZ-6S7B].

17. Scott Shane & Alan Blinder, *Secret Experiment in Alabama Senate Race Imitated Russian Tactics,* N.Y. Times, Dec. 19, 2018, https://www.nytimes.com/2018 /12/19/us/alabama-senate-roy-jones-russia.html [https://perma.cc/99TG-VRK4]; Scott Shane, Alan Blinder, & Sydney Ember, *Doug Jones "Outraged" by Russian-Style Tactics Used in His Senate Race,* N.Y. Times, Dec. 20, 2018, https://www.nytimes. .com/2018/12/20/us/politics/doug-jones-social-media.html [https://perma.cc/BM5T -PCSC]; Craig Timberg, Tony Romm, Aaron C. Davis, & Elizabeth Dwoskin, *Secret Campaign to Use Russian-Inspired Tactics in 2017 Ala. Election Stirs Anxiety for Democrats,* Wash. Post, Jan. 6, 2019, https://www.washingtonpost.com/business/tech nology/secret-campaign-to-use-russian-inspired-tactics-in-2017-alabama-election -stirs-anxiety-for-democrats/2019/01/06/58803f26-0400-11e9-8186-4ec26a485713 _story.html [https://perma.cc/73SB-A7 PS]. A Medium page by Jeff Giesea contains what appear to be six pages of the twelve-page report. Jeff Giesea, BREAKING: *Here's the After-Action Report from the Alabama Senate Disinformation Campaign,* Medium, Dec. 27, 2018, https://medium.com/@jeffgiesea/breaking-heres-the-after-action-report -from-the-alabama-senate-disinformation-campaign-e3edd854f17d [https://perma.cc /LJX7-ZGLT].

Tovo Labs admitted running ads for the group aimed at raising Democratic turnout and depressing Republican turnout, but it claimed it did so using only truthful information, not misinformation. Joohn Choe, of AET-funded Dialectica, admitted to targeting Christian women in Alabama on social media during the campaign to "encourage rejection of Roy Moore on religious grounds while emphasizing the pointlessness of voting pro-life and contrasting it with Alabama's scandalously bad" infant mortality rate. Choe didn't expressly admit to waging a disinformation campaign but said that eventually his "focus shifted from studying disinformation and opposing it experimentally to fighting it wholesale with whatever tools were at hand. Given the state of knowledge I had—that we have, as a society—I concluded that it was the only ethical option available at the time, and I believe it remains so." The activist Matt Osborne was less apologetic about spreading misinformation, calling his Dry Alabama campaign a "smashing success." Joohn Choe, *The Resistance Information Warfare Handbook, Part IV*, Medium, Apr. 2, 2018, https://medium .com/@joohnchoe/the-resistance-information-warfare-handbook-part-iv -a375993f3dc0 [https://perma.cc/XP5V-PW2M]; Jonathon Morgan, *Social Media and the Alabama Special Election*, Medium, Jan. 2, 2019, https://medium.com/@jonathon morgan/social-media-and-the-alabama-special-election-c83350324529 [https://perma .cc/737A-PPAG]; Matt Osborne, *Roy Moore and the Politics of Alcohol in Alabama*, LinkedIn, Aug. 9, 2018, https://www.linkedin.com/pulse/roy-moore-politics-alcohol -alabama-matt-osborne/ [https://perma.cc/YEB4-3JN2]; Tovo Labs, *Proof of Digital Persuasion in Alabama's Senate Race*, Medium, Apr. 7, 2018, https://medium.com /@david.goldstein_4168/https-medium-com-tovolabs-proof-of-digital-persuasion -in-alabama-senate-race-85a517481371 [https://perma.cc/BSG7-GZTV].

18. Elizabeth Garrett & Daniel A. Smith, *Veiled Political Actors and Campaign Disclosure Laws in Direct Democracy*, 4 Election L.J. 295 (2005); Richard L. Hasen, *Chill Out: A Qualified Defense of Campaign Finance Disclosure Laws in the Internet Age*, 27 J. L. & Pol. 557, 570 (2012).

19. Buckley v. Valeo, 424 U.S. 1, 66–68 (1976); 52 U.S.C. § 30121 (2002); 11 C.F.R. § 110.20 (2014).

20. See 52 U.S.C. §§ 30101(9)(A) (2002), 30104(f)(1) (2007), and *Buckley*, 424 U.S. at 44 n. 52 (defining express advocacy); Zachary R. Clark, Comment, *Constitutional Limits on State Campaign Finance Disclosure Laws: What's the Purpose of the Major Purpose Test?*, 2015 U. Chi. Legal F. 527 (2016).

21. Karlene Lukovitz, *Streaming Services Are a "Wild West" for Political Ads, Mozilla Finds*, Video Insider, Sept. 22, 2020, https://www.mediapost.com/publications /article/356119/streaming-services-are-a-wild-west-for-political.html [https://perma .cc/6UB7-BPD4]. See the indictment filed by Special Counsel Robert Mueller, Feb. 16, 2018, at page 20, https://www.justice.gov/file/1035477/download [https://perma .cc/3T8R-U2U3], for the "Hillary is a Satan" example.

22. Richard L. Hasen, *The Ripple Effects of the FEC's Rules on Political Blogging: Why They Will End Up Undermining Limits on Corporation and Union Campaign Finance Activities*, FindLaw, Apr. 5, 2005, https://supreme.findlaw.com/legal-commen tary/the-ripple-effects-of-the-fecs-rules-on-political-blogging.html [https://perma.cc /3WLA-9A7T]; Ashley Balcerzak, *Federal Officials Struggle to Drag Political Ad Rules*

into the Internet Age, Ctr. for Pub. Integrity, June 27, 2018 (updated Oct. 26, 2018), https://publicintegrity.org/federal-politics/federal-officials-struggle-to-drag-political -ad-rules-into-the-internet-age/ [https://perma.cc/7QJZ-UP6F]. The existing rules create an exemption for media corporations, as I discuss more fully below in the context of a foreign spending ban.

23. S. 1356, 116th Cong. (2019), https://www.congress.gov/bill/116th-congress /senate-bill/1356 [https://perma.cc/Z64G-GV2Y].

24. California has temporarily barred the use of anonymous bots for political purposes, an approach that raises more serious constitutional objections than the proposal I suggest. Cal. Bus. & Prof. Code § 17941(a) (2019) ("It shall be unlawful for any person to use a bot to communicate or interact with another person in California online, with the intent to mislead the other person about its artificial identity for the purpose of knowingly deceiving the person about the content of the communication in order to incentivize a purchase or sale of goods or services in a commercial transaction or to influence a vote in an election. A person using a bot shall not be liable under this section if the person discloses that it is a bot"); Steven Musil, *California Bans Bots Secretly Trying to Sway Elections,* CNET, Oct. 1, 2018, https:// www.cnet.com/news/california-bans-bots-secretly-trying-to-sway-elections/ [https://perma.cc/J7GT-PBU2]. Below I argue that courts should outlaw microtargeting of election ads, which would render part of the suggestion here unnecessary.

25. See 11 C.F.R. § 110.11(f)(1) (2014) (exempting from disclosure "(i) Bumper stickers, pins, buttons, pens, and similar small items upon which the disclaimer cannot be conveniently printed [and] (ii) Skywriting, water towers, wearing apparel, or other means of displaying an advertisement of such a nature that the inclusion of a disclaimer would be impracticable").

26. Brown v. Socialist Workers '74 Campaign Comm. (Ohio), 459 U.S. 87 (1982). The FEC has long determined when groups are entitled to such an exemption. See, e.g., Myles Martin, *Advisory Opinion Request 2016-23 (Socialist Workers Party),* FEC, Apr. 21, 2017 (explaining FEC granted renewed partial disclosure exemption for Socialist Workers Party), https://www.fec.gov/updates/advisory-opinion -request-2016-23-socialist-workers-party/ [https://perma.cc/W6DT-5D48]. On the question of who counts as engaging in journalistic enterprises, see the discussion of the foreign spending ban below.

27. Buckley v. Valeo, 424 U.S. 1, 16–18 (1976); Citizens United v. Fed. Election Comm'n, 558 U.S. 310, 366–71 (2010).

28. 52 U.S.C. § 30101(9)(A)(i) (2002) (emphasis added); 11 C.F.R. § 100.155 (2016); 52 U.S.C. § 30101(9)(A)(i) (2002). See Fed. Election Comm'n v. Wisconsin Right to Life, Inc., 551 U.S. 449 (2007) (rejecting under the First Amendment a test for barring nonprofit corporate express advocacy because it required too great an inquiry into the speakers' intent).

29. United States v. Harriss, 347 U.S. 612 (1954); First Nat'l Bank of Bos. v. Bellotti, 435 U.S. 765 (1978).

30. *Citizens United,* 558 U.S. at 368–69; McConnell v. Fed. Election Comm'n, 540 U.S. 93, 234–40 (2003). "Writing for a Court majority of five, Justice Breyer explained a number of purposes served by the section 504 recordkeeping requirements, including that 'recordkeeping can help both the regulatory agencies and the public evaluate broadcasting fairness, and determine the amount of money that individuals or groups, supporters or opponents, intend to spend to help elect a particular candidate.' He recognized that the 'issue request' requirements could impose an administrative burden, and left open the possibility of a challenge to FCC implementing regulations in the future." Richard L. Hasen, *The Surprisingly Easy Case for Disclosure of Contributions and Expenditures Funding Sham Issue Advocacy,* 3 Election L.J. 251, 251–55 (2004) (citations omitted, quoting *McConnell,* 540 U.S. at 239).

31. 11 C.F.R. § 109.21(c), (d) (2010).

32. McIntyre v. Ohio Elections Comm'n, 514 U.S. 334, 358 (1995) (Thomas, J., concurring); Doe v. Reed, 561 U.S. 186, 228 (2010) (Scalia, J., concurring) ("Requiring people to stand up in public for their political acts fosters civic courage, without which democracy is doomed. For my part, I do not look forward to a society which, thanks to the Supreme Court, campaigns anonymously . . . and even exercises the direct democracy of initiative and referendum hidden from public scrutiny and protected from the accountability of criticism. This does not resemble the Home of the Brave"); *Citizens United,* 558 U.S. at 371 (Kennedy, J., majority opinion) ("The First Amendment protects political speech; and disclosure permits citizens and shareholders to react to the speech of corporate entities in a proper way. This transparency enables the electorate to make informed decisions and give proper weight to different speakers and messages"). But see *Doe,* 561 U.S. at 242 (Thomas, J., dissenting) ("The state of technology today creates at least *some* probability that signers of every referendum will be subjected to threats, harassment, or reprisals if their personal information is disclosed"); *id.* at 207–8 (Alito, J., concurring) (describing state's information interest in providing the names of signers of referendum petitions as

"breathtaking" and "chilling," and describing the potential for harassment from disclosed information as "vast"). On the lack of harassment stemming from campaign finance disclosure information, see Hasen, *Chill Out, supra* note 18.

33. Americans for Prosperity Foundation v. Bonta, 141 S. Ct. 2373 (2021) (cleaned up); Richard L. Hasen, *The Supreme Court Is Putting American Democracy at Risk*, N.Y. Times, July 1, 2021, https://www.nytimes.com/2021/07/01/opinion/supreme-court-rulings-arizona-california.html [https://perma.cc/5KKU-RQ5X].

34. Jeffrey Gottfried, *About Three-Quarters of Americans Favor Steps to Restrict Altered Videos and Images*, Pew. Rsch. Ctr.: FactTank, June 14, 2019, https://www.pewresearch.org/fact-tank/2019/06/14/about-three-quarters-of-americans-favor-steps-to-restrict-altered-videos-and-images/ [https://perma.cc/G24M-UKUN]. On the technology to ferret out deep fakes, see Danielle K. Citron & Robert Chesney, *Deep Fakes: A Looming Challenge for Privacy, Democracy, and National Security*, 107 Calif. L. Rev. 1753, 1787 (2019) (expressing skepticism of a technological solution in the short term); *id* at 1784 (discussing dire national security implications of deep fakes); Drew Harwell, *White House Shares Doctored Video to Support Punishment of Journalist Jim Acosta*, Wash. Post, Nov. 8, 2018, https://www.washingtonpost.com/technology/2018/11/08/white-house-shares-doctored-video-support-punishment-journalist-jim-acosta/ [https://perma.cc/MAJ7-8N8B]; Evan Halper, *"Deep Fake" Videos Could Upend an Election—But Silicon Valley May Have a Way to Combat Them*, L.A. Times, Nov. 5, 2019, https://www.latimes.com/politics/story/2019-11-05/deep-fakes-2020-election-silicon-valley-cure [https://perma.cc/A9FV-AE 97].

The "best reasonably available technology" standard would have to be developed, perhaps through Federal Trade Commission regulations, taking into account the cost and efficacy of such technology.

In the meantime, there often will be adequate proof that a particular audio or video of an elected official, candidate, or other public figure has been altered, and that the media portrayal is not a truthful representation. One such example where a fraud was quickly uncovered with conventional technology involved the CNN reporter Jim Acosta. As the *Washington Post* reported: "White House press secretary Sarah Sanders on Wednesday night shared a video of CNN reporter Jim Acosta that appeared to have been altered to make his actions at a news conference look more aggressive toward a White House intern. The edited video looks authentic: Acosta appeared to swiftly chop down on the arm of an aide as he held onto a microphone while questioning President Trump. But in the original video, Acosta's arm appears to move only as a response to a tussle for the microphone. His statement, 'Pardon me, ma'am,' is not included in the video Sanders shared. Critics said that video—which sped up the movement of Acosta's arms in a way that dramatically changed the journalist's response—was deceptively edited to score political points. That edited video was first shared by Paul Joseph Watson, known for his conspiracy-theory videos on the far-right website Infowars." Harwell, *supra*.

35. Citron & Chesney, *supra* note 34, at 1757.

36. Reed v. Town of Gilbert, 576 U.S. 155, 169 (2015) ("It is well established that the First Amendment's hostility to content-based regulation extends not only to restrictions on particular viewpoints, but also to prohibition of public discussion of an entire topic") (cleaned up). Commercial speech is subject to an intermediate standard of scrutiny, and government efforts to require business entities to tell the truth are probably on firmer constitutional footing. CTIA v. City of Berkeley, 928 F.3d 832, 842 (9th Cir.), *cert. denied*, 140 S. Ct. 658 (2019) ("Under *Zauderer* [v. Off. of Disciplinary Couns. of the Supreme Ct. of Ohio, 471 U.S. 626 (1985)] as we interpret it today, the government may compel truthful disclosure in commercial speech as long as the compelled disclosure is 'reasonably related' to a substantial governmental interest, and involves 'purely factual and uncontroversial information' that relates to the service or product provided") (cleaned up). Under *Reed*, a law requiring labeling of deep fakes as altered may well be subject to strict scrutiny because it is a content-based rule (it applies only to altered content that features the name or likeness of a candidate for office) even though it is viewpoint-neutral. See *Reed, supra* (holding that content-based laws are subject to strict scrutiny review).

37. First Nat'l Bank of Bos. v. Bellotti, 435 U.S. 765, 788–89 (1978) ("Preserving the integrity of the electoral process, preventing corruption, and sustaining the active, alert responsibility of the individual citizen in a democracy for the wise conduct of government are interests of the highest importance") (cleaned up); *Citizens United*, 558 U.S. at 339 (2010) (quoting Buckley v. Valeo, 424 U.S. 1, 14–15 (1976)).

38. A.B. 730, 2019–2020 Reg. Sess. (Cal. 2019), available at https://leginfo.legislature.ca.gov/faces/billTextClient.xhtml?bill_id=201920200AB730 [https://perma.cc/8QF6-RFG6], amended California Elections Code Section 20010 until 2023. The quoted language appears in Section 20010(a). The new Section 20010(e) defines "deceptive audio or visual media" as "an image or an audio or video recording of a candidate's appearance, speech, or conduct that has been intentionally manipulated in a manner such that both of the following conditions are met: (1) The image or audio or video recording would falsely appear to a reasonable person to be authentic. (2) The image or audio or video recording would cause a reasonable person to have

a fundamentally different understanding or impression of the expressive content of the image or audio or video recording than that person would have if the person were hearing or seeing the unaltered, original version of the image or audio or video recording."

39. On the difference between deep fakes and cheap fakes, see Dan Patterson, *From Deepfake to "Cheap Fake," It's Getting Harder to Tell What's True on Your Favorite Apps and Websites*, CBS News, June 13, 2019, https://www.cbsnews.com/news/what-are-deepfakes-how-to-tell-if-video-is-fake/ [https://perma.cc/3E3D-WZGZ]; Andrew Sheeler, *California Is Moving to Ban Deepfakes. What Are They, Anyway?*, Sacramento Bee, July 2, 2019, https://www.sacbee.com/news/politics-government/capitol-alert/article232162032.html [https://perma.cc/F4M5-QH8S].

40. In *Cook v. Gralike*, 531 U.S. 510 (2001), the Court considered the constitutionality under the Qualifications Clause of a proposed "Scarlet Letter" ballot provision requiring state officials to label some congressional candidates on the ballot as having "disregarded" or "declined" voter instructions on term limits. The Court rejected the requirement, in part on the basis of the pejorative nature of the ballot descriptions: "In describing the two labels, the courts below have employed terms such as 'pejorative,' 'negative,' 'derogatory,' 'intentionally intimidating,' 'particularly harmful,' 'politically damaging,' 'a serious sanction,' 'a penalty,' and 'official denunciation.'" *Id.* at 524.

41. My proposal is also less intrusive than Professor Rebecca Green's, which "would impose criminal sanction for the knowing manufacture of fake images, audio or other material of an identifiable candidate for public office, published within [a specified number of] days prior to an election, with intent to deceive voters and distort the electoral process." Rebecca Green, *Counterfeit Campaign Speech*, 70 Hastings L.J. 1445, 1456 (2019). She would exempt counterfeit campaign speech clearly labeled as "fake." *Id.* at 1457.

42. McConnell v. Fed. Election Comm'n, 540 U.S. 93, 230–31 (2003) (upholding BCRA § 311, which includes the "Stand by Your Ad" provision); Nicholas Stephanopoulos, *Stand by Your First Amendment Values—Not Your Ad: The Court's Wrong Turn in* McConnell v. FEC, 23 Yale L. & Pol'y Rev. 369, 370–71 (2005).

43. Nat'l Inst. of Fam. & Life Advocs. v. Becerra, 138 S. Ct. 2361, 2375–76 (2018).

44. *Id.* at 2376. "Noting that the disclosure requirement governed only 'commercial advertising' and required the disclosure of 'purely factual and uncontroversial information about the terms under which . . . services will be available,' the Court explained that such requirements should be upheld unless they are 'unjusti-

fied or unduly burdensome.'" *Id.* at 2372 (quoting Zauderer v. Off. of Disciplinary Couns. of Supreme Ct. of Ohio, 471 U.S. 626, 651 (1985)). For an analysis of how lower courts view *Zauderer,* see Valerie C. Brannon, *Assessing Commercial Disclosure Requirements under the First Amendment,* Congressional Rsch. Serv., Aug. 23, 2019, https://fas.org/sgp/crs/misc/R45700.pdf [https://perma.cc/9BM5-VFCG].

45. Arguably the labeling of synthetic videos of candidates as altered on for-profit social media sites is a mixed political and commercial context. But in *Riley v. National Federation of the Blind of North Carolina, Inc.,* 487 U.S. 781, 787–88 (1988), the Supreme Court treated such mixed contexts as meriting the full First Amendment protection afforded to political speech. *Riley,* however, also indicated under the full First Amendment review that it would be constitutional for a state to require professional solicitors for charity to disclose their professional status as a means of combating fraud. See *id.* at 799 n. 11 ("Nothing in this opinion should be taken to suggest that the State may not require a fundraiser to disclose unambiguously his or her professional status. On the contrary, such a narrowly tailored requirement would withstand First Amendment scrutiny"). Perhaps the current Court would not agree with *Riley* on this point. See *id.* at 803–4 (Scalia, J., concurring in part and concurring in the judgment) (agreeing with the Court's opinion except regarding this foot-note: "As to the last two sentences of that footnote, which depart from the case at hand to make a pronouncement upon a situation that is not before us, I do not see how requiring the professional solicitor to disclose his professional status is narrowly tailored to prevent fraud. Where core First Amendment speech is at issue, the State can assess liability for specific instances of deliberate deception, but it cannot impose a prophylactic rule requiring disclosure even where misleading statements are not made").

46. 52 U.S.C. § 30121 (2002).

47. Bluman v. Fed. Election Comm'n, 800 F. Supp. 2d 281, 288–89 (D.D.C. 2011), *aff'd,* 565 U.S. 1104 (2012).

48. Citizens United v. Fed. Election Comm'n, 558 U.S. 310 (2010). Technically speaking, a summary affirmance means only that the lower court reached the correct result, and not necessarily that the reasoning of the lower court is correct. It is hard to see how the Court could have affirmed in this case had it not embraced the self-governance point raised by Justice Kavanaugh in his district court opinion. See Mandel v. Bradley, 432 U.S. 173, 176 (1977) ("summary affirmance is an affirmance of the judgment only, the rationale of the affirmance may not be gleaned solely from the opinion below"). On the tension between the rationales in *Citizens United* and

Bluman, see Richard L. Hasen, Citizens United *and the Illusion of Coherence,* 109 Mich. L. Rev. 581 (2011).

Not everyone accepts democratic self-government as a compelling interest. For example, evelyn douek argues that the problem is one of disinformation, not foreignness, and therefore solutions should not target on the basis of the foreign identity of the speaker: "In a world of globalization and collective action problems, foreigners' speech may well be helpfully informative about matters of public policy." evelyn douek, *The Free Speech Blind Spot: Foreign Election Interference on Social Media,* in *Defending Democracies: Combating Foreign Election Interference in a Digital Age* 265, 279 (Jens David Ohlin & Duncan B. Hollis eds., 2021). douek concedes: "Restrictions on foreign voting, financial contributions and other forms of immediate influence on political representatives or campaigns directly protect the mechanisms of democracy." *Id.* at 284. I do not see how foreign interference on social media or other technology differs meaningfully from financial contributions in terms of improper foreign influence on American campaigns.

Jens David Ohlin defends bans on foreign interference relying on international law and norms that protect the right of each nation's collective right to self-determination: "Foreign interference is a violation of the membership rules for political decision-making, that is, the idea that only members of a polity should participate in elections— not only with regard to voting but also with regard to financial contributions and other forms of electoral participation. Outsiders are free to express their opinions but covertly representing themselves as insiders constitutes a violation of these political norms, which are constitutive of the notion of self-determination, just as much as covertly funneling foreign money to one candidate." Jens David Ohlin, *Election Interference: A Unique Harm Requiring Unique Solutions,* in *Defending Democracies, supra,* at 240.

49. Unlike the complete ban on foreign spending in U.S. elections, federal law before *Citizens United* allowed corporations to raise money from individuals associated with the corporation for a related political action committee, or PAC.

50. Spending to influence an election that appears on the Internet or social media but that lacks words of express advocacy cannot count as an "electioneering communication" (which must be a broadcast, cable, or satellite communication under 52 U.S.C. § 30104(f)(3) (2007)) or an independent expenditure (which must contain words of express advocacy pursuant to the Supreme Court's decision in *Buckley v. Valeo,* 424 U.S. 1 (1976)), 52 U.S.C. § 30101(17) (2002)). The foreign spending ban, however, also prohibits a foreign national, including a foreign government, from

making "an expenditure," 52 U.S.C. § 30121(a)(1)(C) (2002), which includes "any purchase . . . made by any person for the purpose of influencing any election for Federal office," *id.* §30101(9)(A)(i). Money to pay bots or otherwise to spread fake news on Facebook with an intent to influence the U.S. election would appear to be an expenditure under this definition, but such an argument may run into constitutional problems.

51. *Bluman,* 800 F. Supp. 2d at 284. Indeed, three FEC Republican commissioners relied on this dictum from *Bluman* in voting to hold that the foreign spending ban does not apply to ballot measure elections. Fed. Election Comm'n, MUR 6678, *Statement of Reasons of Vice Chairman Matthew S. Petersen and Commissioners Caroline C. Hunter and Lee E. Goodman,* at 2 (Apr. 30, 2015), www.fec.gov/files/legal/murs/current/110432.pdf [https://perma.cc/Q2DM-3A36].

52. Nate Persily and Alex Stamos similarly would limit the foreign campaign ban to ads that expressly mention candidates. Nate Persily & Alex Stamos, *Regulating Online Political Advertising by Foreign Governments and Nationals,* in Stanford Cyber Policy Center, *Securing American Elections* 27, 31–32 (Michael McFaul ed. 2019), https://fsi.stanford.edu/publication/securing-american-elections-prescriptions-enhancing-integrity-and-independence-2020-us [https://perma.cc/2MPR-YZUW].

53. Lamont v. Postmaster Gen. of U.S., 381 U.S. 301, 307 (1965) ("We rest [our opinion] on the narrow ground that the addressee in order to receive his mail [containing 'Communist propaganda'] must request in writing that it be delivered. This amounts in our judgment to an unconstitutional abridgment of the addressee's First Amendment rights"); see also *id.* at 307–9 (Brennan, J., concurring) (noting that the case does not raise the question of whether foreign governments have any First Amendment rights to assert and that the government in its briefs did not raise any compelling interests which could justify infringement on foreign speech, but asserting that the "right to receive publications" is a "fundamental right"); Eugene Volokh, *Can It Be a Crime to Do Opposition Research by Asking Foreigners for Information?* Wash. Post: Volokh Conspiracy, July 12, 2017, https://www.washingtonpost.com/news/volokh-conspiracy/wp/2017/07/12/can-it-be-a-crime-to-do-opposition-research-by-asking-foreigners-for-information/ [https://perma.cc/7JYF-F7DQ].

Volokh's primary argument is that the statute is substantially overbroad in that it covers instances in which foreign nationals might have information relevant to campaigns that campaigns would have a First Amendment right to receive. Volokh, *supra.* One key problem with Volokh's analysis here is that the statute is severable. Title 52 of the United States Code distinguishes between "foreign principals" and other "foreign nationals." 52 U.S.C. § 30121(b) (2002). "Foreign principals" includes a foreign "government." 22 U.S.C. § 611(b)(1) (1995). There seems little doubt that under cases like *Bluman* (recognizing the compelling interest in self-government), Congress has the power consistent with the First Amendment to bar foreign governments from contributing things of value to U.S. election campaigns. The part of the statute barring foreign government interference in U.S. elections is severable and not overbroad. See Richard H. Fallon, *Fact and Fiction about Facial Challenges,* 99 Calif. L. Rev. 915, 953–59 (2011) (describing severability and its relationship to facial challenges). Its application to foreign individuals and nongovernment entities is less certain.

54. Citizens United v. Fed. Election Comm'n, 558 U.S. 310, 351–53; *id.* at 352 ("The media exemption discloses further difficulties with the law now under consideration. There is no precedent supporting laws that attempt to distinguish between corporations which are deemed to be exempt as media corporations and those which are not"); *id.* at 352–53 ("So even assuming the most doubtful proposition that a news organization has a right to speak when others do not, the exemption would allow a conglomerate that owns both a media business and an unrelated business to influence or control the media in order to advance its overall business interest. At the same time, some other corporation, with an identical business interest but no media outlet in its ownership structure, would be forbidden to speak or inform the public about the same issue. This differential treatment cannot be squared with the First Amendment"). But see *id.* at 474 n. 75 (Stevens, J., concurring in part and dissenting in part).

55. Austin v. Michigan Chamber of Com., 494 U.S. 652, 667–68 (1990): "Although all corporations enjoy the same state-conferred benefits inherent in the corporate form, media corporations differ significantly from other corporations in that their resources are devoted to the collection of information and its dissemination to the public. We have consistently recognized the unique role that the press plays in 'informing and educating the public, offering criticism, and providing a forum for discussion and debate.' *Bellotti,* 435 U.S., at 781. See also Mills v. Alabama, 384 U.S. 214, 219 (1966) ('[T]he press serves and was designed to serve as a powerful antidote to any abuses of power by governmental officials and as a constitutionally chosen means for keeping officials elected by the people responsible to all the people whom they were selected to serve'). The Act's definition of 'expenditure' conceivably could be interpreted to encompass election-related news stories and editorials. The Act's restriction on independent expenditures therefore might discourage incorporated

news broadcasters or publishers from serving their crucial societal role. The media exception ensures that the Act does not hinder or prevent the institutional press from reporting on, and publishing editorials about, newsworthy events. Cf. H.R.Rep. No. 93-1239, p. 4 (1974) (explaining a similar federal media exception, 2 U.S.C. § 431(9)(B)(i), as 'assur[ing] the unfettered right of the newspapers, TV networks, and other media to cover and comment on political campaigns'); 15 U.S.C. §§ 1801–1804 (enacting a limited exemption from the antitrust laws for newspapers in part because of the recognition of the special role of the press). A valid distinction thus exists between corporations that are part of the media industry and other corporations that are not involved in the regular business of imparting news to the public. Although the press' unique societal role may not entitle the press to greater protection under the Constitution, it does provide a compelling reason for the State to exempt media corporations from the scope of political expenditure limitations. We therefore hold that the Act does not violate the Equal Protection Clause" (cleaned up).

56. Richard L. Hasen, *Plutocrats United: Campaign Money, the Supreme Court, and the Distortion of American Elections* 124–45 (2016); Sonja R. West, *Press Exceptionalism,* 127 Harv. L. Rev. 2434, 2456 (2014). I offer an extended defense of West's approach in *Plutocrats United.*

57. United States v. Alvarez, 567 U.S. 709, 720–21 (2012).

58. R.A.V. v. City of St. Paul, 505 U.S. 377, 383 (1992) ("These areas of speech can, consistently with the First Amendment, be regulated *because of their constitutionally proscribable content* [obscenity, defamation, etc.]") (original emphasis); Erwin Chemerinsky, *The First Amendment* 5 (2018) ("No matter how appealing the absolute position may be to the First Amendment's staunchest supporters, it is simply untenable. Even one example of an instance where government must be able to punish speech is sufficient to refute the desirability of an absolutist approach. For example, perjury laws or laws that prohibit quid pro quo sexual harassment ('sleep with me or you are fired') both punish speech, but no one would deny that such statutes are imperative"); *id.* at 185–216 (discussing obscenity standards).

59. On the reasons for the actual malice requirement, see the discussion of *New York Times Company v. Sullivan* below. Of course, the government can also engage in speech to counteract false election speech by giving correct information about when, where, and how people vote. Under the government speech doctrine, as the Supreme Court recognized in *Matal v. Tam,* 137 S. Ct. 1744, 1757 (2017), "when a government entity embarks on a course of action, it necessarily takes a particular viewpoint and rejects others. The Free Speech Clause does not require government

to maintain viewpoint neutrality when its officers and employees speak about that venture." The problem is that government counterspeech may not be enough to reach those who consume false election speech and end up disenfranchised.

60. For a skeptical look at the prosecution in the vote-by-text case, see Eugene Volokh, *Are Douglas Mackey's Memes Illegal?*, Tablet Mag.: News, Feb. 9, 2021, https://www.tabletmag.com/sections/news/articles/douglass-mackey-ricky-vaughn-memes-first-amendment [https://perma.cc/2CFF-2TD7?type=image] (quoting 18 U.S.C. § 241 (1996)).

61. For an argument that a broad law against false political speech would violate the First Amendment under even more deferential First Amendment theories, see Clay Calvert, Stephanie McNeff, Austin Vining, & Sebastian Zarate, *Fake News and the First Amendment: Reconciling a Disconnect between Theory and Doctrine*, 86 U. Cin. L. Rev. 99 (2018).

62. See *supra* note 36 (discussing the Supreme Court's ruling in *Reed v. Town of Gilbert*).

63. New York Times Co. v. Sullivan, 376 U.S. 254, 283 (1964); Brown v. Hartlage, 456 U.S. 45, 60 (1982).

64. United States v. Alvarez, 567 U.S. 709, 713, 729–30 (2012). Justice Breyer, in a concurring opinion for himself and Justice Kagan, applied intermediate scrutiny in agreeing the Stolen Valor Act was unconstitutional. Importantly, Justice Breyer recognized that laws punishing false political speech raised difficult questions of balancing, and that counterspeech was the usual appropriate remedy: "I recognize that in some contexts, particularly political contexts, such a narrowing will not always be easy to achieve. In the political arena a false statement is more likely to make a behavioral difference (say, by leading the listeners to vote for the speaker) but at the same time criminal prosecution is particularly dangerous (say, by radically changing a potential election result) and consequently can more easily result in censorship of speakers and their ideas. Thus, the statute may have to be significantly narrowed in its applications. Some lower courts have upheld the constitutionality of roughly comparable but narrowly tailored statutes in political contexts. See, e.g., United We Stand America, Inc. v. United We Stand, America New York, Inc., 128 F.3d 86, 93 (C.A.2 1997) (upholding against First Amendment challenge application of Lanham Act to a political organization); Treasurer of the Committee to Elect Gerald D. Lostracco v. Fox, 150 Mich. App. 617, 389 N.W.2d 446 (1986) (upholding under First Amendment statute prohibiting campaign material falsely claiming that one is an incumbent). Without expressing any view on the validity of those cases, I would also note, like

the plurality, that in this area more accurate information will normally counteract the lie. And an accurate, publicly available register of military awards, easily obtainable by political opponents, may well adequately protect the integrity of an award against those who would falsely claim to have earned it. . . . And so it is likely that a more narrowly tailored statute combined with such information-disseminating devices will effectively serve Congress' end." *Id.* at 738 (Breyer, J., concurring).

Even Justice Alito, dissenting on the constitutionality of the Stolen Valor Act, argued that "there are broad areas in which any attempt by the state to penalize purportedly false speech would present a grave and unacceptable danger of suppressing truthful speech. Laws restricting false statements about philosophy, religion, history, the social sciences, the arts, and other matters of public concern would present such a threat. The point is not that there is no such thing as truth or falsity in these areas or that the truth is always impossible to ascertain, but rather that it is perilous to permit the state to be the arbiter of truth." *Id.* at 751–52 (Alito, J., dissenting).

65. Minnesota Voters All. v. Mansky, 138 S. Ct. 1876, 1889 n. 4 (2018).

66. Hasen, *The Voting Wars, supra* note 13, at 94. A proposed federal law, the Deceptive Practices and Voter Intimidation Prevention Act of 2019, H.R. 3281, 116th Cong. (2019), appears to target those who act with an intent to mislead about when, where, and how people vote, but it requires that such speech be found to be "materially false." Speech that is misleading only would not be illegal under the statute.

67. Philip M. Napoli, *What If More Speech Is No Longer the Solution? First Amendment Theory Meets Fake News and the Filter Bubble,* 70 Fed. Commc'ns L.J. 55, 59 (2018). The article offers a nice history of the development of the counterspeech doctrine at the Supreme Court.

68. The Supreme Court's 2017 decision in *Packingham v. North Carolina,* 137 S. Ct. 1730 (2017), also raises concerns about how excessively broad readings of the First Amendment's application to social media might harm democracy-enhancing efforts. *Packingham* considered a First Amendment challenge to a North Carolina law that made it a crime for a convicted sex offender who had finished serving jail time "to access a commercial social networking Web site where the sex offender knows that the site permits minor children to become members or to create or maintain personal Web pages." *Id.* at 1733. The defendant, who had been convicted in 2002 for having sex with a thirteen-year-old when he was twenty-one, was found guilty of violating the social media statute in 2010 when he posted a message on Facebook thanking God that he had a parking ticket dismissed. *Id.* at 1734.

As the concurring opinion by Justice Samuel Alito explained, the law was so broadly written that it would have made it a crime for a convicted sex offender in North Carolina who had finished serving his sentence to purchase a product on Amazon.com, read a news article on Washingtonpost.com or research medical conditions on WebMD.com. All the justices agreed that the excessively broad law violated the First Amendment. *Id.* at 1741–43 (Alito, J., concurring).

Where the majority and concurrence parted company was in the broad language Justice Anthony Kennedy included in the majority opinion on the First Amendment's application to social media. Justice Kennedy offered a paean to the Internet and social media, calling them a "revolution of historic proportions." He called the Internet in general "and social media in particular" among "the most important places" for the exchange of views. *Id.* at 1735–36.

This is consistent with views Justice Kennedy communicated in a concomitant speech, where he expressed the same optimism Professor Volokh had twenty-six years before about the loss of intermediaries and the power of cheap speech. *Justice Anthony Kennedy Speaks at Salzburg Academy on Media and Social Change,* Salzburg Glob. Seminar, July 25, 2017, https://www.salzburgglobal.org/news/latest-news /article/justice-anthony-kennedy-speaks-at-salzburg-academy-on-media-and-global -change [https://perma.cc/N72L-S7PJ]. There, "Justice Kennedy said, 'Journalists have to begin to understand we are in a new world.' He went onto [*sic*] discuss how conventional institutions and structures were being bypassed as a result of the internet and how individuals were now participating in the revolution of the cyber age. During his lecture, Justice Kennedy also reserved praise for Wikipedia, which he described as one of the most fascinating and inspiring works of modern civilization. He remarked on the vast body of human knowledge which had been collected, describing it as a marvelous tribute to the human spirit. He said, 'The cyber age has tremendous potential, as indicated with Wikipedia. But if it bypasses space and time where there's just this obsession with the present—this neglect of our heritage and history—then our world will change.'" *Id.*

Justice Alito's concurrence noted the loose language in the *Packingham* majority opinion, and he wrote to object to the language's potential to make it more difficult to draft narrowly tailored laws aimed at keeping sexual offenders from making contact with minors: "While I thus agree with the Court that the particular law at issue in this case violates the First Amendment, I am troubled by the Court's loose rhetoric. After noting that 'a street or a park is a quintessential forum for the exercise of First Amendment rights,' the Court states that 'cyberspace' and 'social media in particular' are now 'the most important places (in a spatial sense) for the exchange of views.' The Court declines to explain what this means with respect to free speech law, and the Court holds no more than that the North Carolina law fails the test for content-neutral 'time, place, and manner' restrictions. But if the entirety of the internet or even just 'social media' sites are the 21st century equivalent of public streets and parks, then States may have little ability to restrict the sites that may be visited by even the most dangerous sex offenders. May a State preclude an adult previously convicted of molesting children from visiting a dating site for teenagers? Or a site where minors communicate with each other about personal problems? The Court should be more attentive to the implications of its rhetoric for, contrary to the Court's suggestion, there are important differences between cyberspace and the physical world." *Packingham,* 137 S. Ct. at 1743 (Alito, J., concurring) (cleaned up).

The truth about the benefits and dangers of the Internet and social media probably falls somewhere between Justice Kennedy's and Justice Alito's positions. But Justice Alito is right to be concerned over *Packingham's* loose dicta, which raise dangers for narrowly tailored future laws that might be aimed at fake news and other negative consequences to our democracy flowing from cheap speech and social media.

69. New York Times Co. v. Sullivan, 376 U.S. 254 (1964).

70. Jack Healy, Michael Wines & Nick Corasantini, *Republican Review of Arizona Vote Fails to Show Stolen Election,* N.Y. Times, Sept. 24, 2021; Tierney Sneed, *"The Sickness Is Spreading": MAGA 2020's Amateur Audit-Mania Is Sweeping the Nation,* Talking Points Memo, May 27, 2021, https://talkingpointsmemo.com/news /trump-audit-battleground-states [https://perma.cc/TU7X-S9RF]; Sarah Mimms, *Pro-Trump OAN Reporters Are Blatantly Raising Money for a Bogus Election "Audit" in Arizona,* BuzzFeed News, May 18, 2021, https://www.buzzfeednews.com/article /sarahmimms/arizona-election-results-oan-reporters-fundraising [https://perma.cc /KDG3-KDL3].

71. The quotation is from Berisha v. Lawson, 141 S. Ct. 2424, 2427 (2021) (Gorsuch, J., dissenting from denial of writ of certiorari) (internal quotation marks quoting Prof. Logan omitted); see also *id.* at 2424–25 (Thomas, J., dissenting from denial of writ of certiorari); McKee v. Cosby, 139 S. Ct. 675 (2019) (Thomas, J., concurring in denial of writ of certiorari); David A. Logan, *Rescuing Our Democracy by Rethinking* New York Times v. Sullivan, 81 Ohio St. L.J. 759 (2020).

72. Michael Grynbaum, *Trump Renews Pledge to "Take a Strong Look" at Libel Laws,* N.Y. Times, Jan. 10, 2018, https://www.nytimes.com/2018/01/10/business/media /trump-libel-laws.html [https://perma.cc/7EDM-PFPQ].

73. Yochai Benkler, Robert Faris, & Hal Roberts, *Network Propaganda* 279 (2018).

74. Julie E. Cohen, *Tailoring Election Regulation: The Platform Is the Frame,* 4 Geo. L. Tech. Rev. 641, 657–59 (2020) [https://perma.cc/HUG3-QNFA] (defining and defending interests in anti-factionalism, anti-manipulation, and anti-authoritarianism).

75. For an example of the kind of geographical targeting allowed, such as a congressional district, see the Banning Microtargeted Political Ads Act, H.R. 7014, 116th Cong. 2d Sess. § 325(e)(5) (2020), https://www.congress.gov/bill/116th-congress/house-bill/7014/text (defining "recognized place").

76. Abby Wood and Ann Ravel have proposed a mandatory disclosure regime for microtargeting, including requiring platforms to keep repositories of such microtargeting. Abby K. Wood & Ann M. Ravel, *Fool Me Once: Regulating "Fake News" and Other Online Advertising,* 91 S. Cal. L. Rev. 1223 (2018). As is the case with counterspeech, I am skeptical that disclosure of this information alone will do enough to ameliorate the dangers of such targeted advertising unless the platforms give access to others to target the same recipients.

77. Reed v. Town of Gilbert, 567 U.S. 155, 169 (2015).

78. Barr v. Am. Ass'n of Pol. Consultants, 140 S. Ct. 2335 (2020).

79. Cohen, *supra* note 74, at 662.

80. Manhattan Cmty. Access Corp. v. Halleck, 139 S. Ct. 1921, 1934 (2019); Haley Messenger, *Twitter to Uphold Permanent Ban against Trump, Even If He Were to Run for Office Again,* NBC News, Feb. 10, 2021, https://www.nbcnews.com/business/business-news/twitter-uphold-permanent-ban-against-trump-even-if-he-were-n1257269 [https://perma.cc/VG8K-LRHW].

81. Catie Edmondson & David McCabe, *Congress Will Press Ahead on Military Bill, Defying Trump's Veto Threat,* N.Y. Times, Dec. 2, 2020, https://www.nytimes.com/2020/12/02/us/politics/defense-bill-trump-veto.html [https://perma.cc/78CD-E2Z2] ("With his time in office winding down, the president has become increasingly fixated on the idea of using the popular, must-pass legislation to repeal Section 230 of the Communications Decency Act of 1996, which protects platforms like Facebook and YouTube from being sued over much of the content posted by their users, and how they choose to take that content down"); Sahil Kapur & Dareh Gregorian, *Congress Overrides Trump's Veto for the First Time on Major Military Bill,* NBC News, Jan. 1, 2021 (updated Jan. 2, 2021), https://www.nbcnews.com/politics/congress/congress-overrides-trump-s-veto-first-time-major-military-bill-n1252652 [https://perma.cc/GG8A-9YXL].

The immunity of providers to claims such as libel appears in 47 U.S.C. § 230(c)(1). Section 230(c)(2) gives content providers immunity when they decide to filter or block objectionable content. On this subsection, see Eric Goldman, *Online User Account Termination and 47 U.S.C. § 230(c)(2)*, 2 U.C. Irvine L. Rev. 659 (2012). Most of the attention has been on Subsection (c)(1). Subsection (c)(2), however, is also important. Repeal of that section would entangle platforms in much more litigation over decisions to remove or demote certain election-related speech found to be objectionable.

82. For more on the general debate over Section 230, consumer protection, and privacy, compare Danielle Keats Citron & Mary Anne Franks, *The Internet as a Speech Machine and Other Myths Confounding Section 230 Reform*, 2020 U. Chi. L. Forum 45, https://chicagounbound.uchicago.edu/cgi/viewcontent.cgi?article=1662 &context=uclf, with *CDA 230: The Most Important Law Protecting Internet Speech*, Electronic Frontier Found., https://www.eff.org/issues/cda230 (last visited Dec. 7, 2020). See also Sue Halpern, *How Joe Biden Could Help Internet Companies Moderate Harmful Content*, New Yorker, Dec. 4, 2020, https://www.newyorker.com/tech/annals -of-technology/how-joe-biden-could-help-internet-companies-moderate-harmful -content [https://perma.cc/JD49-FECF].

83. On Justice Thomas's general approach to campaign finance regulation, see Rick Hasen, *Justice Thomas: Leading the Way on Campaign Finance Deregulation*, Election L. Blog, Feb. 24, 2014 (originally published Oct. 8, 2007, at the First Amendment Center), https://electionlawblog.org/?p=58992 [https://perma.cc/LQ5A-6VDY]; on Justice Thomas's criticism of the constitutionality of the Fairness Doctrine, see FCC v. Fox Television Stations, Inc., 556 U.S. 502, 530 (2009) (Thomas, J., concurring) ("I write separately, however, to note the questionable viability of the two precedents that support the FCC's assertion of constitutional authority to regulate the programming at issue in this case. See Red Lion Broadcasting Co. v. FCC, 395 U.S. 367 (1969); FCC v. Pacifica Foundation, 438 U.S. 726 (1978). *Red Lion* and *Pacifica* were unconvincing when they were issued, and the passage of time has only increased doubt regarding their continued validity. The text of the First Amendment makes no distinctions among print, broadcast, and cable media, but we have done so in these cases") (cleaned up).

84. Biden v. Knight First Amendment Inst., 141 S. Ct. 1220, 1222–26 and n. 5 (Thomas, J., concurring). Note 5 of Thomas's concurrence quoted Professor Volokh. On the new Florida law prohibiting social media companies (except those that own a theme park!) from banning candidates, see Brendan Farrington, *Florida Sued over*

Law to Ban Social Media Content Blocking, AP, May 27, 2021, https://apnews.com
article/donald-trump-florida-social-media-media-business-7202f424f2cbdf71df8fe
c2e8cb61d [https://perma.cc/R6XU-W6JC]. On the extent to which Section 230
would preempt *state* laws that would require nondiscrimination by platforms among
users, see Eugene Volokh, *"Does the Government Have the Right to Control Content
Moderation Decisions?",* Reason: The Volokh Conspiracy, Feb. 12, 2021, https://reason
.com/volokh/2021/02/12/does-the-government-have-the-right-to-control-content
-moderation-decisions/ [https://perma.cc/AET6-VVNL].

85. Eric Goldman, *Deconstructing Justice Thomas's Pro-Censorship Statement in
Knight First Amendment v. Trump,* Tech. & Marketing L. Blog, Apr. 12, 2021, https://
blog.ericgoldman.org/archives/2021/04/deconstructing-justice-thomas-pro-censor
ship-statement-in-knight-first-amendment-v-trump.htm [https://perma.cc/GK22
-PMQ2]; Tunku Varadarajan, *The "Common Carrier" Solution to Social Media Censorship,* Wall St. J., Jan. 15, 2021, https://www.wsj.com/articles/the-common-carrier
-solution-to-social-media-censorship-11610732343 [https://perma.cc/YT72-TT9K]
("The situation with Mr. Trump and the social-media giants is different. If they are
monopolies—not 'an easy question,' Mr. [Richard] Epstein acknowledges—the
common-law rule is that 'no private monopoly has the right to turn away customers'");
Reed v. Town of Gilbert, 576 U.S. 155, 169 (2015); Miami Herald Pub. Co. v. Tornillo,
418 U.S. 241 (1974) (rejecting a law requiring newspapers to publish replies to editorials
by people disagreeing with them). Genevieve Lakier's eighteen-tweet analysis of Justice Thomas's position from April 6, 2021 begins at https://twitter.com/glakier/status
/1379445457210990595 and can be viewed in full at https://perma.cc/PJ6Q-6DFV.

For a skeptical look at the common carrier argument from a libertarian perspective, see Matthew Feeney, *Are Social Media Companies Common Carriers?,* Cato
at Liberty Blog, May 24, 2021, https://www.cato.org/blog/are-social-media-companies
-common-carriers [https://perma.cc/NA8F-4DZV?type=image] ("Perhaps [Volokh]
has a persuasive argument for why social media companies should be treated like
common carriers, but as things stand this sounds like an inappropriate comparison.
The telecommunications company you pay provides the only transportation of calls
from your cell phone to another, and it treats all such calls equally. Facebook, Twitter, and the Google-owned YouTube are among many, many options available to
those seeking to connect with others on the Internet's infrastructure. Social media
companies are not analogous to common carrier infrastructure such as a railroad. It
is more accurate to think of these companies as only some of the stops among millions on the Internet's rail network").

Professor Volokh, in a law review article following on Thomas's concurring opinion, argues that platforms are more like telephone companies than media companies, and he is at least open to the idea that these private companies can be compelled to open up their property to content they abhor, not only like telephone companies, but like shopping malls that must let leafletters on their property and universities that must let military recruiters on campus along with other employers under Supreme Court precedent. He believes no one would reasonably associate Trump's speech with Facebook's or Twitter's message if Trump's content were required to remain available on their platforms (tell that to the platforms that faced a barrage of complaints from customers for including Trump's objectionable content in their platform experience). Volokh, like Justice Thomas, draws the line at media companies. He does not believe that Fox News or the *New York Times* could be compelled give access to opponents of their viewpoints. *That* private property is off-limits because it would interfere with the holistic nature of each media organization's speech. Eugene Volokh, *Treating Social Media Platforms Like Common Carriers?*, 1 J. Free Speech L. 377 (2021).

The upshot of the common carrier argument for platforms is the embrace of an ironic de facto media exceptionalism that both Volokh and Thomas attacked in the *Citizens United* context, believing that it is unconstitutional to single out media corporations for special treatment under campaign finance rules generally applicable to corporations. They would treat Fox News better than Twitter because Fox News is a media company—even though in other contexts Volokh has pushed back against the notion that it is possible to fairly distinguish between media and others. Eugene Volokh, *Freedom for the Press as an Industry, or for the Press as a Technology? From the Framing to Today*, 160 U. Pa. L. Rev. 459, 538–39 (2012). Volokh does not view his exception as one limited to the media, but to anyone producing a coherent speech product. Where we differ is over whether social media websites offer a coherent speech product.

The district court in the *NetChoice* case discussed below agreed with my analysis. See also Jack M. Balkin, *How to Regulate (and Not Regulate) Social Media*, 1 J. Free Speech L. 71, 75 (2021) ("Social media curate not only by taking down or rearranging content, but by regulating the speed of propagating and reach of content"); Ashutosh Bhagwat, *Do Platforms Have Editorial Rights?*, 1 J. Free Speech L. 97 (2021); Christopher S. Yoo, *The First Amendment, Common Carriers, and Public Accommodations: Net Neutrality, Digital Platforms, and Privacy*, 1 J. Free Speech L. 463, 505–06 (2021) ("Absent a major change in business practices, social media companies exercise too much discretion over the content they host to be regarded as common carriers or public accommodations").

Volokh points out that this issue can be turned around. Why do progressives (like me) who were skeptical of the Court's protection of corporate power in *Citizens United* now stick up for the free speech rights of private corporations like Facebook and Twitter? I come to this question of platform free-speech rights taking *Citizens United* as a given. If we are going to overturn *Citizens United* and fundamentally rethink the ability of government to rein in corporate speech and power—and for that matter the power of very wealthy individuals to spend money on campaigns—then must-carry requirements for platforms also could be on the table.

86. Henry Olsen, *Opinion: The Critics Are Wrong: Florida's Social Media Law Is a Necessary Protection of Political Speech,* Wash. Post, May 25, 2021, https://www .washingtonpost.com/opinions/2021/05/25/critics-are-wrong-floridas-social-media -law-is-necessary-protection-political-speech/ [https://perma.cc/4737-RUZZ]. On the new conservative fear of the political power of private corporations, see Genevieve Lakier, *The Great Free Speech Reversal,* Atlantic, Jan. 27, 2021, https://www.the atlantic.com/ideas/archive/2021/01/first-amendment-regulation/617827/ [https://perma .cc/GS9Z-AKLD].

87. NetChoice, LLC v. Moody, 2021 WL 2690876 (N.D. Fla. 2021). For further analysis, see Alan Z. Rozenshtein, *Silicon Valley's Speech: The Technology Giants and the Deregulatory First Amendment,* 1 J. Free Speech L. 337 (2021).

88. See Prasad Krishnamurthy & Erwin Chemerinsky, *How Congress Can Prevent Big Tech from Becoming the Speech Police,* Hill, Feb. 18, 2021, https://thehill.com /opinion/judiciary/539341-how-congress-can-prevent-big-tech-from-becoming-the -speech-police [https://perma.cc/898J-88TC]. See also Martha Minow, *Saving the News: Why the Constitution Calls for Government Action to Preserve Freedom of Speech* 147 (2021) ("Treating the large digital platform companies as public utilities would permit regulation, including potentially a new fairness doctrine requiring responsible exercise of the platforms' moderating capabilities or an awareness doctrine assisting users in navigating both the content and their own uses of it"). For a critical response to Krishnamurthy & Chemerinsky, see the comments of Robert Corn-Revere posted in Ronald K. L. Collins, *First Amendment News 287: Bring Back the Fairness Doctrine? Destroying the Internet in Order to Save It,* First Amend. News, Feb. 24, 2021, https://www.thefire.org/first-amendment-news-287-bring-back-the-fairness-doctrine -destroying-the-internet-in-order-to-save-it/ [https://perma.cc/AWG9-NRD2]. For an argument applying the lessons learned from regulating broadcast television to Internet intermediaries, see Gregory P. Magarian, *Forward into the Past: Speech Intermediaries in the Television and Internet Ages,* 71 Okla. L. Rev. 237 (2018).

89. See Tim Wu, *Is the First Amendment Obsolete?*, 117 Mich. L. Rev. 547, 578 (2018) ("To make my own preferences clear, I personally would not favor the creation of a fairness doctrine for social media or other parts of the web. That kind of law, I think, would be too hard to administer, too prone to manipulation, and if it did work too apt to flatten what has made the internet interesting and innovative and therefore counterproductive. But my own preferences are something different than the question of whether Congress has the power to pass such a law under the Constitution. Given the problems discussed in this Essay, and presuming, say, that a firm like Facebook continued to exercise a dominant role over what the population sees and hears, surely Congress has the power to impose some duties designed to safeguard or improve the nation's system of collective self-government, whether for the First Amendment or perhaps for the survival of the republic. I just think it seems implausible that the First Amendment stands for the proposition that Congress, a state, or a city cannot try to cultivate more bipartisanship or nonpartisanship online. The justification for such a law would turn on the trends described above: the increasing scarcity of human attention, the rise to dominance of a few major platforms, and the pervasive evidence of negative effects on our democratic life").

90. For a related proposal requiring platforms to disclose nonneutral content policies, see Luigi Zingales & Filippo Maria Lancieri, *Stigler Committee on Digital Platforms: Policy Brief*, U. Chi. Booth Sch. Bus.: George J. Stigler Ctr., at 14 (Sept. 2019), https://www.chicagobooth.edu/-/media/research/stigler/pdfs/policy-brief---digital-platforms---stigler-center.pdf [https://perma.cc/R6QW-6KVN] ("Platforms should disclose when they voluntarily adopt non-neutral policies for content. For example, if platforms are deliberately demoting content related to specific topics, they should make clear what types of content they are demoting and why. Failure to disclose this information should result in fines or sanctions"); see also *id.* ("Platforms should disclose when they provide specific support or technical assistance to political parties, candidates, or interest advocacy groups, outlining what type of support has been provided and the outcome of this support").

The policy brief is part of a larger study dealing with the role of these platforms in American life and the problems with concentration of power. See *id.* at 10 ("In sum, Google and Facebook have the power of ExxonMobil, the *New York Times,* JPMorgan Chase, the NRA, and Boeing combined. Furthermore, all this combined power rests in the hands of just three people") (boldface deleted). The broader, 336-page final report appears at https://www.chicagobooth.edu/-/media/research/stigler/pdfs/digital-platforms---committee-report---stigler-center.pdf [https://perma.cc/8RXS-5NBK].

91. Jack M. Balkin, *Free Speech Is a Triangle,* 118 Colum. L. Rev. 2011, 2035 (2018). On the political difficulties of using antitrust law to break up the platforms, see Emily Bazelon, *The First Amendment in the Age of Misinformation,* N.Y. Times Mag., Oct. 13, 2020, https://www.nytimes.com/2020/10/13/magazine/free-speech.html [https://perma.cc/4VHJ-WYGK] ("To fend off regulation and antitrust enforcement, the internet platforms spend millions of dollars on lobbying in Washington. They align their self-interest with a nationalist pitch, warning that curbing America's homegrown tech companies would serve the interests of Chinese competitors like TikTok").

For an argument from the left for using antitrust law against the platforms and other large companies, see Zephyr Teachout, *Break 'Em Up: Recovering Our Freedom from Big Ag, Big Tech, and Big Money* (2020); see also Matt Stoller, Sarah Miller, & Zephyr Teachout, *Addressing Facebook and Google's Harms through a Regulated Competition Approach,* Am. Econ. Liberties Project (2020), https://www.economicliberties.us/wp-content/uploads/2020/04/Working-Paper-Series-on-Corporate-Power_2.pdf [https://perma.cc/8XRD-5CZA].

92. Shoshana Zuboff, *You Are Now Remotely Controlled,* N.Y. Times, Jan. 24, 2021, https://www.nytimes.com/2020/01/24/opinion/sunday/surveillance-capitalism.html [https://perma.cc/A7L8-ZEZU]; see also Shoshana Zuboff, *The Age of Surveillance Capitalism* (2019); Cohen, *supra* note 74; see generally Julie E. Cohen, *Between Truth and Power: The Legal Constructions of Informational Capitalism* chs. 1, 6 (2019).

93. Neil M. Richards, *Why Data Privacy Law Is (Mostly) Constitutional,* 56 Wm. & Mary L. Rev. 1501 (2015); Cohen, *supra* note 74, at 641–42 n. 1. For a contrary earlier view, rejected by Richards, that limiting the ability to collect and convey information can violate the First Amendment, see Eugene Volokh, *Freedom of Speech and Information Privacy: The Troubling Implications of a Right to Stop People from Speaking about You,* 52 Stan. L. Rev. 1049 (2000).

Richards argues against a reading of *Sorrell v. IMS Health Inc.,* 564 U.S. 552 (2011), that would view collection of data as an activity protected by the First Amendment. *Sorrell* held unconstitutional a Vermont law that restricted the sale, disclosure, and use of pharmacy records that revealed the prescribing practices of individual doctors. The Court held that the statute was designed to impose a specific content- and speaker-based burden on expression, thereby raising the level of scrutiny, and that the law unconstitutionally burdened such expression and was not justified by Vermont's purported interest in protecting health.

Richards, *supra* at 1506–7, explains: "Before *Sorrell,* there was a settled understanding that general commercial regulation of the huge data trade was not censorship. On the contrary, it was seen as part of the ordinary business of commercial regulation that fills thousands of pages of the United States Code and the Code of Federal Regulations. Nothing in the *Sorrell* opinion should lead policymakers to conclude that this settled understanding has changed. The poorly drafted Vermont law in *Sorrell* discriminated against particular kinds of protected speech (in-person advertising) and particular kinds of protected speakers (advertisers but not their opponents). Such content- and viewpoint-based discrimination would doom even *unprotected speech* under well-settled First Amendment law. As the Court made clear, the real problem with the Vermont law at issue was that it did not regulate *enough*, unlike the 'more coherent policy' of the undoubtedly constitutional federal Health Insurance Portability and Accountability Act of 1996" (cleaned up).

4. Beyond Law

1. Brian Stelter, *Newsmax TV Scores a Ratings Win over Fox News for the First Time Ever*, CNN Business, Dec. 8, 2020, https://www.cnn.com/2020/12/08/media/newsmax-fox-news-ratings/index.html [https://perma.cc/M4V9-7BAG].

2. Richard L. Hasen, *What Happens If Trump Won't Concede*, Slate, Nov. 8, 2020, https://slate.com/news-and-politics/2020/11/trump-concede-threat-legitimacy-biden.html [https://perma.cc/A7DW-YCFT]; Michael M. Grynbaum & John Koblin, *Fox News Helped Fuel Trump's Rise. Now It's Reporting on a Possible Fall*, N.Y. Times, Nov. 4, 2020 (updated Nov. 10, 2020), https://www.nytimes.com/2020/11/04/business/media/fox-news-election-night.html [https://perma.cc/SHS3-EQ9A].

3. Helen Sullivan, *Donald Trump Attacks Fox News: "They Forgot the Golden Goose*,*"* Guardian, Nov. 12, 2020, https://www.theguardian.com/us-news/2020/nov/13/donald-trump-attacks-fox-news-they-forgot-the-golden-goose [https://perma.cc/9RJ4-R487]. Five weeks after the election, after each state had cast its Electoral College votes, Newsmax began referring to Biden as "president-elect." Dominick Mastrangelo, *Newsmax Says It Will Refer to Biden as President-Elect*, Hill, Dec. 15, 2020, https://thehill.com/homenews/media/530272-newsmax-says-it-will-refer-to-biden-as-president-elect [https://perma.cc/3XYF-MG3G]. The same day, however, the network's web page featured a story about Trump touting false claims of rigged voting machines in Michigan. Jeffrey Rodack, *Trump Praises Report on Rigged Michigan Vote*, Newsmax, Dec. 15, 2020, https://www.newsmax.com/politics/michigan-audit-dominion-fraud/2020/12/15/id/1001564/ [https://perma.cc/6KAK-49QT]. OANN refused to call Biden "president-elect" until the January 6, 2021, vote in Congress, claiming, "All of our investigations indicate there was fraud in voting."

Jonathan Easley, *Conservative Outlet OAN Won't Recognize Biden as President-Elect until Congress Certifies,* Hill, Dec. 16, 2020, https://thehill.com/homenews/media /530496-oan-wont-recognize-biden-as-president-elect-until-congress-certifies [https:// perma.cc/9KNQ-RU48].

4. Ben Smith, *The King of Trump TV Thinks You're Dumb Enough to Buy It,* N.Y. Times, Nov. 29, 2020, https://www.nytimes.com/2020/11/29/business/media /newsmax-chris-ruddy-trump.html [https://perma.cc/S68T-WJS7].

5. Zach Montellaro & Elena Schneider, *Trump's Post-Election Cash Grab Floods Funds to New PAC,* Politico, Dec. 3, 2020 (updated Dec. 4, 2020), https://www .politico.com/news/2020/12/03/trump-pac-fundraising-442775 [https://perma.cc /5Y4A-U59B]; Alexis Benveniste & Kaya Yurieff, *Meet Rebekah Mercer, the Deep-Pocketed Co-Founder of Parler, a Controversial Conservative Social Network,* CNN Business, Nov. 16, 2020, https://www.cnn.com/2020/11/15/media/rebekah-mercer -parler/index.html [https://perma.cc/8NHP-EWCD].

6. Nick Corasaniti & Jim Rutenberg, *Republicans Pushed to Restrict Voting. Millions of Americans Pushed Back,* N.Y. Times, Dec. 5, 2020 (updated Jan. 16, 2021), https://www.nytimes.com/2020/12/05/us/politics/2020-election-turnout.html [https://perma.cc/6S5P-6TTS]; Amy Gardner, Jack Dawsey, & Rachael Bade, *Trump Asks Pennsylvania House Speaker for Help Overturning Election Results, Personally Intervening in a Third State,* Wash. Post, Dec. 8, 2020, https://www.washingtonpost .com/politics/trump-pennsylvania-speaker-call/2020/12/07/d65fe8c4-38bf-11eb -98c4-25dc9f4987e8_story.html [https://perma.cc/8HDD-59KX].

7. Nick Corasaniti, Jim Rutenberg, & Kathleen Gray, *As Trump Rails against Loss, His Supporters Become More Threatening,* N.Y. Times, Dec. 8, 2020 (updated Jan. 18, 2021), https://www.nytimes.com/2020/12/08/us/politics/trump-election-challenges .html [https://perma.cc/827A-GSQF].

8. ABC13, *Former Houston Police Captain Charged after Holding Repairman at Gunpoint in Fake Voter Fraud Crusade,* ABC7, Dec. 15, 2020, https://abc7chicago .com/voter-fraud-crusade-lands-former-police-captain-in-handcuffs/8807496/ [https://perma.cc/3BRM-85MD].

9. Russell Muirhead & Nancy L. Rosenblum, *A Lot of People Are Saying: The New Conspiracism and the Assault on Democracy,* preface at x (rev. paperback ed. 2020).

10. David E. Sanger, Nicole Perlroth, & Julian E. Barnes, *Billions Spent on U.S. Defenses Failed to Detect Giant Russian Hack,* N.Y. Times, Dec. 16, 2020 (updated Jan. 2, 2021), https://www.nytimes.com/2020/12/16/us/politics/russia-hack-putin -trump-biden.html [https://perma.cc/KNA5-SVBE] ("Some Trump administration

officials have acknowledged that several federal agencies—the State, Homeland Security, Treasury and Commerce Departments, as well as parts of the Pentagon—were compromised in the Russian hacking. But investigators are still struggling to determine the extent to which the military, intelligence community and nuclear laboratories were affected. The hacking is qualitatively different from the high profile hack-and-leak intrusions that the G.R.U., the Russian military intelligence division, has carried out in recent years. Those G.R.U. intrusions, like the 2016 hacking of the Democratic National Committee, were intended to be short term—to break in, steal information and make it public for a geopolitical impact. . . . Instead it was hoping for long-term access, able to slowly monitor unclassified, but sensitive, government deliberations on a range of topics").

11. Nathaniel Persily, *The Internet's Challenge to Democracy: Framing the Problem and Assessing Reforms* 31 (2019), https://perma.cc/A97Z-72PX ("Although the web is often portrayed as a state of nature for political speech, the platforms are highly regulated environments. Most of the major platforms have rules governing nudity and obscenity, harmful and violent content, harassment, threats, bullying, impersonation, and hate speech, as well as policies against spamming or copyright violations. They take down millions of pieces of content each year. Most such rules from the platforms go well beyond what is required by national laws. Indeed, if such rules were legislated by the government in the United States, almost all would be declared unconstitutional by the courts").

12. Kate Conger, *Twitter Takedown Targets QAnon Accounts,* N.Y. Times, July 21, 2020 (updated July 24, 2020), https://www.nytimes.com/2020/07/21/technology/twitter-bans-qanon-accounts.html [https://perma.cc/MZ4V-B367].

13. Jeremy B. Merrill & Ariana Tobin, *Facebook's Screening for Political Ads Nabs News Sites Instead of Politicians,* ProPublica, June 15, 2018, https://www.propublica.org/article/facebook-new-screening-system-flags-the-wrong-ads-as-political [https://perma.cc/T3FM-TML9]; William Turton, *We Posed as 100 Senators to Run Ads on Facebook. Facebook Approved All of Them,* Vice News, Oct. 30, 2018, https://www.vice.com/en/article/xwyn3q/we-posed-as-100-senators-to-run-ads-on-facebook-facebook-approved-all-of-them [https://perma.cc/4PXF-CFHX]; Patience Haggin & Emily Glazer, *Facebook, Twitter and Google Write Their Own Rules for Political Ads—And What You See,* Wall St. J., June 4, 2020, https://www.wsj.com/graphics/how-google-facebook-and-twitter-patrol-political-ads/ [https://perma.cc/7HY4-XMT4].

So far as I can tell, Facebook has never spelled out in any detail the kind of government regulation it favors. Mark Zuckerberg wrote a 2019 op-ed calling generally for regulations, including those in the area of election integrity. Mark Zuckerberg, *Mark Zuckerberg: The Internet Needs New Rules. Let's Start in These Four Areas*, Wash. Post, Mar. 30, 2019, https://www.washingtonpost.com/opinions/mark-zuckerberg -the-internet-needs-new-rules-lets-start-in-these-four-areas/2019/03/29/9e6f0504 -521a-11e9-a3f7-78b7525a8d5f_story.html [https://perma.cc/8RSV-QYFX]. In contrast, in January 2020 Facebook's director of public management, Rob Leathern, made the following antiregulation statement: "People should be able to hear from those who wish to lead them, warts and all, and . . . what they say should be scrutinized and debated in public." Bill Chappell, *FEC Commissioner Rips Facebook over Political Ad Policy: "This Will Not Do,"* NPR, Jan. 9, 2020, https://www.npr.org /2020/01/09/794911246/fec-commissioner-rips-facebook-over-political-ad-policy -this-will-not-do [https://perma.cc/P6CZ-8BH5].

14. Natasha Lomas, *Twitter's Political Ads Ban Is a Distraction from the Real Problem with Platforms*, Tech Crunch, Nov. 2, 2019, https://techcrunch.com/2019 /11/02/twitters-political-ads-ban-is-a-distraction-from-the-real-problem-with -platforms/ [https://perma.cc/765X-CPBC].

The sheer volume of content on a platform such as Facebook makes real-time content moderation impossible. evelyn douek, *Governing Online Speech: From "Posts-as-Trumps" to Proportionality and Probability*, 121 Colum. L. Rev. 759 (2021).

15. In the midst of a July 2017 speech, Trump tried to hedge a (false) claim of his about signing more bills than any other president at that point in his presidency: "We've signed more bills—and I'm talking about through the legislature—than any President ever. For a while, Harry Truman had us, and now I think we have everybody, Mike. I better say 'think,' otherwise they'll give me a Pinocchio—(laughter)— and I don't like those—I don't like Pinocchios. (Laughter)." Donald J. Trump, *Remarks by President Trump at Made in America Product Showcase*, July 17, 2017 (transcript available at https://trumpwhitehouse.archives.gov/briefings-statements/remarks -president-trump-made-america-product-showcase/ [https://perma.cc/QYV3-HYPU].

16. Zeve Sanderson et al., *Twitter Flagged Donald Trump's Tweets with Election Misinformation: They Continued to Spread Both On and Off the Platform*, 2 Harv. Kennedy Sch. Misinformation Rev. (Aug. 2021) [https://perma.cc/8JF5-ZYNY]; Kayla Gogarty, *Facebook Keeps Touting Its Labels, but Data Suggests Labels Actually Amplified Trump Misinformation*, Media Matters for America, June 2, 2021, https://www .mediamatters.org/facebook/facebook-keeps-touting-its-labels-data-suggests-labels -actually-amplified-trumps [https://perma.cc/4SB3-877T]; Persily, *supra* note 11, at 43 ("Facebook's experience with disputed flags for false stories is a case study in the

difficulty of confronting false claims through mere identification as such. Little evidence exists to support the notion that leaving it up to users to reject propositions, once identified as false, will be enough to shake their belief in the false content. All the more so is this true if evaluation of the asserted claim requires a user to click a button, such as the 'i' button to get more information about it. Most people come to the internet and social media for social reasons; newsgathering is a subsidiary pursuit. The greater the cognitive burden the platform places on users to investigate the truth of an asserted claim, the less likely are users to do so. Moreover, mere identification—especially when it thereby distinguishes the news item from the homogeneously packaged items nearby—only draws attention to the highlighted content, without successfully convincing the user that the content is otherwise dangerous or of low value").

17. Brian Fung, *Social Media Bet on Labels to Combat Election Misinformation. Trump Proved It's Not Enough*, CNN Business, Dec. 8, 2020, https://www.cnn.com /2020/12/08/tech/facebook-twitter-election-labels-trump/index.html [https://perma .cc/RYU7-VR5H]; Mark Bergen & Gerrit De Vynck, *YouTube to Delete New False Election Videos—Even Trump's*, Bloomberg, Dec. 9, 2020, https://www.bloomberg .com/amp/news/articles/2020-12-09/youtube-to-delete-new-false-election-videos -even-trump-s [https://perma.cc/TRC3-EGG7]; Mark Bergen, *YouTube Election Loophole Lets Some False Trump Win-Videos Spread*, Bloomberg, Nov. 10, 2020, https:// www.bloomberg.com/news/articles/2020-11-10/youtube-election-loophole-lets -some-false-trump-win-videos-spread [https://perma.cc/87BS-8M8U].

18. For Facebook's own catalogue of the actions it took before the 2020 U.S. elections, see Facebook, *A Look at Facebook and the US 2020 Elections,* Dec. 2020, https://about.fb.com/wp-content/uploads/2020/12/US-2020-Elections-Report.pdf [https://perma.cc/TL8Y-L8PK].

19. Kevin Roose, *Facebook Reverses Postelection Algorithm Changes That Boosted News from Authoritative Sources,* N.Y. Times, Dec. 16, 2020, https://www.nytimes .com/2020/12/16/technology/facebook-reverses-postelection-algorithm-changes -that-boosted-news-from-authoritative-sources.html [https://perma.cc/96VZ-UZDA]; see also chapter 1. On using political diversity as a signal for quality, see Saumya Bhadani et al., *Political Audience Diversity and News Reliability in Algorithmic Ranking* (ver. 1, July 16, 2020), https://arxiv.org/abs/2007.08078.

20. Ryan Mac & Craig Silverman, *After the US Election, Key People Are Leaving Facebook and Torching the Company in Departure Notes,* BuzzFeed News, Dec. 11, 2020, https://www.buzzfeednews.com/article/ryanmac/facebook-rules-hate-speech

-employees-leaving [https://perma.cc/BL8T-JHLZ]. The emphasis in the text was that of the data scientist in the original email.

21. Mayank Aggarwal, *Twitter Confirms Trump Can Be Banned from Inauguration Day Onwards,* Independent, Dec. 15, 2020, https://www.independent.co.uk/news /world/americas/us-election-2020/trump-twitter-ban-inauguration-biden-b1774105 .html [https://perma.cc/4C6G-DXNP].

22. The next few paragraphs draw from a February 10, 2021, letter I wrote on behalf of a number of scholars and leaders to the Facebook Oversight Board supporting the indefinite deplatforming of Trump from Facebook platforms. The letter is posted at https://www.politico.com/f/?id=00000177-8e40-df6c-abf7-ae726a9b0000 [https://perma.cc/4U56-M3GB].

23. Nick Clegg, *In Response to Oversight Board, Trump Suspended for Two Years; Will Only Be Reinstated If Conditions Permit,* Facebook Newsroom, June 4, 2021, https://about.fb.com/news/2021/06/facebook-response-to-oversight-board-recom mendations-trump/ [https://perma.cc/XH8X-WELQ]. The Oversight Board's May 5, 2021, decision in the case, 2001-001-FB-FBR, is posted at https://www.oversight board.com/decision/FB-691QAMHJ [https://perma.cc/U4PA-CJJJ?type=image]. See also Mike Isaac, *Facebook Oversight Board Upholds Social Network's Ban of Trump,* May 5, 2021, https://www.nytimes.com/2021/05/05/technology/facebook-trump-ban -upheld.html [https://perma.cc/27PP-J37C].

For an optimistic view on the potential for these independent oversight boards, see Kate Klonick, *The Facebook Oversight Board: Creating an Independent Institution to Adjudicate Online Free Expression,* 129 Yale L.J. 2232 (2020). For a letter urging the board to go beyond Facebook's call on deplatforming Trump to consider how the platform's content moderation decisions contributed to the January 6, 2021, violence, see the February 11, 2021, letter submitted to the board by the Knight First Amendment Institute at Columbia University, https://knightcolumbia.org/documents /39b35525do. For the idea of broader social media councils, see David Kaye, *Speech Police: The Global Struggle to Govern the Internet* 122 (2019).

24. Davey Alba, Ella Koeze, & Jacob Silver, *What Happened When Trump Was Banned on Social Media,* N.Y. Times, June 7, 2021, https://www.nytimes.com/inter active/2021/06/07/technology/trump-social-media-ban.html [https://perma.cc/KPK4 -Y6AP]; Neal Rothschild, *Exclusive Data: Trump's Traffic Flop,* Axios, June 4, 2021, https://www.axios.com/trump-blog-social-media-readership-703abeec-49d4 -468b-90e3-7865d43e2486.html [https://perma.cc/E2V8-5C96]; Drew Harwell & Josh Dawsey, *Trump Ends Blog after 29 Days, Infuriated by Measly Readership,* Wash.

Post, June 2, 2021, https://www.washingtonpost.com/technology/2021/06/02/trump
-blog-dead/ [https://perma.cc/RQR9-V5CC].

25. David Kaye, *The False Promise of Banning Fake News,* Freedex, Nov. 25, 2016,
https://freedex.org/2016/11/25/the-false-promise-of-banning-fake-news/ [https://perma
.cc/7VB7-3MCE]; see also Wilton Park, *#FakeNews: Innocuous or Intolerable?,* Feb.
2017, https://www.wiltonpark.org.uk/wp-content/uploads/WP1542-Report.pdf [https://
perma.cc/AJP5-9C6B] (discussing means of combating fake news problem, beginning with fact checking).

26. Kate Conger & Mike Isaac, *In Reversal, Twitter Is No Longer Blocking New
York Post Article,* N.Y. Times, Oct. 16, 2020 (updated Dec. 28, 2020), https://www
.nytimes.com/2020/10/16/technology/twitter-new-york-post.html [https://perma.cc
/W6N3-SD9J].

27. Yochai Benkler, Robert Faris, & Hal Roberts, *Network Propaganda* ch. 6
(2018). They also point out the benefits of fact checking for the majority of the population. *Id.* at 276 ("Despite being ignored by users and outlets on the right, fact-
checking sites serve an important role for the majority of people outside the right").
On traditional media being sucked in by the fringes, see Joan Donovan & Brian
Friedberg, *Source Hacking: Media Manipulation in Practice,* Data & Soc'y, Sept. 4,
2019, https://datasociety.net/library/source-hacking-media-manipulation-in-practice/
[https://perma.cc/D72B-MALR].

28. On the weakness of Facebook's response to the Oversight Board's call for it
to examine its own role in helping foment the January 6 insurrection, see evelyn
douek, *Facebook's Responses in the Trump Case Are Better Than a Kick in the Teeth, But
Not Much,* Lawfare, June 4, 2021, https://www.lawfareblog.com/facebooks-responses
-trump-case-are-better-kick-teeth-not-much [https://perma.cc/6SW9-7QQH]. At the
very least, the platforms need to open up their data more to social science researchers
who can objectively determine the best interventions to combat disinformation. See
Nathaniel Persily & Joshua A. Tucker, *Conclusion: The Challenges and Opportunities
for Social Media Research,* in *Social Media and Democracy: The State of the Field, Prospects for Reform* 313, 322 (Nathaniel Persily & Joshua A. Tucker eds., 2020). Frances
Haugen, a former Facebook product manager, leaked a host of internal company
documents to the *Wall Street Journal* showing the harm Facebook had caused to
its users, including how a tweak in the platform's algorithm increased users' anger
and polarization. The 2021 stories are collected at "The Facebook Files," Wall St. J.,
https://www.wsj.com/articles/the-facebook-files-11631713039.

29. Yochai Benkler, *A Political Economy of the Origins of Asymmetric Propaganda*

in American Media, in *The Disinformation Age: Politics, Technology, and Disruptive Communication in the United States* 43, 47 (W. Lance Bennett & Steven Livingston eds., 2020), https://www.cambridge.org/core/books/disinformation-age/1F4751119 C7C4693E514C249E0F0F997 [https://perma.cc/5P39-855X] [hereafter cited as *The Disinformation Age*].

30. Margaret Sullivan, *Ghosting the News: Local Journalism and the Crisis of American Democracy* 57, 64 (2020).

31. Christopher Ali, *The Merits of Merit Goods: Local Journalism and Public Policy in a Time of Austerity,* 6 J. Info. Pol'y 105, 105 (2016).

32. Sullivan, *supra* note 30, at 39–40; ProPublica, *About the Local Reporting Network* (last visited Dec. 16, 2020), https://www.propublica.org/about/local-reporting -network [https://perma.cc/H7X2-V447].

33. See Sullivan, *supra* note 30, at 61 (on the problematic reliance on billionaires).

34. W. Lance Bennett & Steven Livingston, *A Brief History of the Disinformation Age: Information Wars and the Decline of Institutional Authority* 3, 33–34, in *The Disinformation Age, supra* note 29; Benkler, Faris, & Roberts, *supra* note 27; Benkler, *supra* note 29, at 57.

35. Bill McCarthy, *Fact-Checking Joe Biden's Speech after Electoral College Vote,* PolitiFact, Dec. 15, 2020, https://www.politifact.com/article/2020/dec/15/fact-checking -joe-bidens-speech-after-electoral-co/ [https://perma.cc/MS7W-V3ME] ("'The only decision in the campaign's favor was in Pennsylvania about a three-day extension of a deadline for mail-in voters who had not provided a proper ID with their timely-submitted ballots to cure the defect,' said Stephen Vladeck, a law professor at the University of Texas. That case wasn't about fraud, and it involved a small number of ballots that didn't change the outcome"); Louis Jacobson & Amy Sherman, *Donald Trump Has Lost Dozens of Election Lawsuits. Here's Why,* PolitiFact, Dec. 10, 2010, https://www.politifact.com/article/2020/dec/10/donald-trump-has-lost-dozens -election-lawsuits-her/ [https://perma.cc/L8KM-W3D9]; Lawrence Hurley, *U.S. Supreme Court Swiftly Ends Trump-Backed Texas Bid to Upend Election Results,* Reuters, Dec. 11, 2020, https://www.reuters.com/article/us-usa-election-trump/u-s-supreme -court-swiftly-ends-trump-backed-texas-bid-to-upend-election-results-idUSKBN 28L2YY [https://perma.cc/HS9J-67S9].

36. Rosalind S. Helderman & Elise Viebeck, *"The Last Wall": How Dozens of Judges across the Political Spectrum Rejected Trump's Efforts to Overturn the Election,* Wash. Post, Dec. 12, 2020, https://www.washingtonpost.com/politics/judges-trump

-election-lawsuits/2020/12/12/e3a57224-3a72-11eb-98c4-25dc9f4987e8_story.html
[https://perma.cc/YBD3-H2FC] ("In a remarkable show of near-unanimity across the
nation's judiciary, at least 86 judges—ranging from jurists serving at the lowest levels
of state court systems to members of the United States Supreme Court—rejected at
least one post-election lawsuit filed by Trump or his supporters, a Washington Post
review of court filings found"); Tessa Berenson, *Donald Trump and His Lawyers Are
Making Sweeping Allegations of Voter Fraud in Public. In Court, They Say No Such
Thing,* Time, Nov. 20, 2020, https://time.com/5914377/donald-trump-no-evidence
-fraud/ [https://perma.cc/3NCE-FDDX]. On the debunked claims Giuliani, Ellis,
and other Trump lawyers made in public, see Samantha Putterman, Amy Sherman,
& Miriam Valverde, *Rudy Giuliani, Trump Legal Team Push Conspiracy Theories,
Baseless Claims about 2020 Election,* PolitiFact, Nov. 20, 2020, https://www.politifact
.com/article/2020/nov/20/giuliani-trump-legal-team-push-conspiracy-theories/
[https://perma.cc/B9GA-54HU].

37. Adam Liptak, *Supreme Court Rejects Texas Suit Seeking to Subvert Election,*
N.Y. Times, Dec. 11, 2020 (updated Jan. 15, 2021), https://www.nytimes.com/2020
/12/11/us/politics/supreme-court-election-texas.html [https://perma.cc/AW9V-NEPC];
Associated Press, *AP Sources: FBI Is Investigating Texas Attorney General Ken Paxton,*
Dallas Morning News, Nov. 17, 2020, https://www.dallasnews.com/news/politics/2020
/11/17/ap-sources-fbi-is-investigating-texas-attorney-general-ken-paxton/ [https://perma
.cc/KE5K-VLGR]; Matthew Mosk, Katherine Faulders, & John Santucci, *With Texas
AG Facing Federal Probe, Lawsuit to Help Trump Comes amid Whispers of Pardons,*
ABC News, Dec. 10, 2020, https://abcnews.go.com/Politics/texas-ag-facing-federal
-probe-lawsuit-trump-amid/story?id=74654894 [https://perma.cc/4GXH-3UWH].

38. See Liptak, *supra* note 37 ("Friday's order was not quite unanimous. Justice
Samuel A. Alito Jr., joined by Justice Clarence Thomas, issued a brief statement on
a technical point. But it was nonetheless a comprehensive rebuke to Mr. Trump and
his allies. It was plain that the justices had no patience for Texas' attempt to enlist
the court in an effort to tell other states how to run their elections. The majority
ruled that Texas could not file its lawsuit at all. 'The state of Texas' motion for leave
to file a bill of complaint is denied for lack of standing,' the court's order said. Justice
Alito, taking a slightly different approach, wrote that the court was not free immediately to shut down lawsuits filed by states directly in the court. 'In my view,' he
wrote, 'we do not have discretion to deny the filing of a bill of complaint in a case
that falls within our original jurisdiction'"); Philip Bump, *Trump's Effort to Steal the
Election Comes Down to Some Utterly Ridiculous Statistical Claims,* Wash. Post, Dec.

9, 2020, https://www.washingtonpost.com/politics/2020/12/09/trumps-effort-steal
-election-comes-down-some-utterly-ridiculous-statistical-claims/ [https://perma.cc
/8DPW-QGXG].

39. Sahil Kapur, Julie Tsirkin, & Leigh Ann Caldwell, *McConnell Congratulates
Biden on His Victory as More Republicans Abandon Trump's Fight,* NBC News, Dec. 15,
2020, https://www.nbcnews.com/politics/2020-election/mcconnell-top-republicans
-accept-biden-s-victory-after-electoral-college-n1251250 [https://perma.cc/42DZ-LU5Q]
("In a speech Monday evening, Biden criticized the 17 Republican attorneys general
and 126 Republican members of Congress who signed on to a Texas-led lawsuit to
reject the results in pivotal swing states, and assailed that lawsuit as an 'unprecedented assault on our democracy'"); Jonathan Tamari, *Pennsylvania Congressmen Who
Wanted to Throw Out Their Own State's Votes Still Don't Acknowledge Biden's Win,* Phil.
Inquirer, Dec. 15, 2020, https://www.inquirer.com/politics/election/pa-congressmen
-texas-lawsuit-biden-20201215.html [https://perma.cc/X7CD-5PMR] ("The legal
filing they supported, seeking a drastic remedy that would disenfranchise their own
constituents, repeated misrepresentations about the vote in Pennsylvania. For example, it falsely claimed that Philadelphia and Allegheny Counties disobeyed state law
regarding observers at their vote counts, and that guidance from Secretary of State
Kathy Boockvar for how counties could help voters fix flawed mail ballots was applied unevenly. It was issued statewide").

40. Kapur, Tsirkin & Caldwell, *supra* note 39 ("After weeks of delay, the top
Republican in the Senate, Mitch McConnell, acknowledged on Tuesday that Joe
Biden will be the next president, following an Electoral College vote that officially
certified his win on Monday"); Nicole Via y Rada, *Republicans Who Have Broken
with Trump to Congratulate Biden on His Win,* NBC News, Nov. 10, 2020 (updated
Nov. 23, 2020), https://www.nbcnews.com/politics/2020-election/republicans-who
-have-broken-trump-congratulate-biden-his-win-n1247278 [https://perma.cc/5QVJ
-58GJ] ("Mitt Romney of Utah extended his congratulations to both the president-elect and the vice president–elect on behalf of himself and his wife, Ann, in a
statement on Twitter. . . . Former President George W. Bush also extended his 'warm
congratulations' to Biden, becoming the most prominent Republican to do so")
(cleaned up).

41. Nicholas Fandos, *Senate Republicans Filibuster Jan. 6 Inquiry Bill, Blocking an
Investigation,* N.Y. Times, May 28, 2021, https://www.nytimes.com/2021/05/28/us
/politics/capitol-riot-commission-republicans.html [https://perma.cc/ZB9K-NF6C];
Zach Montellaro, *They Tried to Overturn the 2020 Election. Now They Want to Run the*

Next One, Politico, May 24, 2021, https://www.politico.com/news/2021/05/24/2020
-election-republican-official-races-490458 [https://perma.cc/QA68-25XC]; Richard L.
Hasen, *Republicans Aren't Done Messing with Elections,* N.Y. Times, Apr. 23, 2021,
https://www.nytimes.com/2021/04/23/opinion/republicans-voting-us-elections.html
[https://perma.cc/BJ5L-QB2N].

42. The type of election reforms that could produce more moderate candidates
is the subject of a large literature far beyond the scope of this book. For example, on
the difficult question whether top-two primaries such as that used in California
produce more moderate candidates, see Eric McGhee & Boris Shor, *Has the Top Two
Primary Elected More Moderates?,* 15 Persp. Pols. 1053 (2017), https://doi.org/10.1017
/S1537592717002158. On campaign finance reforms to discourage smaller, potentially
more ideological donors who may help elect more extreme candidates, see Richard H.
Pildes, *Small-Donor-Based Campaign-Finance Reform and Political Polarization,* 129
Yale L. J. F. 149 (Nov. 18, 2019), https://www.yalelawjournal.org/forum/small-donor
-based-campaign-finance-reform-and-political-polarization. On the risk of election
subversion, see Richard L. Hasen, *Identifying and Minimizing the Risk of Election
Subversion and Stolen Elections in the Contemporary United States,* 135 Harv. L. Rev.
Forum (forthcoming 2022).

43. Persily, *supra* note 11, at 49–50 (describing digital literacy efforts and com-
menting on problems with older voters and disinformation); W. Lance Bennett &
Steven Livingston, *The Coordinated Attack on Authoritative Institutions: Defending
Democracy in the Disinformation Age,* 261, 277, in *The Disinformation Age, supra* note
29 ("The problem with media literacy initiatives, no matter how well-intentioned, is
that they assume the disinformation crisis is the result of individual deficiencies
rather than a broken corporate media system and a right-wing propaganda network.
That said, literacy campaigns have a role to play in helping busy and distracted citizens from falling prey to deliberate efforts to deceive"); Ezra Klein, *Why We're Polarized* 89–92 (2020) (discussing motivated reasoning among the most politically knowledgeable and ideologically oriented members of society); Guy-Uriel E. Charles,
Motivated Reasoning, Post-Truth, and Election Law, 64 St. Louis U. L.J. 595 (2020)
(arguing that any "post truth" era is in fact a symptom of partisan-motivated reasoning in a hyperpolarized era); Daniel P. Tokaji, *Truth, Democracy, and the Limits of
Law,* 64 St. Louis U. L.J. 569 (2020) ("Bullshit is deadly to democracy").

44. Cailin O'Connor & James Owen Weatherall, *The Misinformation Age: How
False Beliefs Spread* 63 (2020); David M. J. Lazer et al., *The Science of Fake News,* 359
Sci. 1094, 1095 (2018).

Index